Praise For *No Doctors Required*

I highly recommend *No Doctors Required* as an important resource that teaches readers how to quickly improve their health using the powerful self-care healing methods it shares.

—**Dr. Joseph Mercola,**
Founder of Mercola.com

No Doctors Required is a book that is very needed at this time when the medical system in the USA is becoming less and less capable of truly helping most patients. The practical knowledge and self-care methods Larry Trivieri Jr and over a dozen other acclaimed health experts share in this book can be easily implemented by readers to take command over their own health and well-being. Everyone who wants to understand, gain, and maintain good health will benefit from reading *No Doctors Required* and applying its life-enhancing principles to their lives.

—**Elle Macpherson, entrepreneur, wellness warrior,**
philanthropist, model, Co-Founder of Welleco
(a plant based nutraceutical company specializing in
powdered greens) and most importantly,
mother of two amazing sons.

As a celebrity cancer survivor, health activist, and founder of the Cancer Schmancer Movement, I come in contact with countless authorities in the health space. Few doctors whose paths I've crossed are as brilliant at understanding the body as a system and supporting its ability to function at an optimal level than Dr. Lee Cowden. I have written everything down that he has recommended to me like gospel because I know what a medical genius he is! In *No Doctors Required*, Dr. Cowden and over a dozen other health experts share their expertise with Larry Trivieri Jr to guide you to better health through proven self-care methods most doctors know nothing about. Do yourself a favor and listen to them!

—**Fran Drescher, Actor, Producer, Author,**
Philanthropist, Public Diplomacy Envoy
for Family Health in America.

Larry Trivieri Jr has taken the awesome medical acumen of some of the world's top health experts to the next level in *No Doctors Required*. This book is a testimony of SELF-CARING which is so desperately needed in our more threatening and toxic environment. It is a must read, offering lots of wisdom that anyone can incorporate into improving their daily lives.

—Dr. Stephen Sinatra, cardiologist and
coauthor of the Great Cholesterol Myth

Knowing how to take care of your health has never been more important than it is today. *No Doctors Required* teaches you how to do so on your own, sharing a wealth of powerful self-care methods that can make a dramatic difference in your overall well-being. I am pleased to be a contributor to this book and encourage you to read it and USE IT!

—C. Norman Shealy, MD, PhD,
the father of holistic medicine.

Larry Trivieri is a great writer and *No Doctors Required* is a remarkable book that provides powerful and effective self-care methods that anyone can use to dramatically improve their health and live to a vigorous and disease-free old age, in spite of everything the world and may throw at them. More than ever before, the world needs the information it contains. Read it and put it to good use.

—Dr. Bradley Nelson, author of The Emotion Code
and creator of The Body Code

No Doctors Required is essential reading for anyone who truly cares about their health. Larry Trivieri Jr takes a truly holistic view of health and provide readers with a great checklist to make sure every avenue of your health is on track and a wealth of self-care methods for getting and staying healthier. He and the many acclaimed health experts who contributed to it have really covered every aspect of health and healing. Having suffered from a chronically infected root canal I was especially pleased to read the section on dental toxins.

—Frazer Bailey, Director of the films
E-motion and Root Cause

The Academy of Comprehensive
Integrative Medicine Presents

NO DOCTORS REQUIRED

10 Keys To Creating and Maintaining
Excellent Health Using Proven Self-Care
Methods That Most Physicians Don't Know

To Lucille + Irv —
I hope you like it!
Larry

LARRY TRIVIERI Jr

Foreword by
Dr. Joseph Mercola

gatekeeper press™
Columbus, Ohio

NO DOCTORS REQUIRED:
10 Keys To Creating and Maintaining Excellent Health Using Proven
Self-Care Methods That Most Physicians Don't Know

Published by Gatekeeper Press
2167 Stringtown Rd, Suite 109
Columbus, OH 43123-2989
www.GatekeeperPress.com

This publication is designed to provide accurate and authoritative information in regard to the subject matter covered. It is sold with the understanding that the publisher is not engaged in rendering legal or accounting services. If legal advice or other expert assistance is required, the services of a competent professional person should be sought.

Legal Notice & Disclaimer
This book and the information it contains is not, nor is it claimed to be, a program to treat or diagnose any disease, and is not intended as a substitute for medical care. Neither the author nor the publisher is engaged in rendering professional advice or services to the individual reader. If you suffer from any disease, seek immediate medical attention, and always consult with your physician or other health care provider as appropriate before engaging in any new endeavor related to your health. The author and publisher specifically disclaim all responsibility for any liability, loss or risk, personal or otherwise, which is incurred as a consequence, directly or indirectly, of the use and application of any of the contents in this book. All matters pertaining to your personal health should be supervised by a healthcare professional.

LCCN : 2020952276
ISBN: 9781735212616 (trade paperback)
eISBN: 9781735212609

To our Creator, who has given us life and everything we need to be healthy and whole in accordance with Divine Law.

To my mother, Margaret Mary Moyer Trivieri, who sacrificed every fiber of her being for the sake of her children, grandchildren, and great-grandchildren.

And to you, the Reader. May the information in this book serve you and help to keep you well.

Table of Contents

Foreword

YOUR HEALTH IS your most valuable possession. Ironically, though, the great majority of conventionally trained physicians know very little about what it means to be healthy. During the entire eight or more years of their professional medical education they are given little to no training in preventive health care.

While they may discuss the importance of healthy diet, regular exercise, and adequate sleep, when pressed further most of them cannot help their patients determine the most appropriate diet that they should follow based on each patient's individual metabolism and biochemistry. On average, conventionally trained medical doctorsonly receive 25 total hours of dietary education during the eight years they spend in formal medical training and some get only three hours.

Nor can most doctors truly give adequate exercise advice in terms of which types of exercise are best for each patient. As for sleep, usually the solutions they offer are sleeping pills, which do very little to provide restorative sleep, and are fraught with serious, harmful side effects.

In short, when it comes to these three most basic and essential factors for achieving and maintaining excellent health, the knowledge most doctors have about them is sorely lacking, if not missing altogether. This is true about the other key elements that make up the 10 essential factors that you must know about if you wish to become and stay healthy.

People today simply cannot depend on most doctors to provide them with that knowledge. They need their own how-to guide that helps them to most effectively implement the 10 key factors that are the foundation of lasting vitality so that they can manage and improve their health on their own. **No Doctors Required** is that guide, and the self-care information it shares has never been more important.

It is impossible to overemphasize the importance of why you must make self-care a priority in your life. The reason is both simple and stark—our nation's health care system simply isn't working.

Consider these astounding facts:

- Health care costs in the U.S. now exceed $3.5 trillion per year (about $10,000 per year for each person). As a nation, we spend more money per capita on health-related issues than any other country in the world, yet we continue to rank near the bottom of all non-third world countries when it comes to how healthy our population is.

- More than one-third of our population is chronically ill.

- 60 percent of the population is overweight or obese, and therefore at a much greater than normal risk of developing serious disease conditions, such as diabetes, heart disease, and cancer.

- The number of doctors in the U.S. is shrinking. This is also true of nurses and other health practitioners.

- According to the CDC, healthcare costs account for nearly 20 percent of our nation's GDP. From insurance premiums to deductibles to co-insurance to co-pays to out-of-pocket expenses, being unhealthy usually creates stress and financial strain.

Making matters worse, our health care system is really not a health care system at all. It is a system of *symptom care*. For the most part, all modern conventional medicine is capable of doing is managing chronic disease, not curing or preventing it.

So what can you do?

The best solution is to do all you can to educate yourself about what is necessary to create and maintain good health on your own, and to then take personal responsibility for doing so. And the good news is that doing so is far easier than you likely realize.

This breakthrough guide outlines, in an easy-to-understand and easy-to-implement way, the 10 most essential factors you need to incorporate into your life in order to safeguard your health and the health of your loved ones.

In the pages that follow you will learn proven-to-work, self-care tips and techniques you can immediately put to use to achieve greater vitality and well-being. These are the same self-care approaches that the contributing integrative physicians have used to keep their patients healthy for so long. By implementing these approaches into your life and the lives of your loved ones, you also can achieve the same benefits that they enjoy, such as:

- Balanced energy
- Enhanced immunity
- Improved gut health
- Excellent cardiovascular and other health values
- Sharp mental function
- Good muscle strength and flexibility
- High level emotional health and well-being
- Very low levels of stress.

The life-saving information in **No Doctors Required** has been skillfully compiled by the author, Larry Trivieri, as he interviewed some of the best integrative medical doctors and medical researchers in the United States, all members of the Academy of Comprehensive Integrative Medicine. These doctors shared with Larry their self-help "pearls" of knowledge that they have used to keep their patients alive and well for decades after the allopathic conventional doctors sent those patients home to die. It is Larry's artful "translation" of the knowledge and experiences of the contributing doctors and researchers into everyday language that makes this book so powerful.

Unlike other books focused only on how to treat disease, **No Doctors Required** is an authoritative guide-book that also shows you how you and your loved ones can avoid becoming sick in the first place. The information it imparts is more critical than ever. It is also the first book to receive the imprimatur of the Academy of Comprehensive Integrative Medicine, the organization to which I am proud to belong.

I am also proud to say that Dr. Cowden, who is a co-founder of the Academy and a contributor to this book, is my personal physician. He is also a long-time friend and served as one of my initial natural medicine mentors. Because I can personally attest to the benefits his approach to health provide, I highly recommend **No Doctors Required** to you. Take the information it contains to heart and apply it to your own daily life. If you do so, I can promise you that it will make a positive difference in your life.

Dr. Joseph Mercola

For more than 23 years, Dr. Joseph Mercola has dedicated himself to educating others about proven natural and integrative health care methods through Mercola.com, the world's most visited natural healthcare site. Dr. Mercola is also the New York Times bestselling author of numerous health books, including KetoFast: Rejuvenate Your Health with a Step-by-Step Guide to Timing Your Ketogenic Meals; Fat For Fuel: A Revolutionary Diet to Combat Cancer, Boost Brain Power, and Increase Your Energy; and EMF*D - 5G, WiFi.& Cell Phones: Hidden Harms and How to Protect Yourself.

Introduction

I MAGINE BEING ABLE to ask more than a dozen leading physicians and health experts, all of whom specialize in keeping their patients healthy rather than waiting for them to get sick, what you needed to do to also stay healthy, have more energy, and remain disease-free.

Now imagine being able to distill down what all of their recommendations had in common and then create your very own self-care program to achieve and maintain excellent health on your own, without having to depend on your doctor.

I wrote this book so that you can do exactly that.

Beginning in 1992, when I met my friend and mentor, the late Burton Goldberg, and helped him create the landmark single-volume encyclopedia *Alternative Medicine: The Definitive Guide* I have had the very good fortune of being able to meet, interview, and learn from literally hundreds of world-class healers. In every case, they emphasized the importance of proper self-care methods, and why self-care is the foundation of individual good health.

Among the most skillful and accomplished healers I have come to know over the years is Dr. W. Lee Cowden, who was a major contributor to the Guide, as well as to this book. Because of his expertise in a wide range of holistic and integrative therapies, Dr. Cowden has for years been sought out by other physicians to learn more about his methods. In 2008, Dr. Cowden co-founded the Academy of Comprehensive Integrative Medicine (ACIM). I consider the ACIM to be the premier organization of its kind, which is why the recommendations you will find in *No Doctors*

Required comes from Lee and other physicians and health experts who are ACIM members. I am very grateful to each of them for coming together in this book to share their knowledge and self-care recommendations so that you can improve your own health (and the health of your loved ones) in the comfort of your own home.

2,500 years ago, Hippocrates, the Father of Western Medicine, wrote, "The greatest medicine of all is teaching people how not to need it." This is best accomplished by learning how to prevent disease instead of waiting for its onset to treat it. Preventing illness before it can start is also the single best way there is for you to avoid all of the costs—which go far beyond monetary expenses alone—associated with the medical treatment of disease. A complete self-care health program that addresses each of the ten most important keys necessary for becoming and staying healthy is the foundation upon which true disease prevention is built. This book is designed to empower and guide you in how to create such a program and put it to optimal use.

What You Will Learn

To get where you want to go in terms of your health, you need to know as much as you can about how healthy you are right now. Chapter 1 is designed to help you do so. In it you will find detailed health self-assessment questionnaires. By going through them you will have a much clearer idea about the current state of your health, physically, mentally, emotionally, spiritually, and with regard to your environment. You'll also learn your current health status with regard to your social life. This is important, since your relationships with others can have a direct bearing on your health, both positively and negatively.

Then, in order to go even deeper, you will learn about essential medical tests that most conventional doctors either ignore or are not informed about. Many of these tests are inexpensive, and all of them provide important information about where on the spectrum of health you are in ways that more common conventional medical tests often fail to determine. You will learn how you can order these tests for yourself in many cases, and how to evaluate your test results based on optimal health ranges, which in many cases are much different than the so-called "normal" ranges most doctors rely upon.

The rest of the book guides you through the steps and methods you need to follow for each of the other 10 key elements that must be part of effective self-care. You will learn:

- How to easily know which foods and beverages you most require to become and stay healthy, and how to reduce chronic inflammation, the underlying cause of most disease.

- How to further improve and fine-tune your diet based on your unique biochemical individuality and needs.

- A simple self-testing method you can use to determine if you are being affected by food allergies or sensitivities.

- How and why your "gut" health determines your overall health (including the health of your brain) and what you must and can do on your own to improve your gastrointestinal health.

- A breakthrough supplement that has scientifically been proven to not only heal the lining of the GI tract to prevent "leaky gut" syndrome, but to also counteract and repair the harmful effects of glyphosate (RoundUp) and other harmful pesticides and insecticides that are so prevalent in our nation's food supply.

- What you need to know about choosing nutritional supplements, including which ones are most important and effective and which ones to avoid.

- The best self-care methods you can use to minimize and detoxify from the effects of the environmental toxins that we are all exposed to each day in our food, homes, and places of work.

- Easily implementable strategies and self-care techniques you can use to optimize your mindset and beliefs, reduce stress, and how to find and free yourself from trapped emotions that are literally stored in your body.

- Energy-boosting self-care methods, including a powerful four minute-or-less exercise routine that you can perform anytime and anywhere without the need for equipment that is proven to significantly increase energy, improve aerobic capacity, tone muscles, and increase muscle strength.

- A wealth of self-care strategies and techniques you can use to achieve deeper levels of truly restorative sleep.

- The importance of spiritual health and how you can deepen your connection to God in ways that will also significantly improve your health and overall well-being.

And much more, including how to put everything together to create your very own impactful self-care health program.

Final Thoughts and Tips Before You Get Started

There are many health books on the market today that promise you vibrant health in at little as a few weeks or months. *No Doctors Required* is not that type of book. While I have no doubt that you will start to experience greater levels of health, energy, and happiness soon after you begin putting what you are about to learn to regular good use, don't expect to achieve all of the health gains you may desire all at once.

Although as a nation we seem to prefer quick fixes, the truth is that creating and maintaining excellent overall health is a lifelong journey. There is always one more step to take, and one more thing we can learn along the way. The key is to be persistent and to make your health a priority each day.

Applying what you will learn in this book is not difficult, even though much of the information its contributors and I share may be new to you. Take your time as you begin to implement what you learn. Don't try to do everything at once. You will get much better, longer lasting results if you act as the tortoise, not the hare. Go slow and steady.

And by all means enjoy yourself. The more you can make your self-care routine enjoyable instead of a chore, the more likely you will be to continue committing to and benefiting from it. As you do so, celebrate your gains. You'll deserve to.

CHAPTER 1

The First Key: Knowing How Healthy You Are Right Now

T HE BEST WAY to reach your destination is to start by knowing where you are. In terms of health, this means starting with an accurate assessment of how healthy you are currently.

Most people, including most physicians, actually do not know what it means to be healthy. Are you one of them? More importantly, are you healthy?

How you answer that question most likely depends on whether or not you are currently suffering from an illness or have a chronic ailment or nagging condition that never quite goes away. If you do not, then you probably consider yourself to be healthy. That's because today the term *health* is commonly understood to only mean being disease- and symptom-free. Yet the true definition of health is far more than the mere absence of symptoms. Member physicians of the Academy of Comprehensive Integrative Medicine (ACIM) recognize that true health means being healthy and whole in body (both your physical body and your external environment, which so powerfully influences your body), mind (including habitual emotions and beliefs), and spirit (having a connection with God or the Divine and harmonious family and social relationships).

Unlike most physicians, ACIM physicians assess how well their patients are in each of the above categories. Rather than simply focusing on their patients' symptoms, they go much deeper in their assessments, looking at their patients' diet, lifestyle choices, daily stressors, mental and emotional states, and other related factors, including their commitment to their own health. In addition, these physicians will often employ various diagnostic tests that are often overlooked by conventional physicians in order to gain a complete overview of their patients' health.

If possible, it is recommended that you seek out an ACIM member physician who can help you stay healthy. However, the focus of this book is on what you can do on your own without a doctor to maintain and improve your health. With that in mind, the remainder of this chapter is designed to help you gain an accurate picture of your current health status, along with indications of what areas of your life you may need to focus on in order to achieve greater levels of vitality and overall well-being. You will also learn about important medical tests you should consider, most of which you can order on your own.

Your Self-Assessment Intake

One of the most renowned and pioneering holistic, integrative physicians in the world is C. Norman Shealy, MD, PhD. Dr. Shealy began his career as an acclaimed neurosurgeon, and has developed numerous innovative protocols for managing and reversing pain, depression, stress, and many other health conditions. Many of these protocols are increasingly being integrated into hospitals and medical practices all across the United States.

According to Dr. Shealy, less than five percent of all Americans meet the following criteria for good health:

- Normal body weight (having a body mass index, or BMI, between 18 and 24; you can quickly and easily calculate your BMI at www.bmi-calculator.net)
- Nonsmoker

- Consuming a minimum of five daily servings of fruits and vegetables
- Exercising at least 30 minutes five days a week.

In his book, *Blueprint For Holistic Healing,* Dr. Shealy wrote, "If all Americans had these habits, within twenty-five years, average American life would be one hundred instead of the current seventy-eight...true health is virtually impossible without these habits."

Do you possess the above four essential habits for good health? Answering that question honestly and without self-judgment is the first step you must take to determine whether or not you are doing all you can to be healthy.

In another of his many books, *Living Bliss,* Dr. Shealy outlines "10 Smart Steps To Keep You Alive (and Well!)," explaining that the more than 30,000 patients with whom he shared them were able to overcome pain and depression by following them, and that 85 percent of them "got back on a solid path to wellness". In addition to the four healthy habits above, the remaining 10 steps are:

- Getting an adequate amount of restful sleep each night.
- Practicing self-regulation such as autogenic training for at least 20 minutes each day.
- Maintaining a positive attitude toward yourself, your life, and others.
- Developing a strong social network of friends and loved ones.
- Enjoying intimacy with a loving partner to relieve tension and increase oxytocin levels.
- Assisting a healthy diet with appropriate high-quality nutritional supplements.

How many of these additional healthy habits have you incorporated into your life? Don't worry if you have not done so or are unfamiliar with some of the above concepts. You will learn how you can easily make them a part of your self-care health regimen in the chapters that follow. For now, simply note your answers because they provide clues about what areas of your life you most need to address.

The following questionnaires can further help you determine how healthy you are. "If you want to see if you are making progress in the right direction over time," Dr. W. Lee Cowden, co-founder of the Academy of Comprehensive Integrative Medicine, advises, "photocopy the questionnaires, put your answers on the photocopied version, date it, save it, and then weeks or months later answer the newly-photocopied questionnaires from this book again (without looking at your previous answers) and then compare those answers to your previous answers. You can then focus your subsequent efforts on areas where you have not made the desired progress."

A Body/Mind/Spirit Self-Test Questionnaire

The following questions can help you further assess your current health status. Answer them Yes or No.

Body: (Physical and Environmental Health)

___ 1. Do you maintain a healthy diet?

___ 2. Is your water intake adequate (at least 1/2 ounce per pound of body weight)?

___ 3. Are you within 20 percent of your ideal body weight?

___ 4. Do you feel physically attractive?

___ 5. Do you fall asleep easily and sleep soundly?

___ 6. Do you awaken in the morning feeling well rested?

___ 7. Do you have more than enough energy to meet your daily responsibilities?

___ 8. Are your five senses functioning well?

___ 9. Do you take time to enjoy your daily experiences?

___ 10. Does your sexual relationship feel gratifying?

___ 11. Do you engage in exercise regularly (at least 30 minutes/5x week)?

___ 12. Do you have good endurance or aerobic capacity?

___ 13. Are you physically strong?

___ 14. Do you do some stretching exercises?

___ 15. Are you free of chronic aches, pains, ailments, and diseases?

___ 16. Do you have regular bowel movements?

___ 17. Are you free of any drug or alcohol dependency?

___ 18. Do you live and work in a healthy environment with respect to clean air, water, and indoor pollution?

___ 19. Do you regularly spend time in nature?

___ 20. Do you have an awareness of your vital life force energy?

Mind: (Mental and Emotional Health)

___ 1. Do you have specific goals in your personal and professional life?

___ 2. Do you have the ability to concentrate for extended periods of time?

___ 3. Do you use visualization or mental imagery to help you attain your goals or enhance your performance?

___ 4. Do you believe it is possible to change for the better?

___ 5. Can you meet your financial needs and desires?

___ 6. Is your outlook basically optimistic?

___ 7. Are your thoughts/self-talk about yourself more supportive than critical?

___ 8. Does your job make use of your best talents?

___ 9. Is the work you do enjoyable and fulfilling?

___ 10. Are you willing to take risks or make mistakes in order to succeed?

___ 11. Are you able to adjust beliefs and attitudes as a result of learning from your experiences?

___ 12. Do you have a sense of humor?

___ 13. Do you experience peace of mind and tranquility?

___ 14. Are you free from a strong need for control or the need to be right?

___ 15. Are you able to fully experience (feel) painful emotions such as fear, anger, sadness, and hopelessness?

___ 16. Are you aware of and able to safely express such emotions?

___ 17. Do you take time to relax, or make time for hobbies and play?

___ 18. Do you experience joy?

___ 19. Do you enjoy high self-esteem?

___ 20. Is your sleep free of disturbing dreams?

Spirit: (Spiritual and Social Health)

___ 1. Do you actively commit time to your spiritual life, making time for prayer, meditation, or reflection?

___ 2. Do you listen to and act on your intuition?

___ 3. Are creative activities a part of your work or leisure time?

___ 4. Do you feel a connection to God, Spirit, or Higher Power?

___ 5. Are you grateful for the blessings in your life?

___ 6. Are you able to let go of your attachment to specific outcomes and embrace uncertainty?

___ 7. Do you take time away from work to rest and nurture yourself?

___ 8. Do you operate from a win-win philosophy when deciding the best course of action for a given situation?

___ 9. Do you feel your life has a sense of purpose?

___ 10. Are playfulness and humor important to you in your daily life?

___ 11. Are you able to forgive yourself and others?

___ 12. Do you experience intimacy, besides sex, in your committed relationships?

___ 13. Do you have one of more close friendships with someone you can confide in or speak openly with?

___ 14. Do you or did you feel close to your parents?

___ 15. If you have experienced the loss of a loved one, have you fully grieved that loss?

___ 16. Have your experiences of painful life challenges enabled you to grow spiritually?

___ 17. Do you donate to charities or volunteer your time to help others?

___ 18. Do you feel a sense of belonging to your "tribe" or community?

___ 19. Do you experience unconditional love?

___ 20. Do you enjoy spending time socializing with others?

The more Yes answers you have in each of the above categories, the more likely it is that you are doing well within them. Your No answers are indications of where you need to make improvements.

Assessing Your Levels of Chronic Stress and Depression

Chronic stress and depression are both common in our society today. Yet it is not unusual for people who suffer from these conditions to not be aware of the extent that they do so. For that reason, Dr. Sergey Sorin, MD, DABFM, who, along with Dr. Shealy, oversees the Shealy-Sorin Wellness Institute in Springfield, Missouri, recommends answering the following two questionnaires to determine to what degree depression and/or stress may be affecting you.

The first questionnaire is known as the Zung Self-Rating Depression Scale, which was developed by William W. Zung and first published more than 50 years ago.

Zung Self-Rating Depression Scale

For each of the 20 questions below, check the frequency which best describes how often you felt or behaved this way during the past several days as follows: V= Very little of the time, S= Some of the time, L= Large-part of the time, or M= Most of the time.

___ 1. I feel downhearted and blue.

___ 2. Morning is when I feel the best.

___ 3. I have crying spells or feel like it.

___ 4. I have trouble sleeping at night.

___ 5. I eat as much as I used to.

___ 6. I still enjoy sex.

___ 7. I notice that I am losing weight.

___ 8. I have trouble with constipation.

___ 9. My heart beats faster than usual.

___ 10. I get tired for no reason.

___ 11. My mind is as clear as it used to be.

___ 12. I find it easy to do the things I used to do.

___ 13. I am restless and can't keep still.

___ 14. I feel hopeful about the future.

___ 15. I am more irritable than usual.

___ 16. I find it easy to make decisions.

___ 17. I find I am useful and needed.

___ 18. My life is pretty full.

___ 19. I feel that others would be better off if I were dead.

___ 20. I still enjoy the things I used to.

Scoring Your Answers

For questions 1, 3, 4, 7-10, 13, 15, and 19, Very little of the Time (V) = a score of 1, Some of the Time (S) = a score of 2, Large-part of the Time (L) = a score of 3, and Most of the Time (M) = a score of 4.

For questions 2, 5, 6, 11, 12, 14, 16-18, and 20 the score numbers are reversed, with Very-little of the Time (V) = a score of 4, Some of the Time (S) = a score of 3, Large-part of the Time (L) = a score of 2, and Most of the Time (M) = a score of 1. Add up your total score.

If you scored 45 or above, you may indeed be prone to depression, with the highest scores indicative of greater severity. The lower your score is below 45, the less likely it is that depression is a factor affecting your health.

The Holmes-Rahe Social Readjustment Rating Scale

Drs. Shealy and Sorin also include the Holmes-Rahe Social Readjustment Rating Scale as part of their patients' overall personal stress assessments. This scale was developed in 1967 by psychiatrists Thomas Holmes and Richard Rahe following a study they conducted to determine whether or not stress contributed to physical illness. They surveyed over 5,000 medical students, asking them if they had experienced any of 43 life events (listed below) during the previous two years. They "weighted" each life event with a specific value for stress and found that the more of these life events the students had experienced, and the higher the total of each weighted event was, the more likely it was that illness would follow in the near future.

To take this test, circle the mean values that correspond with any life events listed below that you have experienced during the past two years.

Death of spouse	100
Divorce	73
Marital separation	65
Jail term	63

Death of a close family member	63
Personal injury or illness	53
Marriage	50
Fired at work	47
Marital reconciliation	45
Retirement	45
Change in health of family member	44
Pregnancy	40
Sexual difficulties	39
Gain of new family member	39
Business readjustment	39
Change in financial state	38
Death of close friend	37
Change to different line of work	36
Change in number of arguments with spouse	35
Mortgage over $20,000	31
Foreclosure of mortgage or loan	30
Change in responsibilities at work	29
Son or daughter leaving home	29
Trouble with in-laws	29
Outstanding personal achievement	28
Spouse begin or stop work	26
Begin or end school	25
Change in living conditions	24
Revision of personal habits	23
Trouble with boss	20
Change in work hours or conditions	20

Change in residence	20
Change in schools	19
Change in recreation	19
Change in church activities	18
Change in social activities	17
Mortgage or loan less than $20,000	16
Change in sleeping habits	15
Change in eating habits	15
Vacation, especially if away from home	13
Christmas, or other major holiday stress	12
Minor violations of the law	11

Add the above scores for the life events that apply to you.

Scores between 11 and 150 indicate a low to moderate chance of becoming ill in the near future, scores between 151 and 299 indicate a moderate to high chance (50%) of becoming ill, while scores of 300 and above indicate a high to very high risk (80%) of becoming ill within two years.

If your overall scores on the above tests indicate you are depressed, chronically stressed, or at a high risk for becoming ill, you need to take immediate action to reverse matters, which the rest of this book will empower you to do. Many of the stresses and risk factors for disease we face are in fact lifestyle choices over which you have complete control (if you are a smoker, you may need professional assistance in order to successfully quit). Decide to make better, healthier choices today. With time and commitment you will soon find your levels of stress diminishing, along with corresponding improvements in your health and mood.

Recommended Medical Tests

Although the above self-assessments can offer a more accurate indication of your current health status, they usually are not enough to provide you with a complete picture.

In the remainder of this chapter, you will learn about specific blood tests that you should consider having annually. Many physicians are unaware of some of these tests or simply fail to consider them for their patients. That's unfortunate, since all of these tests are extremely useful for detecting imbalances in your body that can lead to disease if they are left unchecked. While you can have your doctor order them for you, in most states in the U.S., you can also order them online via a number of reputable, high quality labs without the need for a doctor's prescription. Once you purchase the test, you will receive a lab requisition by email to print and take with you to a designated local lab where a sample of blood, etc. can be obtained from you. In some cases, you will be sent test kits for the tests you select and then, if necessary, you will go to a local partner facility that will collect your samples and send them back to the company for analysis.

Many of these tests are also available through the Life Extension Foundation (LEF). For more information, visit www.lef.org and click on the Lab Testing link. You will find the contact information for the other labs in the Resources section of this book.

Conventional Blood Tests

Even if you consider yourself to be in a state of good health, it's still wise to schedule a yearly checkup with your physician to know if and when there may be a need to make changes in your diet or other lifestyle factors. During such checkups, most doctors will likely order the following tests for you.

CBC blood test: The CBC (complete blood count) test measures the amount of red and white blood cells, plus platelets in your blood.

BUN blood test: BUN stands for "blood urea nitrogen". This test helps physicians assess kidney function. Elevated BUN levels are an indicator of possible kidney damage or disease.

Creatinine blood test: Creatinine is a waste product produced by your muscles and excreted by your kidneys. The creatinine test is usually ordered in conjunction with the BUN test to compare the ratio level of each substance. Healthy ratios of BUN to creatinine range from 10-1 to 20-1. Ratios above this range indicate a lack of blood flow to the kidneys, which can be an indicator of congestive heart failure, gastrointestinal bleeding, or chronic, low-grade dehydration, while ratios below this range can be signs of malnutrition or liver problems.

Glucose blood test: This test is used to determine your fasting blood sugar (glucose) level. For accurate results, you will need to fast for at least eight hours before the test is administered, and also refrain from drinking anything that contains sugar, including fruit juices. "It is acceptable to drink water during this eight-plus hour fast," Dr. Cowden says. Normal fasting blood glucose levels range from 70 to 100 mg/dL, although ideal levels are between 70 to 85 mg/dL. Levels above 100 mg/dL are indicators of prediabetes, while readings above 125 mg/dL indicate diabetes. Levels below 70 mg/dL are signs of hypoglycemia (low blood sugar), and can also be signs of underactive thyroid and/or adrenal gland function, pituitary gland disorders, or possible kidney or liver disease.

Lipid Panel: This test measures your HDL, LDL, total cholesterol, and triglyceride levels, all of which are markers for both cardiovascular health and disease. It is preferable to do a water fast for 12 hours before a blood lipid panel is drawn, Dr. Cowden advises. While this test remains important, cholesterol levels alone are not enough to accurately assess heart health. In addition, elevated LDL and total cholesterol levels often result in conventional MDs prescribing statin drugs for their patients, the consequences of which can be very dangerous.

25-hydroxy-vitamin D, or 1,25-dihydroxy vitamin D: These tests are used to determine vitamin D levels in your bloodstream.

Liver blood tests (ALT/AST/ALP/GGT): Assessing liver function is very important. One way for doing so is to measure liver enzymes known as *aminotranferases*. Two of the most common liver enzymes as alanine aminotransferase (ALT) and aspartate aminotransferase (AST). Elevated ALT and AST blood levels are indications of impaired liver function, liver damage or disease. Normal ranges of ALT and AST vary somewhat from lab to lab but are usually between 7 and 56 units and 5 to 40 units, respectively, per liter of blood serum.

"Alkaline phosphatase (ALP) is produced by liver bile ducts and by bone," Dr. Cowden explains. "If it is elevated, you could then do an alkaline phosphatase isoenzyme test to determine the source of the elevated ALP. The ALP isoenzyme from the bile duct source can increase because of inflammation in the bile ducts (cholecystitis), or from cancer in the liver, or from the biliary system. although this is less common. The ALP isoenzyme from bone can be elevated in children with rapid growth rates, in someone healing a bone fracture, in someone with more severe forms of arthritis or osteomyelitis, and when cancer is present in the bone."

Gamma-Glutamyl-Transferase (GGT) is an enzyme made in the liver bile ducts, kidneys and a few other organs. The GGT test measures the amount of GGT in the blood. It was originally used to screen for liver damage and the effects of alcoholism. When GGT is elevated, it often signifies inflammation in the liver bile ducts. If GGT is in the upper end of the normal range or above normal, there is an increased risk from several causes, so these causes for elevation should be further investigated. Alcohol consumption and taking of acetaminophen and various other pharmaceutical drugs, as well as infections in the liver and bile ducts, can result in elevation of ALT, AST, ALP and/or GGT. "Normal GGT levels in men range up to 70 U/L (units per liter), while normal levels for women range up to 45 U/L," Dr. Cowden says. "Ideal levels are less than 16 U/L for men, and less than 9 U/L for women."

Prothrombin Test: Also known as a PT or INR, this blood test is used to determine how well your body's blood clotting factors are working. It is used when people either bleed (including bleeding from the gums) or bruise easily, experience swollen or painful joints, or when blood clotting occurs when it shouldn't. It is also administered before surgical procedures, and ordered for women who experience heavy menstrual periods. Usually, it is administered in conjunction with another test known as the partial thromboplastin time test (PTT) to provide a more complete picture of what happens when a person forms blood clots.

In addition to analyzing the body's blood clotting performance and detecting bleeding or clotting disorders, these tests can be helpful in screening for liver problems, vitamin K deficiencies, immune diseases, certain types of cancer, such as leukemia.

Uric Acid Test: Uric acid is a waste product formed by the body's metabolism, or break down, of purines, which are found in meat, fish, and certain grains and legumes. Uric acid is also produced as cells die. Once produced, your body excretes it, primarily through urination.

The uric acid test is a blood test used to determine uric acid levels. In women, uric acid levels are considered elevated at any measurement about 6 mg/dL, while in men elevated levels are measurements above 7 mg/dL. Elevated uric acid levels can be an indication of gout, risk of kidney stones and other types of kidney disease, and cancer.

Other Medical Tests You Should Consider

In addition to the above blood tests, the following tests are also recommended. Be aware that many physicians will not suggest these tests unless you specifically ask for them. In many cases you can now order these tests on your own, as well.

Comprehensive Metabolic Panel (CMP): This test includes blood measurements of BUN, creatinine, glucose, ALP (alkaline phosphatase), ALT and AST. It also measures blood levels of albumin, calcium, carbon dioxide (bicarbonate), chloride, sodium, potassium, total bilirubin, and protein. The CMP test is very useful for assessing the your body's overall health metabolism, and chemical balance, and overall kidney and liver function. It can also be used to screen for various conditions, including diabetes, kidney disease, liver disease, and bone disease.

Comprehensive Vitamin and Mineral Panel Tests: These tests measure vitamin and mineral levels in the bloodstream to determine both vitamin and mineral deficiencies and excesses. Both of these tests can be measured with urine as well as blood.

Thyroid Panel: The thyroid panel test measures three thyroid hormones—T3, T4, and TSH. T3 is the active form of T4 and helps cells make use of digested food to create energy, rather than storing food as fat. T4 (thyroxine) can be bound with protein or remain unbound in the body. TSH (thyroid-stimulating hormone) is a hormone secreted by the pituitary gland that stimulates the thyroid to produce T4 and ultimately T3.

The thyroid panel blood test helps doctors determine how well the thyroid is functioning and screens for symptoms of both an overactive and underactive thyroid (hyperthyroidism and hypothyroidism, respectively), and Hashimoto's disease, an autoimmune disease that is the primary cause of hypothyroidism if it persists.

APOE4: The APOE4 test can determine if you are genetically predisposed to develop Alzheimer's disease or dementia. APOE is a gene that everyone has two copies of, receiving one copy from each parent. There are three variant APOE genes, which are known as alleles. They are APOE2, APOE3, and APOE4. The combination of these paired alleles determines your APOE genotype. Of the three, APOE2 is the rarest, and research shows that carrying even one copy can reduce your risk of developing Alzheimer's by as much as 40 percent. The most common APOE allele is APOE3. Research thus far indicates that APOE3 does not influence Alzheimer's risk.

Carrying even one copy of APOE4 has been shown to increase the risk for Alzheimer's by as much as 300 percent, while carrying two copies can increase the risk by 12-fold. Moreover, the presence of even one copy of APOE4 can also lower the age in which the disease first begins to develop.

It is estimated that between 10 to 15 percent of the human population carries at least one copy of APOE4. Given the risk it poses for Alzheimer's, it is a good idea to be tested to learn if you are one of them. To do so, you will need to take a gene, not a blood, test.

One of the easiest ways to obtain this test is through the company 23andMe ,which has been approved by the Food and Drug Administration (FDA) to provide genetic information for ten health risks, including APOE4 and Alzheimer's. You can find more information about the tests 23andMe offers by visiting their website (www.23andme.com).

It's important to stress that even if you are a carrier of the APOE4 gene it does not mean that you are fated to develop Alzheimer's or dementia. APOE4 is far from the only causative factor associated with these diseases. Moreover, it can only lead to Alzheimer's if it is "turned on" or triggered by a poor diet or other unhealthy lifestyle habits. Fortunately, there is much that you can do to significantly reduce your risk of developing Alzheimer's regardless of whether or not you are a carrier, starting with the self-care recommendations in this book.

B12 and Folic Acid (Folate) Tests: Many people today are deficient in B vitamins, most especially B12 and folic acid, which is why you should consider being tested to determine your blood levels of these vital nutrients. You can request these tests on their own, and they may also be included as part of the comprehensive vitamin panel test covered above. "If the B12 is low, methyl-B12 or hydroxy-B12 or adenosyl-B12, but not cyanocobalamin, should be used to correct the deficiency," Dr. Cowden says. "If the folate level is low, 5-methyl-tetrahydro-folate (5-MTHF) is the best supplement to correct the deficiency."

Homocysteine: Homocysteine is a non-protein-derived amino acid in the blood. Homocysteine levels are strongly influenced by your diet, as well as genetic factors. B vitamins such as vitamins B6 and B12, along with the active form of folate (5-MTHF) are necessary to help break down homocysteine in the body. A deficiency of these vitamins can cause an unhealthy increase in homocysteine. Elevated blood levels of homocysteine are indications of an increased risk of coronary heart disease, atherosclerosis, blood clots, heart attack, stroke, and systemic inflammation in the body.

The homocysteine test is useful for diagnosing malnutrition, folate and vitamin B12 deficiencies, and genetic defects in intracellular methylation enzymes. It can also help detect cardiovascular disease risk.

hs-C-reactive Protein (CRP) and Fibrinogen: These inexpensive tests measure the amount of the pro-inflammatory markers high sensitivity C-reactive protein, or hs-CRP, and fibrinogen in the bloodstream, and can be used to detect chronic inflammation and to monitor your progress as you work to reduce inflammation levels in your body. The hs-CRP test can also be used to determine your risk of heart disease and stroke.

Any hs-CRP reading above 3.0 mg/L is an indication of chronic inflammation. The higher the reading, the more likely it is that systemic chronic inflammation is present. The optimal hs-CRP level for men is anything under 0.55 mg/L, while for women it should be under 1.5 mg/L.

Fibrinogen is a protein that acts as a blood clotting agent. Like CRP, it is also a useful marker for determining the presence of chronic inflammation. In both men and women, the optimal fibrinogen level is between 295 - 370 mg/dL.

Hemoglobin A1C (A1C): The hemoglobin A1C test measures the average amount of glucose in the bloodstream over an 8 to 12 week time period. It is a far more accurate marker for diabetes (both type I and type II) and prediabetes than the blood glucose test mentioned above. Moreover, it can be administered without the need for fasting.

This test measures the thickness of the amount of glucose that is bound to the blood's hemoglobin, a protein found inside the red blood cells that transports oxygen to your cells, tissues, and organs, and which gives blood its red color. There are different types of hemoglobin, but its main form is hemoglobin A.

When glucose binds with it, hemoglobin gets a "coating" of sugar attached to it. The coat thickens as the amount of glucose in the blood increases. Since the A1C test measures your glucose levels over a three-month time period, it provides a much more accurate reading of how high your glucose is, compared to the snapshot glimpse provided by the blood glucose test.

A healthy A1C reading is 5.6 percent or lower. Readings between 5.7 to 6.4 percent indicate prediabetes, while readings above 6.4 percent are an indication of diabetes. Elevated A1C readings have also been linked to a variety of other serious health conditions, including heart disease, stroke, nerve damage, kidney disease, and eye damage which, if left unchecked, can result in blindness.

Ferritin Test: This test screens for iron overload and excess free iron (unbound iron in the blood). While iron plays many important roles in the body, as Stephen Sinatra, MD, a world-renowned cardiologist and a pioneer in the field of metabolic cardiology, explains, "Too much iron can cause oxidative stress and can be toxic."

Dr. Sinatra recommends that serum ferritin levels be checked to screen for iron overload and possible inborn genetic errors of metabolism, such as hereditary hemochromatosis, which is characterized by an accumulation of dangerously high levels of iron. "That's why any male over the age of 18 should never take iron in a multivitamin because, again, iron accumulates in the body," he adds.

The ferritin test measures iron storage in the body. While ferritin ranges between 200 to 300 ng/mL are considered normal by laboratories for both women and men, an ideal range is between 30 and 80 ng/mL for men and non-menstruating women, according to Dr. Cowden. (Menstruating women are more likely to suffer from iron deficiency than iron overload.)

High levels of ferritin are indications of an increased risk for chronic diseases (heart attack, stroke, dementia and even cancer) due to excess stored iron (ferritin).

Both excess stored and unbound levels of iron tend to rise as we age. This is especially true for middle-aged men and postmenopausal women. Fortunately, you can easily reduce excess iron levels by donating blood a few times each year, exercising regularly, and reducing your intake of red meat.

Mg RBC: Magnesium is vitally important to overall health, yet most people are chronically deficient in magnesium.

In a standard serum (blood) test, magnesium levels often appear as normal, leading doctors to tell their patients they do not need to increase their magnesium levels. What many doctors fail to understand is that magnesium levels in the serum is much less important than the levels of magnesium inside red blood cells, which is where magnesium is most needed in order for it to carry out its hundreds of important functions. The Mg RBC test measures the amount of magnesium inside the red blood cells and is a far more accurate measurement of your body's overall magnesium status.

The normal range for magnesium inside red blood cells is between 5.0 to 7.0 mg/dL. Levels of 5.5 mg/dL or higher are more optimal.

MTHFR: MTHFR is an abbreviation for a gene that codes for an enzyme called *methylenetetrahydrofolate reductase*. This enzyme produces 5-methyl-tetra-hydro-folate (5MTHF) in our cells, which is important for converting homocysteine into methionine. As mentioned above, homocysteine is toxic and the body needs methionine for proper metabolism and muscle growth and to make S-adenosyl-methionine (SAMe), the body's most important methylator.

People with a mutation of MTHFR may have difficulty eliminating toxins from the body. In addition, mutations in the *MTHFR* gene have been linked to thrombosis and heart disease, and can lead to blood clots, stroke, embolism, and/or heart attacks. MTHFR mutations can also be a factor in elevated homocysteine levels. The risk of birth defects and difficult pregnancies can also be increased when MTHFR mutations are present.

A blood test can be used to determine whether or not you have a MTHFR mutation. If you do, don't despair. There are a number of effective options you can use to address this issue, starting with supplementing with a bioavailable form of folic acid called methyl-folate (a fermented folic acid). You should also consume more folate-rich foods, such as asparagus, avocado, broccoli, lentils and other legumes, spinach and other leafy green vegetables, and bright-colored fruits.

Comprehensive Female or Male Hormone Panel: This test is available either as a single blood draw or a spit test in which saliva is collected multiple times over a 24-hour period. Blood and/or saliva samples are then sent to a lab for testing.

Hormone panel tests on saliva or blood typically measure the cycling and production of cortisol, DHEA, estradiol, pregnenolone, progesterone, and testosterone. Blood only is used to test thyroid hormones and sex hormone binding globulin (SHBG).

Once you know your hormone levels, you can then work with a physician trained in the use of hormone balancing to bring your hormones into balance, if necessary. Adopting the self-care recommendations in this book will also help you keep your hormone levels balanced and healthy.

DHEA: Dr. Shealy considers DHEA to be "the single most important chemical in evaluating health and longevity." He and Dr. Sorin have both found low DHEA levels to be associated with a wide range of diseases, ranging from anxiety and depression, autoimmune and immune disease, cancer, chronic fatigue, dementia, diabetes, heart disease, high blood pressure, low libido, and obesity, among others. In his book, *Life Beyond 100*, Dr. Shealy wrote that 100 percent of thousands of patients he tested at his clinic had DHEA levels that were "at best, fair to low", and 50 percent were found to have serious DHEA deficiency, regardless of the disease they presented with.

DHEA levels are highest in early adulthood, and then begin to decline around age 30, when the body begins to convert DHEA into DHEA-sulfate (DHEA-s). DHEA-s is the form of DHEA that most doctors who use hormone tests screen for. Dr. Shealy and Dr. Sorin recommend measuring DHEA levels, as well. The lab they recommend for ordering this test is Quest Diagnostics Nichols Institute. You contact them at: Quest Diagnostics Nichols Institute, 33608 Ortega Hwy, San Juan Capistrano, CA 92675. Phone: (800) 642-4657.

VAP Test: The VAP (Vertical Auto Profile) test is one of the most accurate blood tests you can use to determine your risk for developing heart disease and stroke. Unlike the conventional cholesterol panel covered above, which only measures HDL, LDL, total cholesterol, and triglyceride levels and is only capable of identifying 40 percent of people at risk for heart disease or stroke, the VAP test provides a far more comprehensive look at your cholesterol profile. It not only more accurately and directly measures LDL ("bad") cholesterol, it also measures what is known as LDL pattern density. This is crucial, because smaller, denser LDL patterns can increase the risk of arterial plaque and heart disease by as much as 300 percent.

Just as importantly, the VAP test screens for and measures the following:

- Very-Low-Density Lipoprotein (VLDL), the main carrier for triglycerides. An elevated VLDL level can be another significant risk factor for heart disease. There are three types of VLDL, VLDL1, VLDL2, and VLDL3. Of these VLDL3 is the smallest types and poses the greatest risk.

- Non-HDL Cholesterol (the total of LDL and VLDL levels combined). Elevated levels of non-HDL cholesterol are a better measurement of heart disease risk than LDL levels alone.

- Lipoprotein(a), or Lp(a), a genetic risk factor for heart disease. Lp(a) is more dangerous than other types of cholesterol, and does not respond to traditional cholesterol-lowering drugs.

- LDL Size Pattern. LDL particles vary in size, ranging from small, dense "Pattern B" particles to larger, less dense "Pattern A" particles. Smaller LDL particles are associated with an increased risk for heart disease, insulin resistance, and diabetes.

- HDL subfractions HDL2 and HDL3, which also provide better indications of heart disease risk. HDL2 is large and buoyant, and is the most protective form of HDL cholesterol. Low levels of HDL2 with normal or above normal levels of LDL can increase the risk of heart disease. In addition, HDL3 is not as protective as HDL2.

- Intermediate-Density Lipoprotein (IDL), another genetic risk factor for heart disease.

- Real LDL, a measurement of the actual cholesterol circulating in your body. Real LDL is calculated by subtracting Lp(a) and IDL from LDL.

The VAP test is also effective for detecting metabolic syndrome, another significant risk factor for heart disease, stroke, and type II diabetes.

The Brain Gauge—Measuring The Health Of Your Brain

Brain health and functioning is too often overlooked by physicians until a patient begins to exhibit signs of cognitive decline or has suffered from a concussion or other types of traumatic brain injury (TBI). At that point, cognitive testing may be recommended. Expensive diagnostic screening tests, such as a functional magnetic resonance imaging (fMRI) or a SPECT scan, may also be used to examine the physical shape of the brain and any possible anomalies in its structure. The results of such tests will then be used by physicians to determine the best possible course of treatment.

As with all other aspects of your health, monitoring your brain health to detect early signs of potential diminished brain function makes much better sense than waiting for actual decline to set in and advance before it is treated. Thanks to an innovative device known as the Brain Gauge, you now can effectively monitor your brain health at home as often as you wish in as little as 15 minutes each time.

The Brain Gauge is the result of over 20 years of research conducted by Mark Tommerdahl, PhD, associate professor at the University of North Carolina at Chapel Hill. Dr. Tommerdahl's interest in measuring brain health began in the 1980s when he was working as analysis engineer at a neurophysiology lab while pursuing his PhD and studying patterns of brain activity in response to tactile (touch) stimulation. "These patterns can be extremely complicated, but they're also very robust and very redundant," Dr. Tommerdahl explains. "In other words, there are very repeatable brain response patterns to specific types of stimuli. I was interested in looking at how different interactions occurred between different regions of the brain."

Based on his work at that time, Dr. Tommerdahl hypothesized about how brain patterns could be altered based on neurological insults and other types of stimuli. "We tested this hypothesis with pharmacological insults and surgical insults in nonhuman primates as well as some other animal models," he says. "And we have a fair amount of success developing an understanding of how those patterns of brain activity were altered or would be altered under different types of insult."

Beginning in 2004, Dr. Tommerdahl conducted sensory experiments with human subjects using tactile stimulators and looking at how those sensory experiments correlated with the animal experiments. "We found very good correlation, but at the time we were using tactile stimulators that weighed about a hundred pounds. It was a lot to carry around, making conducting the tactile experiments very difficult."

Dr. Tommerdahl continued his experiments and a few years later, a conversation with another UNC professor, Bob Dennis, PhD, led them to begin work together. "I told Bob that if we could deliver stimuli to two places on the skin and deliberate with high fidelity, we could probably answer a lot of questions about many neurological disorders and about brain health." Dr. Dennis was convinced Dr.

Tommerdahl was right and offered to help. Their collaboration led them to develop the world's first portable tactile stimulator. "It weighed about 15 pounds and allowed us to stimulate people's skin in two places and studied the interaction between the stimulation and the brain pattern responses," Dr. Tommerdahl says. "That study was sponsored by a grant from the U.S. Army to study autism. We achieved some significant findings with that. We then started looking at chronic pain, alcoholism, and then concussion and TBI in the sports concussion field and after a couple of years in that field we had significant data."

As their research continued, so did outside research funding, including from the Office of Naval Research's BLAST program, and the joint National Football League General Electric Head Health Challenge. Eventually, Drs. Tommerdahl and Dennis cofounded the company Cortical Metrics and developed the Brain Gauge, a tactile stimulator device that looks similar to a computer mouse and connects to any desktop or laptop computer. Today, brain research using the Brain Gauge is being conducted at more than 50 prestigious universities around the world besides UNC, including Harvard, Duke. Johns Hopkins, Cornell, Mount Sinai School of Medicine, the University of Michigan, and MIT, among others.

The Brain Gauge measures changes in information processing in the brain and delivers rapid, reliable, objective assessments of brain health at a very low cost. The Brain Gauge method takes advantage of the relationship between the nerves in the finger tips and the interactions that take place in the individual's brain that result from the vibration. These interactions in the brain characteristically deteriorate when brain health declines or the brain is injured, and improve with recovery.

The Brain Gauge delivers mechanical vibrations to two finger tips placed over two sensors. During each test, the two sensors will "buzz" your fingertips in a specific way. The app that comes with the device asks questions about what you felt, and then analyzes your responses using clinically-proven neuroscience. In less than 15 minutes, you can complete a comprehensive brain health assessment and gain valuable insight into your mental fitness based on a measurement of eight essential components of brain health: Speed, Focus, Fatigue, Accuracy, Sequencing, Timing Perception, Plasticity, and Connectivity. After each session, you will also receive a comprehensive mental fitness score called your cortical metric. Although the science is based on a large number of complex interactions between these two areas, Brain Gauge is an easy to use test, similar to a game, with easy to interpret results, making it the quickest and most accurate way to assess your current level of mental fitness and to track improvements to it over time.

Another exciting benefit offered by the Brain Gauge is its ability to measure and track how effective your diet, any supplements or medications you may be taking, and any medical treatments you are receiving, are based on how your brain responds to them for better or worse. It can also measure and monitor how well you sleep, and monitor symptoms of chronic pain, and indicate signs of neurological and neuro-developmental issues. In addition, because the Brain Gauge tests are adaptive, they will keep you challenged and engaged, even as your cognitive skills improve.

The Brain Gauge Home model is available for outright purchase ($499.00) or on a subscription contract for as low as $19/month for a six-month contract, or $29 for a month by month contract. The Brain Gauge Home model offers unlimited testing for up to five users and there are no long-term commitments for users who chose a subscription plan. For more information about Brain Gauge, visit www.corticalmetrics.com.

CHAPTER 2

The Second Key:
Putting Out the Fire of
Inflammation and Discovering
The Diet That Is Most Right For You

I N THIS CHAPTER, you are going to learn how and why you must safeguard yourself against chronic inflammation and how discovering and adopting the diet that is most appropriate for you is perhaps the most essential step you can take to eliminate this most serious threat to your health. There is no "one size fits all" diet for everyone. You are a unique individual with specific dietary and nutritional needs. Therefore, the key to healthy eating is finding and then following the diet that is most suitable to you. This chapter will empower you to do exactly that, without having to rely on a doctor.

You may currently suffer from some degree of chronic inflammation and not be aware of it. Yet, if you experience any sort of lingering health challenge, you can be sure that persistent inflammation is involved.

Under normal circumstances, inflammation acts as a natural healing mechanism in your body. It is short-lived and acts as a vital immune response. Without it, your body could not act to heal wounds, burns, or other injuries, nor could it protect you from harmful bacteria, viruses, and other microorganisms. This type of inflammation response is known as acute inflammation. Once wounds, burns, etc heal, or the harmful microorganisms are dealt with, the inflammatory response will subside. However, when the inflammation response becomes chronic, meaning when it does not subside as nature intended, it sets the stage for a wide variety of health problems to occur.

"Chronic inflammation that is not controlled by the body is a major part or cause of a number of diseases," explains William Pawluk, M.D., a well-known integrative and ACIM member physician based in Baltimore, Maryland". "Uncontrolled inflammation causes accumulated molecular damage that is largely responsible for aging. Immune system imbalance, especially over-activity, causes the body to start attacking its own tissues resulting in chronic inflammation. This is seen most commonly in arthritis, autoimmune diseases, and certain cancers."

Chronic inflammation typically occurs when an acute inflammation response fails to heal or resolve an injury or infection, but it can also occur in the absence of injury or infection. When it does so, it is almost always due to a variety of other factors, all of which act as stressors in the body that trigger an ongoing inflammation response. One of the most significant of these stressors is an unhealthy diet.

Left undetected or ignored, chronic inflammation will usually continue to progress to the point where it manifests as a disease condition. In the process, the compounds and immune cells that play a role in acute inflammation can start to change, eventually causing ongoing damage to healthy organs and tissues in your body.

Because chronic inflammation usually does not present with the obvious symptoms characteristic of acute inflammation, it often goes undiagnosed by conventional physicians despite its harmful effects, which can be life-threatening. In 2011,the Centers for Disease Control and Prevention (CDC) noted chronic, low-level inflammation contributes to the onset and progression of at least seven of the ten leading causes of death by disease in the United States: heart disease, cancer, chronic lower respiratory disease, stroke, Alzheimer's disease, diabetes, and kidney disease. Since then, the range of disease conditions caused by chronic inflammation has continued to expand. ACIM and other integrative physicians teach their patients that unless and until chronic inflammation is properly dealt with and eliminated, the diseases it can cause cannot and will not be healed.

The Dietary Link

When chronic inflammation occurs, the body's immune system becomes locked into an "on" position, continuing to operate as if the body is facing harmful infections and/or has been injured in some way, when in actuality neither of those issues is present. A primary factor that causes the immune system to become "stuck" in this "on" position is an unhealthy diet. Such diets can even include otherwise healthy foods to which you may be sensitive or allergic.

Most of the causes of chronic inflammation originate and consequently wreck havoc in your gut. Research continues to establish how closely interrelated immune function is to the health of the body's overall gastrointestinal system. Suboptimal gastrointestinal function results in diminished immune function while simultaneously triggering and maintaining the body's inflammatory response.

"Our foods can either be inflammatory or anti-inflammatory," Dr. Pawluk says. "We need to decrease our intake of inflammatory foods and increase our intake of anti-inflammatory foods. Foods such as conventionally-produced red meat and refined carbohydrates cause inflammation in your body, so eliminating or reducing them in your diet can keep you healthier."

Examples of inflammation-promoting diets include those that are high in sugars and carbohydrates (particularly simple, or "white" carbohydrates such as breads, pastas, and white rice), foods and beverages containing artificial sweeteners and colorings, unhealthy oils and trans-fatty acids, excessive amounts of conventionally-produced meats and dairy products, and other foods that have an acidifying effect in the body once they are metabolized. These foods are especially inflammation-promoting in diets that lack healthy saturated fats and fresh fruits and vegetables. Inadequate water intake throughout the day can also cause or worsen chronic inflammation, as can an excessive consumption of grains.

Eating batter-fried or barbequed foods or starchy foods, especially if they are over-cooked, is another common cause of chronic inflammation. Such foods unleash what are known as advanced glycation end products (AGEs) into the bloodstream. AGEs are formed by an unhealthy binding of dietary sugars with body proteins and fats. Besides triggering inflammation, they also generate free radicals, causing free radical damage and oxidative stress on the body's tissues and organs. The consumption of fast, or "junk", foods is another significant trigger of chronic inflammation. "Fast foods are called that because they speed you to your grave," Dr. Cowden says.

"Avoiding such foods, while increasing your intake of anti-inflammatory foods is an important strategy for reducing and preventing chronic inflammation," Dr. Pawluk states. "The body needs its own high levels of anti-inflammatory support molecules, called antioxidants, which act to keep chronic inflammation under better control, not allowing it to become worse, while also slowing down the aging process. One of the best ways to maintain high levels of antioxidant, anti-inflammatories in the body is through daily nutrition. You are what you eat. Eating foods and nutrients that nature has provided, and are readily available, will go a long way to keeping you healthy."

High on the list of foods Dr. Pawluk recommends eating regularly are avocadoes, organic berries (especially blueberries, strawberries, blackberries and raspberries), wild-caught fish (cod, halibut, mackerel, lake and river trout, salmon, sardines, and snapper), cruciferous vegetables (broccoli, Brussels sprouts, and cauliflower), mushrooms, tomatoes, and, as a treat, dark chocolate with 70 percent or more cacao. He also recommends organic olive oil, organic green tea, and the spice turmeric.

Unhealthy Foods and Beverages

The first step to maximizing your diet's ability to improve and maintain your health is to know what foods and beverages you need to avoid. Regardless of your unique biochemical makeup, you need to eliminate the following types of foods and drinks altogether.

Genetically Modified Foods (GMOs): Also known as genetically engineered (GE) or bioengineered (BE) foods, GMOs are widely found in America's food supply, and the number of different foods that are becoming genetically modified continues to increase. Until recently, GMOs were limited to plant foods. Now, however, GMOs are moving into animal food products, as well, starting with GMO salmon, which the Food and Drug Administration (FDA) has approved for human consumption.

Although the FDA and the US Department of Agriculture (USDA continue to insist that GMO foods are safe for human consumption, this fact has never been established with long-term human safety studies, while various animal studies indicate the potential GMOs have to cause or increase the risk of cancer and other serious diseases.

From 1999 to 2013, scientists from 29 countries signed on to an open letter that was submitted to the United Nations, the World Health Organization (WHO), and the United States Congress demanding a moratorium on the further release of GMOs into the environment because they were "extremely concerned about the hazards of GMOs to biodiversity, food safety, human and animal health" (The letter can be read at www.i-sis.org.uk/list.php).

A subsequent report entitled *Ban GMOs Now*, written by Dr. Mae-Wan Ho and Dr Eva Sirinathsinghji, published by the organization Science and Society, further outlined the dangers GMOs pose to human health, the world's food supply, and biodiversity in general. (You can read an executive summary of this report, and download the entire document, at www.i-sis.org.uk/Ban_GMOs_Now.php). Thus far, the recommendations made in the open letter and this report continue to be ignored by government agencies and the manufacturers of GMOs.

GMO foods harm the body in a number of ways because the DNA these foods contain are foreign to the body and cannot be effectively digested when consumed. Thus, GMOs can trigger serious, even life-threatening allergic reactions and autoimmune diseases, and trigger ongoing inflammation. ACIM physicians routinely find that the health of their patients quickly and significantly improves once they eliminate GMO foods from their diet.

Avoiding GMO foods requires diligence, however. It also means avoiding certain foods altogether, such as corn and soybeans, both of which are almost entirely genetically modified if grown in the United States. Moreover, corn and corn-derivatives such as corn starch and corn syrup, especially high fructose corn syrup, are common additives in most canned, boxed, and other types of packaged and processed foods. In addition, GMO corn and soybeans are both used to feed livestock, poultry, and farm-raised fish by most commercial meat, poultry, and fish producers due to how inexpensive they are.

Most cottonseed grown in the US is also genetically-modified, and is also used to feed livestock for the same reason. These are just some of the reasons you should always choose meats and poultry derived from grass-fed, pasture-raised animals, and also opt for wild-caught fish that are low in mercury (see below).

A recent food entry you should also be aware of and avoid is the Impossible Burger, so named because it mimics actual hamburgers in appearance, texture, and taste. Its manufacturer, Impossible Foods, touts it as an eco-friendly alternative to burgers derived from conventionally raised livestock, which typically require approximately 30 pounds of herbicide-laden corn and soy for every pound of hamburger produced. But as Dr. Joseph Mercola points out, grass-fed cattle never eat corn or soy, only grass that is free of herbicides. Another worrisome aspect of the Impossible Burger is that it is made from GMO soy. Not only is GMO soy not healthy for you, but, as Dr. Mercola also notes, GMO soy crop production "is associated with resistant super weeds and super pests and uncontrollable cross contamination" and takes a significant toll on the environment. Thus, claims that the Impossible Burger is somehow eco-friendly are highly suspect.

To learn more about the Impossible Burger, read Dr. Mercola's analysis on his website (https://articles.mercola.com/sites/articles/archive/2019/06/26/impossible-burger.aspx).

Foods Laced With Antibiotics and Growth Hormones: It's a sad reality that all conventionally raised livestock and poultry in the U.S. today are laced with growth hormones and antibiotics before they are slaughtered to enter our nation's food supply. The same thing is true for many farm-raised fish. Growth hormones are used to accelerate the growth of these animals, typically at twice their natural rate, in order to get their food products to market faster. These same animals are also laced with antibiotics in order to protect them from the unnatural diets they are fed, and to mitigate infectious illnesses they are more susceptible to due to the unsanitary, overcrowded, "factory farming" conditions in which they are raised. In fact, since 1993, even cow's milk and other dairy products derived from conventionally raised cows has been found to contain growth hormones, including IGF-1, which is known to increase the risk of cancer. Conventionally raised livestock also have higher levels of stress hormones which flood their system before they are slaughtered.

All of these harmful substances enter your body whenever you eat foods derived from animals and fish raised this way. To maintain and improve your health, you need to avoid consuming such foods whenever possible. "Also educate other family members and friends and encourage them to educate their friends about the harmful effects of GMO foods and conventionally-produced animal-derived foods so that they can learn how to avoid these Franken-foods," Dr. Cowden advises. "You pay only a little bit more for healthy foods than for Franken-foods but you can save much more in subsequent healthcare costs if you eat only healthy foods. If enough of the American public buy healthy foods instead of Franken-foods, the big corporations producing the Franken-foods will possibly go out of business or change to producing healthy foods. If we can't get the US Congress to pass legislation to protect us, then we can 'vote' at the grocery store by how we spend our money."

Foods Laced With Pesticides and Herbicides: Each year nearly eight billion pounds of pesticides are sprayed world-wide on conventionally grown food crops, with the most prevalent use among developed nations being in the U.S. Alarming amounts of herbicides are used, as well. They are also used on the feed given to conventionally raised livestock and poultry. Meats from conventionally raised livestock on average contain five times (500%) the amount of pesticides found in nonorganic vegetables, while nonorganic butter has up to 20 times (2,000%) the amount of pesticides of nonorganic vegetables.

Pesticides and herbicides, when ingested, pose serious health risks because of the various ways they disrupt the body's natural healing systems. One of the primary health risks they cause is "leaky gut syndrome" because of how they perforate the inner lining of the gastrointestinal (GI) tract. When this occurs, undigested food particles and the harmful chemicals they contain pass from the GI tract into the bloodstream, causing systemic inflammation, allergic and autoimmune reactions, and increasing the risk for cancer and other serious illnesses.

Like GMOs, chemical pesticides and herbicides have never been tested for long-term human safety. In the past few decades, one of the most harmful and prevalent pesticides that has entered our nation's food supply is glyphosate, the main ingredient in RoundUp and other commercial weedkillers. Unlike other pesticides and herbicides, many of which, at least to some extent, can be washed off from conventionally grown fruits and vegetables, glyphosate penetrates inside food crops and cannot be washed off. Eating glyphosate-laced foods wreaks havoc in your body and increases your risk for certain cancers.

The use of glyphosate is now so prevalent that human population studies have found that virtually all Americans have glyphosate residues in their bodies. Glyphosate has also been found in 70 percent of our nation's drinking water and even in the air we breathe. Fortunately, thanks to the discoveries of ACIM physician Dr. Zach Bush, we now know that nature itself has provided the means for effectively protecting us from glyphosate, using a product Dr. Bush developed called ION*Gut Health. You will learn more about ION*Gut Health and the important health benefits it provides in Chapter 3.

Given the higher levels of pesticides and herbicides found in nonorganic meats and butter, if you are on a budget, Dr. Cowden recommends spending your money first on organic meats and butter, followed by organic fruits, and then vegetables. If you cannot avoid buying nonorganic fruits and vegetables, focus on those that have the lowest amount of pesticide/herbicide content. You can find lists of these foods by visiting the website of the Environmental Working Group (EWG.org), starting with their free annual report *Shopper's Guide To Pesticides in Produce*™. EWG also provides other resources that can help you make healthier food buying choices, as well as information about how you can help get rid of glyphosate in our food supply.

If you do buy nonorganic produce, be sure to clean them before eating. According to research published in the *Journal of Agricultural and Food Chemistry*, one of the most effective ways of doing so is to make a solution of water and baking soda, which was found to be the most thorough way of cleansing pesticide residues on apples (nonorganic apples typically have a high pesticide residue content). Simply combine one ounce of baking soda (be sure it does not contain aluminum) with 100 ounces of water and soak your produce in this solution for 15 minutes, then rinse and pat dry.

Another way to have organic, fresh greens for your meals is to grow them inside your home near a window in potting soil. Methods for doing so are described in the book *Year-Round Indoor Salad Gardening* by Peter Burke. "Doing this will be more nutritious than eating salad-makings from the grocery store harvested many days or even weeks before you buy them and will cost about 90 percent less," Dr. Cowden says.

Processed Foods: Processed foods are any foods that contain artificial food additives and preservatives. They include all packaged foods, fast foods, and nonorganic snacks. While preservatives can and do preserve the shelf life and sell-by dates of such foods, their chemical nature can be harmful to the body, triggering inflammation, damaging cellular DNA, and disrupting hormone balance, thus increasing your risk of chronic degenerative diseases. The same is true of artificial food additives.

One of the most prevalent preservatives is monosodium

glutamate (MSG), which is also labeled as "textured protein", "soy protein isolate", or "natural flavoring", and other seemingly innocent designations. Other common preservatives and additives are aspartame (Equal and NutraSweet), saccharin (Sweet'N'Low), sodium nitrate, sucralose (Splenda), BHT, BHA, potassium bromate, carrageenan, food dyes, and other so-called natural food colorings. For the sake of your health, do your best to avoid processed foods altogether.

Dairy Products: Nonorganic milk, butter, and other dairy products contain high levels of antibiotics, growth hormones, and pesticides. And even if they did not, humans are still not suited for consuming them. (Organic butter, yogurt, and yogurt products such as kefir can be exceptions, depending on whether or not your system can tolerate them.) This truth becomes evident when you examine the effect dairy products have on your body's lymphatic system. (You will learn more about your lymphatic system, why it is so important for your health, and how you can keep it healthy in Chapter 5.) Regular consumption of milk and other dairy products causes the lymphatic system to become clogged, thus impairing its functioning.

Milk and other dairy products also create excess mucus in the body, especially within the intestines, lungs, and sinuses, and often results in chronic acidity, taxing the body's pH-balancing mechanisms. Chronic acidic buildup in the body's cells, tissues, and organs can lead to a wide range of serious health conditions.

For all of the above reasons, eliminating, or at least minimizing, your consumption of dairy products is another wise choice you can make for your health. Unsweetened coconut milk, almond milk and macadamia nut milk are good-tasting milk substitutes that can be used for recipes. Coconut yogurt, almond yogurt, and Kite-Hill almond cheeses are also good dairy substitutes.

Farm-Raised Fish/Fish High in Heavy Metals and Other Toxins: While fish can be a healthy addition to your overall diet, it's important to avoid consuming fish that are high in mercury and other heavy metals and toxins, and to avoid farm-raised fish because of the antibiotics, food dyes, and other harmful substances they contain, and the unnatural, pesticide-laden diets they are fed.

As pollution continues to take a toll on our world's oceans, rivers, and lakes, fish ingest heavy metals (especially mercury) and other toxins, and also are irradiated as they swim through waterways contaminated with nuclear waste. This is especially true of shellfish and larger bony fish, all of which should only be eaten sparingly. The best seafood choices are smaller fish such as sardines, anchovies, and wild-caught salmon. To see which fish have the lowest levels of mercury and other heavy metals, take advantage of the free report entitled *The Smart Seafood Buying Guide* created by the Natural Resources Defense Council. It is available at www.nrdc.org/stories/ smart-seafood-buying-guide. In addition, when you do eat fish, consider taking a heavy metal-binding supplement such as modified citrus pectin or cell-wall-cracked chlorella immediately after your meal.

Sugar and Simple/Refined Carbohydrate ("White") Foods: The average American consumes 150 pounds of simple or refined sugar each and every year. This equates to more than 40 teaspoons of sugar a day. Sugar's many harmful effects include increasing the risk of heart disease, weakening the immune system and increasing susceptibility to infection, stimulating excessive insulin production, increasing the production of harmful triglycerides, diminishing mental function, increasing feelings of anxiety and depression, increasing the risk of cancer, and increasing systemic yeast overgrowth (candidiasis).

To eliminate sugar from your diet, it is important that you read food labels, since sugar is a common ingredient in packaged foods in the forms of fructose, sucrose, corn syrup, lactose, and maltose. In general, foods that are canned, processed, or cured are also likely to be high in sugar. Healthy sugar substitutes include small amounts of raw, organic honey, stevia extract, monk fruit sweetener (also known as Lo Han Guo extract), and, if eaten sparingly, dark chocolate. "Dark chocolate sweetened with only stevia or monk fruit is best," Dr. Cowden says.

Refined carbohydrates act in much the same way that sugar does when consumed and metabolized in your body, and should also be avoided. The most common health risks when these foods, which include white breads, pastas made from white flour, instant mashed potatoes, white rice, chips, and sugar laden commercial cereals, are consumed on a regular basis are excessive insulin production, excessive fat storage, and elevated blood sugar levels.

Hydrogenated Oils, Trans Fats, and Excessive Omega-6 Oils: Certain fats are essential for good health. Unfortunately, many people, instead of eating foods rich in healthy fats, consume harmful fats such as trans-fatty acids and hydrogenated fats, which have been linked to a host of disease conditions, including arteriosclerosis, heart attack, angina, cancer, kidney failure, and obesity. Trans-fatty acids and hydrogenated fats are commonly found in margarine, cooking fats, commercial peanut butter, commercial cereals, and packaged foods.

Omega-6 oils are a different story. Unlike trans- and hydrogenated oils and fats, omega 6 essential fatty acids (EFAs) are good for us if taken in the correct amounts, as are omega-3 EFAs. All fats that naturally occur in foods are good for us, whereas trans, or partially hydrogenated, fats, which are manmade, are not.

EFAs are vital for good health. They make up part of the body's cell membranes and are particularly concentrated in the adrenal glands, brain cells, eyes, nerve cells, and the sex glands. Without enough EFAs, your body cannot adequately produce enough energy, regulate hormone production and proper nerve function, maintain brain health, and maintain the proper functioning of its musculoskeletal system. EFAs are not produced by your body and must be obtained through the foods you eat or as omega oil supplements.

Both omega-3 and omega-6 EFAs are found in unsaturated fats and oils. The problem with unsaturated fats lies in how prevalent they have become, disrupting the balance between the omega-3 and omega-6 oils.

For much of human history, the dietary balance between omega-3 and omega-6 fatty acids was approximately 1:1. This healthy ratio is what nature intended. Today, that ratio has been skewed to between 1:8 to 1:15, and for some people it's as much as 1:25. In fact, researchers have established that at least 9 percent of the total amount of calories consumed by the average American today come from polyunsaturated fats high in omega-6 fatty acids. That research also established that omega-6s begin to create toxicity in our bodies when they exceed 4 percent of our total daily caloric intake.

One of the main reasons why most people are consuming far too much omega-6 oils is because of how widespread the use of the vegetable oils that contain them has become. These oils include canola oil, corn oil, cottonseed oil, grapeseed oil, peanut oil, rapeseed oil, rice brain oil, safflower oil, soybean oil, sunflower oil, vegetable oil, and wheat germ oil. Because these oils are cheaper alternatives to healthier oils such as flaxseed, walnut, and olive oil (oils that are high in omega-3 fatty acids, especially the first two), they are staple ingredients in many canned and packaged foods. Because of their lower cost, these oils are also used by most restaurants and other dining establishments in the United States.

The biggest health threat posed by excess omega-6 oil consumption is chronic inflammation and oxidation within the tissues and organs of the body. To protect yourself against this problem use omega-6 oils sparingly, if at all, when you cook or bake at home, and check the labels of canned and packaged foods when you go shopping. For cooking, Dr. Cowden recommends using coconut oil or white palm kernel oil, which are fully saturated and cannot form trans-fats or oxidized fats when cooked.

Foods Packaged In Plastic: To some degree, you are most likely ingesting plastic on a regular basis, especially if you drink from plastic water bottles, eat foods packaged or wrapped in plastic (plastic wraps), or placed in plastic food containers, because the plastic they contain leaches into food and beverages. Seafood is also a source of plastic because of the high amounts of plastics now found in our oceans. Another plastic contaminant is bisphenol-A (BPA), an ingredient found in the linings of canned food and some plastic bottles.

Plastic contains chemicals, including BPA and phthalates, which disrupt the body's endocrine (hormone) functions because of how they mimic estrogen, poison insulin receptors in the cells, and increase the risk for a serious illnesses, including cancer.

To safeguard your health, avoid canned and other plastic stored food and don't drink from plastic bottles.

Sodas and Other Unhealthy Beverages: It should go without saying that any health conscious person should not consume soda. In addition to the many health risks soda consumption causes, the chemicals and artificial flavorings soda contains have been linked to depression and neurological conditions. Moreover, although drinking soda may seem to quench your thirst, in reality soda is dehydrating.

Other beverages you should avoid are commercial, nonorganic fruit and vegetable juices (which are high in sugar and sodium, respectively), commercial sports drinks, nonherbal teas, and alcohol.

General Guidelines For Healthy Eating

Creating a diet that supports good health and protects against disease starts with following these guidelines.

Eat Plenty of Fresh Fruits and Vegetables: A variety of fresh fruits and vegetables (ideally organic) should be a daily staple of your diet because of the rich supply of vital nutrients, enzymes, and fiber they supply.

Vary Your Healthy Meals: Many people are deficient in essential nutrients because they routinely eat a limited variety of foods meal after meal. Not only does such "diet monotony" limit nutrient intake, it also can lead to food allergies and sensitivities, both of which are common, yet frequently undiagnosed. Varying your meals, preferably on a 4-day rotational basis, reduces the risk for such conditions, and will increase your nutrient intake.

Eat Organic Foods: Whenever possible, choose organic fruits and vegetables, as well as wild caught fish and free-range meats and poultry food free of the hormones and antibiotics. If possible, also cultivate relationships with farmers in your areas who grow organic foods.

Maximize Your Intake of Essential Omega-3 Fatty Acids: Contrary to popular belief, all of us require fat in our diet, including saturated fats. Fats act as your body's energy reserves, and serve as a primary form of insulation, helping to maintain healthy body temperature, build cell membranes, assist in transporting oxygen, aid in the absorption of fat-soluble vitamins, and protect against inflammation. Fats also help nourish the skin, nerves, and mucous membranes.

The best sources of fat in the diet are essential fatty acids (EFAs), particularly omega-3s. As mentioned, many people have an excess of omega-6s in their diet, compared to omega-3s, so maintaining a proper balance between the two is important. Good sources of omega-3 EFAs include herring, mackerel, sardines, wild-caught salmon, wild game, flaxseed and flaxseed oil, walnuts and walnut oil, and pumpkin seeds.

Eat Fiber-Rich Foods: The standard American diet supplies no more than a third (and often even less) of the amount of fiber necessary for optimum health and to reduce the risks for heart disease, high blood pressure, certain types of cancer (especially colon and rectal cancer), diabetes, constipation, hemorrhoids, gall bladder disease, and gastrointestinal conditions such as colitis and diverticulitis. Good sources of fiber include fruits, vegetables, bran, rolled oats, brown rice, and other complex carbohydrates.

Make Fermented Foods A Regular Part Of Your Diet: Fermented foods help the body's GI tract replenish healthy, immune-supporting bacteria. A healthy human gut contains numerous different species of friendly bacteria. Many people today rely on probiotic supplements to help maintain healthy bacteria. However, at best these supplements contain no more than a dozen or so strains of bacteria, such as acidophilus or bifidus. By contrast, fermented foods contain hundreds of different strains of healthy bacteria. Excellent fermented food choices include sauerkraut, kimchi, organic pickles, miso and tempeh, which are staple foods in a number of Asian cultures.

Add Sprouted Foods To Your Diet: Sprouted foods are made by germinating seeds, nuts, beans, and grains. During the sprouting process the amount of nutrients the chosen foods contain can increase by as much as 15 times over their original nutrient content due to increased metabolic activity. Moreover, the sprouting process breaks down the nutrients, making them much easier for the body to use. To learn more about sprouts and how to make them, Dr. Cowden recommends the book, *Year-Round Indoor Salad Gardening* by Peter Burke.

Sprouted foods should always be eaten raw, either by themselves or added to salads or as a side dish to healthy meals.

Minimize Caffeine: While caffeine in moderation (one to two cups of coffee per day) is harmless and provides a variety of health benefits, too much regular caffeine consumption can contribute to a wide range of health problems, and can decrease platelet stickiness, thus interfering with the blood clotting process. It can also cause a loss of calcium and other minerals in the body.

Minimize, But Don't Eliminate, Your Salt Intake: A certain amount of salt is required by your body in order to carry out its many functions. When salt intake is excessive, however, water is drawn into the bloodstream, increasing blood volume, which can increase blood pressure levels, and impair the lymphatic system's ability to eliminate cellular waste matter. Additionally, many brands of commercial salt lack iodine (which is essential for proper thyroid function) and other essential trace minerals. When you do use salt, choose sea or Celtic salt, both of which are rich in such co-factor minerals.

Avoid Drinking With Your Meals: Drinking while eating dilutes stomach acid and digestive enzymes, impairing digestion. Drinking cold beverages while you eat also causes the blood vessels in your GI tract to constrict, negatively impacting their ability to absorb the nutrients food contains. If you must have drink with your meals, it's best to drink either warm water with lemon or warm, organic, herbal teas.

Chew Your Food Thoroughly: Digestion begins in your mouth as food comes in contact with saliva, which begins the breakdown of food. Chewing food thoroughly aids this process. Rather than counting each time you chew, simply keep chewing until each bite of food is almost liquid before you swallow it. This simple step can go a long way toward improving and maintaining your digestion.

Eating To Maintain Your Body's Acid/Alkaline (pH) Balance

Health is all about balance. Inside of your body's cells, tissues, and organs this means having balanced pH levels.

Though this vital aspect of health is often ignored by doctors, the concept of acid-alkaline balance is not new. In 1933, Dr. William Howard Hay wrote a book entitled *A New Health Era*, in which he stated, "[W]e depart from health in just the proportion to which we have allowed our alkalis to be dissipated by introduction of acid-forming food in too great amount."

Acid-alkaline balance is determined by measuring pH. In the body, pH refers to the relative concentration of hydrogen ions in blood, urine, and saliva. It is a measurement of the acid-alkaline ratio of the body's fluids and tissues. When this ratio is balanced, good health results. When pH levels are imbalanced, proper absorption and utilization of nutrients is interrupted, which impairs cellular energy production, setting the stage for disease.

pH is measured on a scale of 0 to 14. A pH of 7 is considered neutral. A pH reading below 7 is an indication of acidity, and readings above 7 indicate an alkaline condition. In order to thrive, your body's blood chemistry needs to be slightly alkaline, with a pH of 7.365.

Many doctors and health researchers dismiss the importance of eating in a way that supports pH balance, pointing out that the body's own homeostatic mechanisms maintain blood pH levels on their own. This is true. However, what these critics ignore is what the body must do in order to cope with a diet consisting primarily of acid-producing foods and beverages. To neutralize their acidifying effects, your body must call on its stores of the acid-quenching minerals calcium, magnesium, and potassium, all of which play hundreds of other important roles in your body. Eating primarily acidifying foods depletes your body of these vital minerals. Conversely, eating mostly alkalizing foods, replenishes your body's supply of these minerals since they, and many other important nutrients, are found in abundance in alkalizing foods.

The acidifying, alkalizing, or neutral effects produced by foods and beverages are far more significant, in terms of your health, than their pH values prior to their consumption. For example, a number of foods that are acidic in nature, such as certain citrus fruits and vinegars, have an alkalizing effect in the body once they are digested and metabolized. Knowing the effects foods and beverages will have on your pH levels is a key to choosing your foods wisely.

Acidifying foods, beverages, and condiments include alcohol, breads, caffeine products (chocolate, coffee, black tea), fish, most grains, legumes, meats and poultry, milk and dairy products, all refined and processed foods, most seeds and nuts, soda, sugars and artificial sweeteners, tap water, and yeast products.

Alkalizing foods and beverages include all green vegetables, most colored vegetables, cold-pressed oils (flaxseed, olive, coconut, avocado, hemp), sprouts, certain fruits and nuts, herbs and spices, and mineral water. These should make up the biggest portions of every meal you consume. The foundation of every alkalizing meal is plenty of fresh vegetables (ideally organic), which should always be part of lunch and dinner. Raw vegetables also make an ideal snack food during the day.

You should eat a certain amount of raw vegetables every day, while lightly steaming or sautéing the rest. This will ensure that the rich supply of enzymes vegetables contain are not destroyed by overcooking. Enzymes are found in all fresh fruits and vegetables and play an essential role in healthy digestion. When enzymes are deficient in your diet, your body is unable to properly digest and assimilate the foods you eat, setting the stage for further health problems. Enzymes are inactivated and destroyed when vegetables are cooked in temperatures over 118 degrees Fahrenheit, and in some cases as low as 108 degrees.

Most people do well on a diet consisting of between 60-80 percent of foods that are alkalizing. It is also important to eat more alkalizing foods at every meal, rather than eating all your alkalizing foods at one or two meals, and eating acidifying foods the rest of the day. This includes snacks.

However, not all people will benefit from following the above recommendations. The late Nicholas Gonzalez, MD, found that many of his patients were genetically too alkaline and thus required more acid-producing foods, including red meat, in order to balance their tissue pH and maintain their health. Dr. Gonzalez's finding is one more reason why it is so important to know and eat according to your unique biochemistry. Fortunately, there is an easy and accurate test you can do on your own to determine if the foods you eat are supporting your body's tissue pH balance.

The Saliva pH Test: You can measure your saliva pH by using pH testing strips. They are available at your local pharmacy, health food store, and online retailers (make sure the strips have a measurement range between 5.5 to 8.0 pH in 0.2 increments). Saliva pH testing conducted six to eight hours after a meal can help you discover if the foods you ate caused pH imbalance in your body. Here's how to perform the test.

Once you are done eating, thoroughly brush and floss your teeth. Then wait at least six hours, and do not drink anything except water, abstaining from water completely during the last hour. (**Note:** A person with average digestion will take 8 hours to clear beef and other meats from their stomach, so they can still be getting an "alkaline tide" effect on their saliva pH from the meat still in their stomach 6-8 hours after the meal is over.)

To start the test, first spit three times into a sink or toilet. Then spit onto a pH strip, making sure your fingers do not come in contact with the area of the paper you spit on. Wait 15 seconds. The paper will turn a shade of yellow, green, or blue, depending on what your saliva pH is. Compare the color to the numbers on the color-coded chart that is included with the pH strip container. The number that your pH paper color result corresponds to is the pH of your saliva.

A healthy reading will be at or close to 7.0 (between 6.8 and 7.2). Readings below or above this range indicate that the foods you ate may be negatively affecting your pH. If you are in doubt about which foods in the meal you ate are the culprits, you can repeat the test in the same manner, waiting at least six hours after you eat each of the suspected foods separately before testing. Keep a record of your saliva pH measurements so that you can determine if your food choices over time are moving you closer to a reading of 7.0, or if they should be avoided because they are not doing so.

(**Note:** "Eating foods that are allergens will usually cause an acidic saliva pH below 6.8 even though such a food might create alkalinity in most other people," Dr. Cowden notes. An easy yet effective self-care method you can use to test if foods act as allergens when you consume them is known as the Coca Pulse Test discussed later in this chapter.)

To determine your body's baseline pH, perform the saliva pH test first thing in the morning, ideally after fasting for at least 12 hours overnight, and before you eat or drink anything. Performing this test regularly will help you know how well your food choices are supporting your health.

Water—The Ultimate Health Elixir

One of the easiest and most powerful things you can do for your health is to drink adequate amounts of water each and every day.

Water is the medium through which all of your body functions occur. Most doctors, however, rarely consider whether or not their patients are meeting their daily water requirements. Making matters worse, the standard American diet further interferes with the numerous functions that water helps your body perform. The end result is that many people are today chronically dehydrated and don't know it. Instead, they and their doctors often mistake the symptoms of chronic dehydration for various illnesses that they then seek to treat medically. In many cases, rather than medical treatments, all that is necessary is for patients to resupply their bodies with the water they need.

One of the easiest and most accurate ways to know if you need to drink more water is to monitor your urine. Your urine should be clear and almost colorless, resembling unsweetened lemonade. If you are slightly to moderately dehydrated, your urine will generally be yellow. If you are severely, or chronically, dehydrated, your urine will appear orange or dark-colored and rust-like.

(**Note:** Urine can change color due to the use of vitamins and other nutritional supplements, often appearing bright yellow when such supplements are used.)

Most people will do well drinking at least one-half ounce of water for every pound of their body weight (example 75 ounces of water for a person who weighs 150 pounds). To get started, begin each day with a glass of water. For further benefit, you can add fresh-squeezed lemon juice. Then wait at least 20-30 minutes before having breakfast. "Stop drinking water from 30 minutes before the meal until 30 minutes after the meal, but drink two ounces of water every 15 minutes for the rest of the day," Dr. Cowden advises. "Drinking smaller amounts of water more often is more hydrating than drinking large amounts less frequently."

The Importance Of Only Drinking High Quality Water: It is essential that you only drink pure, filtered water. Avoid tap water because most tap water contains toxins, such as chlorine and fluoride (both of which have been linked to cancer despite being approved as tap water additives by government regulatory agencies), asbestos, lead and other heavy metals, pesticides and herbicides, plastics, various other industrial toxins, and residues from antibiotics and other pharmaceutical drugs. In addition, harmful microorganisms, including parasites and viruses, are commonly found in tap water.

In place of tap water, consider investing in a high-quality reverse osmosis (RO) water filtration system. Reverse osmosis effectively filters out the harmful toxins in tap water. Although such units may seem expensive, their cost pales in comparison to the harm that is caused by continuously drinking unfiltered tap water.

Reverse osmosis systems are also a healthier and more cost-effective solution than drinking bottled water. Studies have shown that many brands of bottled water are no healthier than tap water, and many are less healthy. In addition, the chemicals in plastic bottles can leach into the water, and empty water bottles now pose a serious threat to our environment. Over the long run, you'll pay far less for a reverse osmosis system and replacement filters compared to the accumulative cost of buying bottled water. Since the reverse osmosis process removes all minerals from the water, you should add trace minerals to the RO water before drinking it.

Another alternative is to invest in a water distiller. Be aware that such devices can increase your electricity costs due to the time it takes for water to be distilled. Since the distillation process strips out both healthy and harmful minerals tap water contains, consider adding trace mineral drops to distilled water before drinking.

If you are often on the go, invest in a non-disposable, eco-friendly water bottle so that you can take your pure, filtered water from your home with you. Remember to keep it tightly capped between drinks.

Tailor-Making Your Diet—Two Important Factors To Consider

What constitutes a healthy diet for one person is often not ideal for another person. There are a number of factors that need to be assessed in order to effectively customize the diet that will best support your health and unique biochemical needs. Two of the most important are determining whether or not you have food allergies and sensitivities, and knowing your metabolic type.

Food Allergies and Sensitivities

Most people have food allergies or sensitivities because of factors such as genetic predispositions and the toxicity of our nation's food supply. The difference between food allergies and food sensitivities is one of degree. Allergic reactions to foods tend to be more severe and noticeable, while the symptoms of food sensitivities are more subtle. Both food allergies and sensitivities can sap your health if they are ignored or undetected.

Three effective self-care methods for detecting food allergies and sensitivities are keeping a food journal, going on an elimination diet and noticing how you feel after you reintroduce suspected foods and beverages, and performing the Coca pulse test.

Food Journal: Writing down the foods and beverages you consume at each meal, along with any symptoms you experience after eating, can help detect food allergies and sensitivities. Bear in mind though that, while some symptoms may appear within only 20-30 minutes after a meal, it can sometimes be two to three days before others become apparent, especially if you are constipated or have a slow transit time between when food is eaten and its waste products are eliminated.

Experiencing fatigue after eating a normal size meal is usually a sign that you may be allergic or sensitive to something you ate. There are many other ways that food allergy symptoms can manifest, however, so note any and all other symptoms you may experience after meals, and their intensity and duration.

An Elimination Diet: Once you have compiled a list of foods that you suspect may be causing you problems, eliminate them from your diet for at least a month. Then reintroduce them to your diet one at a time, waiting at least three days before you eat another suspected food. This way enough time will pass for potential symptoms to present themselves. If they do, avoid eating the offending food from that point on.

"Most people develop allergies or sensitivities to foods that they eat frequently," Dr. Cowden explains. "Therefore, it can be beneficial to switch to a 4-day rotational diet plan, especially while trying to regain health. In such a plan, for example, if you eat a beef steak once or twice today, you should not eat anything with beef in it (veal, hamburger, meat-sauce, etc.) for the next three days, but then you can have beef again four days later."

The Coca Pulse Test: This test was developed by Arthur Coca, MD, and is another effective way to sleuth out food allergies and sensitivities. Before you eat, sit in a chair and relax for five minutes. Then check your pulse rate by placing your finger on either of your carotid arteries, which run alongside your neck. Count the number of pulses you feel for 60 seconds. That is your pulse rate in beats per minute.

Then eat your meal. Fifteen minutes after you finish eating, repeat the pulse test. Avoid all physical activity during this time, as well as upsetting conversations, and don't watch TV, especially the news, during the meal and for 15 minutes afterwards. If your pulse rate after you eat increases by ten beats or more per minute most likely at least one of the foods you ate is an allergen. This is even more likely if your pulse rate has increased by 15 beats or more. You can then narrow down your results by repeating the Coca test before and after you eat each one of the foods separately over the next few days.

This test works for all food groups except for nightshade vegetables. To determine if you are allergic to nightshades use the elimination diet technique above.

Beware of Lectins: It may seem hard to believe that nutritious whole foods like beans, grains, nuts—even certain fruits and vegetables— could pose a threat to your health, but they *can*. That's because such foods contain an abundant type of sticky proteins called *lectins*. And while the primary purpose of these proteins is to bind to carbohydrates in order to protect plants from threats by predators, their effects on the *human* immune system harmful. In binding with sugars on the surface of your gut, lectins can trigger reactions ranging from bloating, weight gain, chronic fatigue, celiac disease, irritable bowel syndrome, and sinus problems, to the worsening of a whole host of immune diseases, including lupus, rheumatoid arthritis, fibromyalgia, and more.

Lectins can cause problems because of how they bind to carbohydrate molecules located on the surface of red blood cells (RBCs). Lectins often bind to two red blood cells at the same time, causing them to clump together. This prevents the bound RBCs from entering the capillary beds to provide oxygen to other cells. Capillaries are tiny, thin blood vessels that connect arteries to the veins. Red blood cells are intended to travel through them in single file. When lectins bind them together this is not possible. As a result, not only are RBCs prevented from delivering oxygen to other cells, but the cells, deprived of oxygen, aren't able to produce energy efficiently. In addition, lactic acid begins to build up in the body's tissues, leading to impaired metabolic function that can cause disease.

Lectin-containing foods include all beans, grains, eggplant, lentils, peas, peppers, potatoes, taro, tomato extracts (but not tomatoes themselves), wheat, wheat germ, and fruits such as artichokes, jackfruit, limes, mango, and watermelon. Certain spices, such as allspice and cinnamon also contain lectins.

To reduce the risk of lectin foods causing RBC clumping, consider taking digestive enzymes such as bromelain 30 minutes before and during meals. Also, cooking beans and legumes overnight, or even for one hour in a pressure-cooker, can reduce the harmful effects of these foods on red blood cells.

Brain Gauge: Because of the way it can quickly and accurately monitor how your brain responds to the foods and beverages you consume, the Brain Gauge, which you learned about in Chapter 1, is another effective tool you can use to determine if you have existing food allergies or sensitivities.

"If you're looking at whether or not removing gluten or anything else from your diet might be beneficial, the Brain Gauge can definitely help in that regard because it can reveal if what you are consuming is offensive to your neurological health," Dr. Mark Tommerdahl, co-developer of the Brain Gauge says. "You can use it to track and see if you are getting better from removing things from your diet based on the effects they have on your brain. It gives you feedback much quicker than if you just wait for symptoms to develop and then go away. And if you do find something, you can track your recovery to see if your diet is actually making your brain health better."

Your Metabolic Type

The concept of specific diets based on a person's individualized needs is not new. In fact, it originated thousands of years ago as a central tenet of both traditional Chinese medicine (TCM) and Ayurveda. This concept was further developed and advanced in the 1960s by William Donald Kelley, DDS, and is known as the Metabolic Typing diet.

Dr. Kelley developed metabolic typing after he was diagnosed with late-stage pancreatic cancer and told by his physician that he only had 60 days to live. Kelley rejected that prognosis and sought to cure himself. He did so and was cancer free two months later after changing his diet and taking high doses of pancreatic enzymes between meals. (You will learn more about the health benefits of this special class of enzymes in Chapter 3.)

Kelley recognized early on that the dietary changes he made for himself would not necessarily benefit everyone else. Continuing his research, he concluded that a person's diet needs to be tailored to each individual's unique metabolism in order to maintain the equilibrium of the autonomic nervous system, which is comprised of two main branches, the sympathetic and parasympathetic nervous systems. It was Kelley's view that the autonomic nervous system has the greatest impact on a person's metabolism, which he defined as the sum total of all the chemical reactions that occur inside the body.

Kelley was able to show that people metabolize foods differently and that they have different rates of cellular oxidation, meaning that people's cells convert food into energy at different rates. But cellular oxidation, which is often considered the cornerstone of other metabolic typing diets, was only one aspect of Kelley's more comprehensive approach to metabolic typing.

Dr. Kelley identified three main metabolic types: sympathetic-vegetarian (carbohydrate type), parasympathetic-carnivore (protein type), and sympathetic-parasympathetic balanced. He further broke down each of these types into four subsets, for a combined total of 12 metabolic types, each based on an individual's overall characteristics.

According to Kelley's research, in general, sympathetic-vegetarian types do best following a diet that is comprised of 60 percent carbohydrates, 25 percent protein, and 15 percent fat, whereas the diet of parasympathetic-carnivore types is comprised of 40 percent protein, 30 percent carbohydrates, and 30 percent fat. People in the sympathetic-parasympathetic balanced category do best on a diet consisting of 50 percent carbohydrates, 30 percent protein, and 20 percent fat. These ratios vary, however, depending on which subset a person is in. Some people also require most of their diet to be comprised of raw, or uncooked, foods compared to people of other metabolic types.

Once Kelley determined which metabolic type a patient was, he prescribed a specific diet along with various nutritional supplements and other health recommendations, including coffee enemas, for that person. In this way, he was able to help many people diagnosed with late stage, inoperable cancer to fully recover. Despite the good he did, he faced ongoing harassment from the medical establishment throughout his career.

One of the significant advantages of knowing and eating according to your metabolic type is that doing so helps to keep your tissue pH balanced, thereby protecting against poor health. Employing the saliva pH test discussed above is also a good way of determining whether you are eating foods that are most appropriate for your metabolic type.

Testing yourself for food allergies and sensitivities is also important, because of the possibility that you may be having unhealthy reactions to foods even if they are otherwise right for your type.

Another fact to be aware of is that your metabolic type can change over time as your health continues to improve, especially if you have been an adrenal-exhausted sympathetic type and your adrenal glands are now recovering. As your health improves, the foods and nutrients you need to maintain your health may also change.

Helpful Questions: To help you better determine if the foods you are eating support your health, ask yourself the following questions:

- Do you experience hunger soon after meals containing certain foods?

- Does eating certain foods leave you satiated?

- How does eating certain foods make you feel afterwards? Tired? Irritable? Energetic? Happy?

- Do you consistently experience flatulence or other gastrointestinal issues after eating certain foods?

Overall, how you feel after you eat a food or combination of foods is the best indicator of whether or not what you ate is healthy for you.

A complete discussion of Dr. Kelley's work is beyond the scope of this book. For a more in-depth look at the 12 metabolic types Dr. Kelley identified, visit https://drkelley.info/dr-kelleys-metabolic-typing. *Dr. Kelley's Self-Test for the Different Metabolic Types*, along with his book *One Answer For Cancer* are also recommended. Printed versions of both of these books are difficult to find and can sell for over $100 online. You can obtain digital copies of both of them, as well as online recordings (both audio and video) for a fee of $47 at www.oneanswertocancer.com.

Dr. Joseph Mercola has also created a metabolic questionnaire that, while not as extensive as Dr. Kelley's, is still very helpful. It is free and available at products.mercola.com/nutritional-typing, and also comes with a downloadable ebook of healthy recipes.

By following the guidelines and employing the self-care tests that you learned about in this chapter you will start to notice consistent and ongoing improvements in your health and overall well-being. The key is to put what you now know into action.

CHAPTER 3

The Third Key: Optimizing The Health Of Your Gut

Y OU CAN FOLLOW all of the healthy eating recommendations you learned about in Chapter 2, but if the foods you eat are not fully digested and the nutrients they contain don't reach your cells the way nature intended, your health will still be compromised. That is why it is vital to do all that you can to optimize the health of your gut (your body's gastrointestinal, or GI, tract). In this chapter, you will learn how to do so.

Your Body's "Second Brain"

In addition to digesting foods and liquids and eliminating wastes and toxins, the gastrointestinal tract can be likened to your body's "second brain" due to the enteric nervous system that is located in the linings of the esophagus, stomach, and small and large intestines. Research conducted in the last few decades reveals that the enteric nervous system acts as a single entity, brimming with neurotransmitter proteins. (Neurotransmitters send nerve impulses from nerve cells to other cells and are essential for your body to be able to perform its many functions.) These proteins are produced by cells that are identical to those found in the brain, and this complex circuitry enables this "GI brain" to mimic actual brain function in that it is able to act independently, learning, remembering, and producing so-called "gut feelings."

All of these processes are part of the overall operation of your body's autonomic nervous system (ANS). The nerve endings that are attached to the linings of the GI tract provide nerve impulses that stimulate the operation of the various organs and glands within your body. The type of stimulation that the ANS is able to provide to your organs and glands is a direct reflection of the health of your GI tract.

The Microbiome and How Disease Occurs in the Gut

Healthy functioning of the GI tract depends in large part on the health of the gastrointestinal lining. The health of the GI lining, or intestinal walls, depends in turn on a coating of intestinal bacteria. Hundreds of distinct species of bacteria exist within the GI tract. These friendly bacteria, also known as *flora*, form a protective shield that covers the intestinal walls and prevents harmful and damaging toxins, "non-friendly" bacteria, viruses, and other microorganisms, from passing through the GI lining into the body's bloodstream. These flora also enable vital nutrients and fluids to pass through the GI lining into the body's cells, tissues, and organs.

So long as these flora are present in sufficient numbers and remain unharmed, the overall functioning of the GI tract remains intact. However, if they are subjected to repeated exposure to harmful substances, then the white blood cells within the microvilli that also line the GI tract go into attack mode. In cases in which healthy flora are temporarily exposed to harmful substances, the white blood cells are soon able to resolve the problem by attacking and eliminating these substances. But when chronic exposure to such substances occurs, the effort of the white blood cells to dispose of them can irritate and inflame the lining of the GI tract.

This ongoing assault of harmful substances, combined with the irritation and inflammation, diminishes the defensive capacities of the friendly flora, making the intestinal walls increasingly permeable. When this occurs, toxins, abnormal proteins, and other harmful substances can pass through the walls into the bloodstream. This is known as "leaky gut syndrome."

If this process continues unchecked, the stage is set for disease to occur, first within the GI tract itself, and then, potentially, in other areas of the body. Healthy bacteria are forced to contend with unhealthy bacteria, leading to a condition known as *dysbiosis* that results in the proliferation of harmful flora from the lower colon, where they are normally kept in check by friendly bacteria, into other areas of the GI tract and into the bloodstream.

In addition, further damage is caused by the spread of free radicals that are produced as a side effect of the chronic inflammation besieging the GI tract. This can cause impaired digestion and malabsorption of essential nutrients. Eventually, this creates a vicious circle in which the body is not only under attack from within the GI tract, but also unable to mount an effective defense because it is no longer able to obtain sufficient nutrients.

In recent years, scientists' views of the GI tract and the microorganisms it contains have changed due to ongoing discoveries about the environment in which these microorganisms collectively exist, known as the *microbiome*. What scientists have discovered is that more than half of the human body is actually not human at all. According to the latest scientific evidence, only 43 percent of our bodies' total cell count is comprised of human cells. The larger (57%) amount consists of cells of the microorganisms that live on our skin, inside our mouth and nasal passages, and, primarily, within our gut.

In a discussion about the microbiome (*The Second Genome*, BBC Radio 4. April 10, 2018), Ruth Ley, PhD, Director of the Department of Microbiome Science at the Max Planck Institute for Developmental Biology, stated that "your body isn't just you" when explaining how essential a healthy microbiome is to human health. In that same discussion, Rob Knight, PhD, of the UC San Diego added, "We're finding that these tiny creatures [in the microbiome] totally transform our health in ways we never imagined until recently."

Scientists have also discovered that the microorganisms that comprise the microbiome have a genome that far exceeds the human genome. The human genome is composed of approximately 20,000 genes that work together to provide our bodies with the genetic instructions they need to develop and function. By contrast, the microbiome contains between two to 20 million genes that comprise a second genome within us that augments and directly influences our human genome.

In light of these discoveries, scientists are finding that health is greatly dependent on having a balanced microbiome, and that an unhealthy microbiome is a primary cause of chronic inflammation and a wide variety of diseases. In addition, scientists now know that the microbiome in the gut produces approximately 90 percent of the "feel good" neurotransmitter serotonin in the body, with only 10 percent being produced by the brain. The microbiome is also responsible for calorie extraction from foods that supplies the body with energy. An unhealthy microbiome fails to produce energy from food efficiently, while also failing to produce adequate amounts of serotonin.

The following self-care measures can help you maintain or restore healthy microbiome and overall gut function.

Conscious, Stress-Free Eating

In Chapter 2, you learned how Dr. Kelley's pioneering research that led to the development of Metabolic Typing also led him to determine that it is the autonomic nervous system (ANS) that has the most influence over a person's metabolism.

The ANS is made up of two sub-branches—the sympathetic and parasympathetic nervous systems. Research by Dr. Kelley and others has established that complete digestion can only occur when our bodies are in a parasympathetic dominant state, meaning one that is calm, relaxed, and at rest. Eating when our bodies are in a sympathetic dominant state, a state of stress characterized by "fight or flight" chemical reactions in the body, compromises digestion, causing inadequate nutrient intake and impaired gut health.

To ensure that you are not in a sympathetic dominant state when you eat, eliminate distractions such as looking at your cell phone, watching TV, or otherwise placing your attention outside of your meal itself. Try not to eat when you are in a hurry or on the run. Take time to savor and enjoy your meals, chewing each bite thoroughly in a relaxed manner.

Also avoid eating whenever you are in an upset or excited state. Avoiding upsetting conversations with others during meals is also important.

You can also take a few moments before eating to practice a stress relaxation technique. One effective method that Dr. Cowden teaches his patients to do four times a day (before each meal, and again at bedtime) is to sit comfortably while gently holding your left thumb and index finger with your right hand. As you do so, breathe deeply and easily in through your nose and out through your mouth. Close your eyes and imagine yourself in a place of comfort and relaxation. Continue this technique for four minutes, or until you feel more relaxed.

Finally, before you eat, take a moment to say a prayer of thanks, blessing your meal with the intention that it will provide you with good health and abundant energy. Numerous studies have found that expressing gratitude in this manner enhances our ability to maximize the benefits we receive from our meals.

Food Preparation and Food Combining

How you prepare the foods you eat can impact your gut health for better or worse, as can the combinations of foods you eat during the same meals.

How you cook your food plays a significant role in how much nutrition you will derive from it. The best cooking methods are baking, boiling, sautéing and steaming foods. Grilling and frying should be used sparingly because these methods can create toxic substances called advanced glycation end products, or AGEs, which have been linked to accelerated aging and many chronic degenerative diseases. If you do choose to grill or fry, use healthy oils that do not quickly oxidize. One of the best choices is organic, cold-pressed, unrefined coconut oil.

In general, the less foods are cooked, the more nutrients they contain. This includes vital enzymes and certain vitamins, which are destroyed when foods are overcooked or cooked at high temperatures. For this reason, you should always try to include both raw and lightly cooked organic vegetables with your meals.

The cookware you use is also important. Avoid using aluminum, stainless steel, and most nonstick pots and pans. When heated, particles from aluminum pots and pans leach into foods and get absorbed by the body. Aluminum is a toxic metal that has been linked to dementia and other neurological conditions. Similarly, the use of heated stainless steel cookware over time releases particles of nickel, another toxic metal. Many nonstick pots and pans, such as those that are Teflon-coated, release plastic into foods when they are heated, as well as toxic gases. Healthier cookware options include ceramic metal cookware, and porcelain and glass (Pyrex and Corning) products, although they are more prone to breaking if they are dropped.

You also need to pay attention to how you combine foods, especially if you suffer from food allergies (see Chapter 2) or low stomach acid production. The principle of food combining is based on how the foods you eat are digested. For example, when you eat foods that are primarily high in proteins, such as meat, fish, or poultry, your body will digest it in the stomach. To do so effectively, your stomach needs to create a temporary highly acidic environment (pH 1-3).

By contrast, digestion of foods high in starchy carbohydrates begin in the mouth as you chew them and is completed in the small intestines. This process requires a much less acidic or mildly alkaline environment (pH 5-10).

Combining protein-rich foods with starchy carbohydrate foods during meals such foods forces your body to attempt two opposite tasks—digesting the protein foods in a highly acidic environment, while simultaneously digesting the starchy carbohydrates in an environment that is mildly alkaline, or at least much less acidic. The end result is that both food groups end up partially undigested, leaving your body unable to obtain the full supply of nutrients they contain. Moreover, the undigested remnants will buildup in your colon, where they will decompose and ferment, creating toxins and mucus.

These food-combining guideline will make your meal choices easier and healthier.

1. Eat protein-rich foods (meats, fish, poultry, dairy) away from starchy carbohydrates (potatoes, yams, breads, wheat products and other grain products).

2. Non-starchy carbohydrate vegetables (green, leafy, and colored vegetables), on the other hand, can be combined with either protein-rich foods or starchy carbohydrates. Such vegetables will not interfere with the digestion of either proteins or starchy carbohydrates.

3. Fruits are best eaten alone at least 45 minutes prior to other meals, and several hours after a previous meal. (With the exception of avocados and tomatoes, both of which can be included with meals.) It is also a good idea to eat only one type of fruit at a time.

4. Avoid drinking water or other beverages with your meals, especially meals featuring protein-rich foods, so as not to dilute the digestive juices needed to breakdown solid foods.

5. To further aid your body's digestive process, make sure you chew your food thoroughly before swallowing.

Take Care Of Your Liver

Your liver plays a vital role in supporting healthy digestion and maintaining overall gut health. It is also responsible for performing over 500 essential functions, including processing food, aiding in the assimilation of vital nutrients, and converting glucose from foods into glycogen, a primary energy source for your body.

Your liver is also the most internal important organ for detoxification of both internal waste products and external environmental pollutants. Due to the continued proliferation of environmental toxins, along with poor diet, alcohol consumption, the regular use of pharmaceutical drugs, and other factors, it is constantly under siege.

There are a variety of effective self-care steps you can take to help improve liver function, beginning with following the healthy eating recommendations in Chapter 2, as well as the other guidelines in this chapter. In addition, you need to also:

Avoid the use of commercial household cleaners and other products that are high in chemicals. This includes aerosol sprays, commercial laundry and dishwashing detergents, table polish, floor cleaners, and commercial cosmetics and hair dyes. Nontoxic alternatives to such products can be found at your local grocery or health food store.

Avoid exposure to secondhand smoke, and if you smoke, seek help so that you can quit.

Unless your doctor tells you otherwise, avoid the use of prescription and over-the-counter drugs. All drugs, when used regularly place a major burden on your liver.

Spice up your diet with turmeric. Turmeric is rich in curcumin, a compound that can protect the liver from a variety of chemical toxins. (You can also supplement with curcumin extracts.)

Avoid the use of pesticides and commercial insect spray repellents in your lawn and yard.

Support liver function using nutritional supplements. Certain supplements have been scientifically proven to aid liver function, including natural vitamin E (avoid synthetic versions), omega-3 oils, alpha-lipoic acid, liposomal glutathione, and acetyl-L-carnitine. Milk thistle is another excellent supplement aid as long as it is taken with liposomal glutathione.

Adopt An Antifungal Diet

One of the most overlooked causes of disease is fungal (including yeast) overgrowth in the body, along with mycotoxins, which are poisonous substances emitted by fungi. Once fungi and mycotoxins enter the organs or the bloodstream they can wreak havoc on your health.

One of the world's foremost experts on fungi and mycotoxins and the harm they can cause is Doug Kaufmann, an independent nutritional researcher, author of 12 books, including *The Fungus Link: An Introduction to Fungal Disease*, and host of the daily television show Know The Cause, which is broadcast throughout the U.S. on the WGN America network, and to 200 countries around the world.

Doug's research in this area began when he became ill in 1971 after serving as a U.S. Navy Medical Corpsman attached to the 7th Marine Division in Vietnam. At the time, he thought his symptoms, which continued to plague him into the 1980s, were due to food allergies. When he read a research paper in 1980 that explained how certain foods can change the terrain of the GI tract to cause "leaky gut syndrome", Doug realized the role fungi played in his own condition. After spending years studying the clinical effects of pathogenic fungi on the body, Doug created a specific antifungal diet known as the Kaufmann One Diet, which enabled him to successfully treat himself without the use of drugs, simply by eliminating the foods and other substances that fungi and yeasts feed upon once they enter the body.

"The Kaufmann One Diet has two tiers; Kaufmann 1 and Kaufmann 2," Doug explains. "Each tier, or phase, was designed with this idea in mind: Fungi and yeasts can become parasitic organisms on and inside our body, causing health problems that can be difficult to diagnose. Often and unknowingly, we feed these parasites via our diet. Fungi crave sugar, and if you have a fungal infection, their cravings often become your cravings. Sugar does not simply come in the form of candy, soda and other obvious junk foods. The carbohydrates from grains, potatoes, corn and corn products, certain fruits, breads, pasta, alcohol and other staples of the standard American diet are just as effective at feeding a parasitic fungal organism.

"For many, the Kaufmann One Diet begins as a test: Do your symptoms subside or cease after following the diet for 30 or 60 days? Does your brain fog clear? Does the chronic pain, fatigue or general malaise dissipate? Does the weight fall off? If so, you may have discovered that fungi and yeasts are a root cause of the health problems you have been experiencing."

During phase 1 of the Kaufmann One Diet, you eliminate all sugar, artificial sweeteners, grains, breaded meats, coffee, tea, and alcohol from your diet. You also abstain from consuming pistachios, peanuts and peanut-containing products, mushrooms, salad dressings and yeast-containing products. Potatoes, legumes, yams, and butter-substitute products, such as margarine, are also eliminated.

Allowed foods and beverages during phase one include eggs, free range poultry, wild caught seafood, grass fed meats (beef and lamb), yogurt (plain and organic), butter, sour cream, filtered water, fresh-squeezed lemonade sweetened with stevia, fresh-squeezed vegetable juices, avocados, berries, green apples, limes and lemons, and all nonstarchy vegetables. You can also consume cold-pressed and organic coconut oil, and flax seed, olive, and grape seed oils. Raw nuts and seeds, and unpasteurized apple cider vinegar, are also permitted.

"When beginning the Kaufmann One Diet, some people might experience an exacerbation of their symptoms initially, and some might experience flu-like symptoms or other intense discomfort," Doug warns. "This reaction is known as a Herxheimer reaction, and is usually the result of fungal die-off and their poisonous byproducts being released into your system. This is temporary, and it may be a good sign that you've taken the first step towards better health—ridding your body of health-destroying, parasitic fungal organisms.

"Still, for others, the results may not be so quick or so dramatic. In either case, please give the diet time to work. Your health problems likely did not develop overnight, and any solution will not likely resolve your problems overnight, either."

You should stay on the Kaufmann One Diet until your symptoms disappear and your health noticeably improves. Once that happens, you can "graduate" to the Kaufman Two Diet and begin to slowly reintroduce foods such as brown rice and legumes, while still avoiding sugar and other harmful foods.

"Many physicians now tell me that the Kaufmann One Diet alone works quickly for their patients, while others with more deeply imbedded fungal conditions may require both 'starving the fungi' with my diet and simultaneously killing the fungus with anti-fungal medications and/or the proper supplements" Doug says.

To find out more, visit Doug's website, www.knowthecause.com.

Addressing Imbalanced Stomach Acid Production

When you eat, your stomach secretes hydrochloric acid (HCl) to help the body break down food. This causes the pancreas to secrete bicarbonate, a form of alkalizing salt that neutralizes, or buffers, HCL after it performs its function. If HCl is not neutralized it can interfere with pancreatic enzymes that are also necessary for proper digestion. Poor diet, vitamin deficiency, and chronic environmental, emotional, and illness-induced stress can interfere with this process. Low stomach acid production disrupts the body's entire digestive system, causing acid-alkaline imbalance and poor absorption of vitamins and minerals essential for good health.

The most common symptom of this imbalance is heartburn, due to over-acidity. Other symptoms include nausea, cramping, gas, bloating, constipation, diarrhea, undigested food in stool, bad breath, brittle and dry hair, skin and nails. Low stomach acid can also lead to diabetes, arthritis, malnutrition, and other conditions, including cancer.

Research published as early as the 1960s, in peer-reviewed medical journals show that in most cases of abnormal HCl production, *too little* HCl is being produced, not *too much*. This is especially true as we get older. ACIM physician Steven W. Hines, ND, NE, founder and director of Hope Wellness Center in San Angelo, Texas, and its treatment facility in Ciudad Acuňa, Coahuila, Mexico, reports that he has found even ten-year-old children who are not producing sufficient amounts of stomach acid. "I have seen hundreds of gastric reflux cases," he says, "and 95 percent of them are solved with more stomach acid, not less."

"If you do not have enough stomach acid you have food allergies," Dr. Hines continues. "Stomach acid is the GI tract's sterilizer. When digestion is normal you have lots of stomach acid, you denature the proteins and antigens in the food you eat so it no longer causes an immune response. Everybody that has any type of degenerative disease has allergies."

When HCl is deficient, certain foods, especially proteins, are only partially digested. This leads to fermentation of undigested food particles in the stomach and intestine, causing stress and inflammation of the small intestine, and impairing your body's ability to absorb and metabolize nutrients.

To address and prevent low stomach acid production Dr. Hines recommends taking a broad spectrum digestive enzyme with every meal, and supplementing with mastic gum and DGL (de-glycyrrhizinated licorice). "Mastic gum and DGL both act like a tonic for the GI tract," he says. "And mastic gum also protects against H. pylori, the most common cause of stomach ulcers."

Another supplement Dr. Hines recommends is a high quality glutamine product. "Glutamine is the predominant fuel of the cells in the small intestine," he says. "To regenerate the gut quickly, take two to three grams of pharmaceutical grade L-glutamine per day."

Dr. Hines also recommends supplementing with potassium (400 mg twice a day). "If your body doesn't have enough potassium it can't produce stomach acid," he points out. In addition, he recommends zinc (25 mg/day), and magnesium (250-1,000 mg/day, but not the oxide form). For people who have had their gallbladder removed, supplementation of bile salts with each meal is also essential because bile acids are necessary to emulsify fats and fat soluble nutrients. *Saccharomyces boulardii*, available as supplement called Florastor, can also improve gastrointestinal function, according to Dr. Hines, especially for people who have taken antibiotics because this "friendly yeast" can stop the spread of *Candida albicans* and other harmful types of yeast in the gut in little as three days. It is also helpful in cases of C-Difficile. In addition, *Saccharomyces boulardii* promotes production of IgA (immunoglobulin A), a primary antibody in the GI tract that provides an extra layer of immune support to defend against infection. Dr. Hines recommends taking three capsules twice a day.

Another effective tool to address low stomach acid is betaine HCl. "We use betaine to supplement the amount of stomach acid patients have," Dr. Hines explains. "It helps to bring stomach acid levels up to proper levels, and helps the stomach to start creating its own healthy amounts of acid."

Betaine HCL also acts as a methyl donor, helping your body to make better use of the B vitamins folate and B12. Taken with each meal, especially with high protein meals, betaine can aid the stomach in reaching its ideal pH (1.5-2.0). "When we get the stomach acid to 1.5 pH, it triggers hormones that tell the liver to produce bile, and the pancreas to produce digestive enzymes and secrete bicarbonates," Dr. Hines explains. "The digestion process normalizes, and the supplemental stomach acid from betaine kills any residual H. pylori remaining in the stomach, eliminating heartburn/acid reflux. When we get the stomach sterilizing itself and triggering all of these digestive functions, the entire body functions better."

Dr. Hines offers these instructions for using betaine HCl:

Use capsules containing 649 mg (10 grains) of betaine HCl along with pepsin in a 1:3000 ratio. Take one capsule at the beginning of the first meal, then add one capsule with each subsequent meal until you feel a warmness in your stomach toward the meal's end or within ten minutes after the meal. If no warmth is felt with the first capsule, take two capsules with your second meal. Continue to follow this pattern, up to a maximum of seven capsules with each meal.

Once you feel warmth or a slight burning/indigestion sensation in the stomach, you have gone over the amount needed. At your next meal, take one less capsule. This will be the dosage you need until you feel warmth again. For example, if you feel warmth in the stomach at four capsules, then back down to three capsules with each meal. If you reach seven capsules with no feeling of warmth in the stomach do not increase the dosage any higher. This is the maximum dosage.

Do not take betaine with small snacks, such as an apple or banana, but only with high-protein meals, such as meat. Also limit your water intake during meals to 4-6 ounces so as to not dilute stomach acid. Make sure to spread your dosage throughout the entire meal, allowing time between each capsule, so as to not dump a full load of stomach acid into your body all at once.

"Eventually, you will feel warmth again at your normal dose," Dr. Hines says. "This is good. It means your stomach is beginning to normalize stomach acid production, so take one less capsule at your next meal. If you later feel warmth again, back off one more capsule. You will wean off the supplement entirely as your body heals and produces a natural amount of stomach acid."

To help others improve their gut health, Dr. Hines created the DVD tutorial *Learn How to Treat Yourself: Digestion and Digestive Disorders*. It is available through the Hope Wellness Center (www. hopewellness.com).

Enzymes

Enzymes are a class of proteins that are responsible for catalyzing every single chemical reaction that occurs in your body. Vitamins, minerals, hormones, and various other substances in your body cannot be activated without enzymes.

There are many types of enzymes. To support gut health and digestion, two classes—plant-derived digestive enzymes and pancreatic enzymes—can significantly aid digestion when taken with meals. Pancreatic enzymes offer additional important benefits when taken away from meals.

Plant-Derived Enzymes: Plant-derived enzymes, which are often used as digestive enzymes, are found in all uncooked plant foods and are essential for proper digestion and the body's ability to break down and utilize the proteins, fats, and carbohydrates contained in foods. However, the enzyme activity in foods are often impaired due to food production methods such as the widespread use of pesticides and herbicides, pasteurization, genetic engineering, and irradiation.

Cooking at high heat destroys enzymes in foods, as does the use of microwaves, and enzymes can be further depleted by drinking fluoridated water. Because of these factors, most people suffer from undiagnosed enzyme deficiencies.

Taking plant-derived enzymes with your meals helps ensure proper digestion and improves absorption of the nutrients they contain. Such enzymes also spare your body from having to call on its own internal enzyme supply, resulting in less bodily energy being needed for digestion. This frees that saved energy to be used for other purposes, such as maintaining overall metabolic function. Research has shown that the regular use of plant-derived enzymes with meals not only enhances digestion, but also helps prevent and reverse a variety of gastrointestinal problems while also boosting immune function.

Caution: There are four categories of plant-derived enzymes— protease, which digests proteins; amylase, which digests carbohydrates: lipase, which digests fats, and cellulase, which digests soluble fiber. However, these types of enzymes, which are commonly found in plant-derived enzyme products, are secreted from a class of fungi known as Aspergillus, most commonly from *Aspergillus niger* and *Aspergillus oryzae*. Since Aspergillus causes mold, the possibility exists that the use of these plant-derived enzymes obtained from Aspergillus fungi can cause problems for people who are immune-compromised or otherwise susceptible to allergic reactions to Aspergillus.

Based on the research of Doug Kaufmann and others about the health-damaging effects of mold and fungi, using plant-derived enzymes that are obtained from Aspergillus is not recommended. Healthier enzyme options include bromelain, papaya leaf or papain, serrapeptase, lumbrokinase, nattokinase, and using ox bile to absorb fats. You can buy these products at your local health food store, and online.

Pancreatic Enzymes: Pancreatic enzymes are derived from animals, usually pigs. They are also produced by the pancreas, which is responsible for producing important hormones, especially insulin.

Like plant enzymes, pancreatic enzymes aid digestion. However, their greater benefits are derived when they are taken away from meals, as was first shown by the English scientist John Beard.

Beginning in 1902, Beard worked with a surgeon to inject pancreatic extracts directly into cancerous tumors, with considerable success. Dr. William Kelley was influenced by and furthered Beard's research when he developed his Metabolic Typing Diet. Pancreatic enzymes played an important role in helping the patients Dr. Kelley treated recover from cancer.

Besides preventing and improving gastrointestinal problems, pancreatic enzymes offer other significant benefits because of how they function with the GI tract and the bloodstream. Not only can they enhance digestion when taken with meals, when taken away from meals they enter directly into the bloodstream, where they go to digest foreign particles, viruses, and other harmful microorganisms in the gut, and undigested protein molecules that can cause leaky gut syndrome.

Taking pancreatic enzymes away from meals helps protect your gut against the various agents that cause GI disease, while simultaneously boosting your overall immune function. Pancreatic enzymes have also been shown to clear internal scar tissue caused by inflammation, and to help protect against a variety of inflammatory disease conditions, including atherosclerosis and heart disease, and viral infections.

Pancreatic enzymes are not as commonly found in health food as plant enzymes are. They are also more expensive. Still, given the benefits they provide, they should be considered as a first line of defense against GI problems and other health conditions. You can purchase them online at Amazon.com and other websites. High quality brands include those from the companies Nutricology and Nutrizyme from American Nutriceuticals.

Prebiotics, Probiotics, and Fermented Foods

As mentioned, proper functioning of your GI tract depends on the bacteria in your gut, specifically "friendly" bacteria, also known as probiotic bacteria. *Probiotics* means "pro life." The benefits of probiotic bacteria begin at birth when they first start to colonize the GI tract of newborns after the baby comes through the birth canal. This is particularly true in infants who are breast-fed and not born by C-section.

Human breast milk contains an abundant supply of a particular class of probiotics known as *bifidobactera*, which are essential for the proper development of babies' digestive and immune systems. Lack of bifidobacteria during early childhood can cause allergies and poor absorption of nutrients. There should be at least several hundred, and in some individuals several thousand, other species of friendly bacteria in the gut besides bifidobacteria, but various factors, especially antibiotic ingestion (from eating antibiotic-tainted meats or taking antibiotic prescriptions), reduce the number of species of probiotics found in the gut.

In addition to supporting digestive function, probiotics play many other important roles sustaining gut health, and help produce various substances that kill or deactivate harmful, disease-causing bacteria, viruses, and yeasts. Probiotics also help to reduce high cholesterol levels and recycle estrogen to reduce the likelihood of osteoporosis and to minimize symptoms of menopause. In addition, probiotics have been shown to aid in the treatment of various other disease conditions, including acne, allergies, cystitis, eczema, rheumatoid arthritis, gout, migraine headaches, and even depression.

Many people are lack enough of these friendly bacteria due to poor diet, modern-day food production techniques, an over-reliance on antibiotics and other pharmaceutical drugs, and other factors, including chronic stress, excess mucus production, poor gut transit time (the time it takes food waste products to be eliminated from the bowels; gut transit time can be too fast or too slow), and impaired hormonal function. Probiotic deficiencies also occur as we age.

Because they are alive, friendly bacteria need to eat. They get their sustenance from the foods that are rich in *prebiotics*, substances that "feed" and stimulate the growth and activity of friendly bacteria.

Instead of being digested by your body, prebiotics from food are digested by the bacteria. Commercial farming and food-production methods, such as sterilization and the use of preservatives and other chemicals and food additives, have greatly reduced the useable prebiotic content of foods that make up the standard American diet.

You can replenish your body's supply of friendly bacteria by eating foods that stimulate their growth in the GI tract. Organic yogurt with active probiotic cultures can help replenish friendly bacteria, but other foods can be even more helpful. They include fermented foods, such as kimchi, miso and tempeh. Sauerkraut is another excellent choice, as is drinking kefir, which is produced by adding kefir grains to milk and allowing the mixture to ferment. During this fermentation process, lactose in milk is broken down, making kefir suitable even for people who are lactose intolerant.

Eating foods rich in prebiotics can also help. Such foods are also good sources of fiber and include asparagus, bamboo shoots, broccoli, Jerusalem artichokes, sunflower seeds, leeks and onions. Whole grains, such as barley, oats, and wheat, also contain prebiotic compounds, but because of the risk such foods have for triggering fungal overgrowth, they are best avoided, or at least minimized in your diet.

If these dietary measures alone are not enough to boost friendly bacteria levels, consider using inulin. Inulin is a type of fiber found in chicory root and in some of the prebiotic foods mentioned above. Research shows that inulin acts as an excellent aid to digestion because it stimulates the growth of healthy gut bacteria, particularly *Bifidobacteria* and *Lactobacilli*. Inulin also helps to slow overall digestion, thereby enhancing the absorption of nutrients from food. Inulin increases stool bulk and promotes regularity, as well, helping to eliminate waste products from food faster and more efficiently. Insulin supplements are available in both capsule and powder form. Powdered inulin may be preferable for most people because it easily dissolves in water to make a drink you can consume once a day. A typical dose is 3,000 mg.

While probiotic supplements can also be used, you should rely on your diet, especially the regular consumption of fermented foods, to maintain and replenish the supply of healthy gut bacteria, because probiotic supplements only contain a few strains of friendly bacteria, while food sources help the body produce far more strains that are more aligned with the gut's ecosystem of bacteria.

Stay Physically Active

Regular exercise and other forms of physical activity can further improve digestion and overall gut health, and positively affect the microbiome, while a lack of regular physical activity can disrupt gut health.

Regular exercise benefits the GI tract by:

- Reducing transit time of food though the intestines, resulting in more regular bowel movements.
- Increasing healthy gut bacteria, especially the strains of lactobacillus and bifidobacteria.
- Decreasing harmful bacteria in the GI tract.
- Increasing bacteroidetes, a strain of gut bacteria that has been shown to increase metabolism and reduce the risk of excess weight gain and obesity.
- Decreasing another class of bacteria called firmicutes that can raise the risk of obesity and promote sugar cravings.

In addition, regular physical activity and exercise has been found to increase the production of healthy, short-chained fatty acids (SCFAs) within the GI tract. This is important because beneficial bacteria in the gut feed off of SCFAs. In addition, SCFAs enhance brain health and immunity while reducing the risk of gastrointestinal disorders, metabolic syndrome, and other health conditions.

Try to exercise or otherwise engage in physical activity for at least 30 minutes every day. One of the easiest ways to do so is to take a daily 30-minute walk. Doing so will aid your digestion and improve overall gut health and function.

Dr. Hines' Modified Specific Carbohydrate Diet

Dr. Hines has had great success helping his patients recover from a wide spectrum of gut issues and other illnesses by placing them on the diet he created called the Modified Specific Carbohydrate Diet (MSCD). He developed MSCD as a less restrictive version of the Specific Carbohydrate Diet popularized by the late Elaine Gottschall.

One of Dr. Hines' patients was Laura Schroeder, a long-term sufferer of Lyme disease whose condition was drastically improved after adopting MSCD and being treated by him. Schroeder had been plagued for years with extreme joint and neurological pain brought about by her struggle with Lyme disease. "Within four days of being on the diet, my joint pain of all those years began to disappear," she says. Following her successful recovery, Schroeder joined the Hope Wellness Center staff and teamed with Dr, Hines to write *The Road to Health: Overcoming Chronic Illness through Nutrition* in order to help others recover from chronic illness, just as she did.

"Dr. Hines didn't create the MSCD to be a one-and-done deal; it's meant to become an eating lifestyle," Schroeder explains. "Our approach is one of progression, beginning strictly, then adding foods back into the patient's diet as the digestive tract heals and the immune system function improves. The progressive nature of the diet is designed to lead patients to a lifestyle of healthy eating, one not limited by what they can and can't eat, but by what they choose to eat based on their new perspective about health and nutrition."

"The initial three-month phase of the MSCD is a strict diet that contains zero artificial anything, no grains, and no sugar," Dr. Hines says. "It's a no-disaccharide diet. Disaccharides are a class of carbohydrates and sugars such as lactose, maltose and sucrose. During this initial phase, people eliminate all sources of corn, potatoes, and all grains, including wheat, barley, oats, and rye. The purpose of this phase of the MSCD is to heal the GI tract and minimize the inflammatory process, while at the same time normalizing peristalsis, inhibiting the growth of yeast, and avoiding the most common allergens associated with the standard American diet."

A significant advantage of the MSCD is that it's flexible and fully-customizable, meeting the specific needs of each person. Dr. Hines customizes the diet for each patient, based on lab results, known food allergies, and specific diagnoses. He trains his patients to "listen to your gut" so that they can begin to tweak the diet based on what foods they can and can't tolerate.

Checkpoints on the diet are at months three, six, nine and twelve. These checkpoints give patients the opportunity to evaluate their health and see if there are foods they can add back into their diet, or if there are additional foods they need to remove. If at three months patients see a significant improvement in health, they can begin to add back foods that were previously not allowed in the beginner phase. The same is true at the subsequent three-month checkpoints. "However, remember that everybody responds differently," Schroeder notes. "If you've had a chronic illness for awhile and you have a lot of damage to repair, it might take longer than three months to reintroduce some food. That's okay. Be patient. Don't reintroduce something back into your diet just because you're at the three-month mark. Listen to your body."

A complete explanation of the MSCD and how to implement it is explained in *The Road To Health*. The book is available to order at www.hopewellness.com. Schroeder serves as a Nutritional Consultant for Dr. Hines' patients and can be contacted with questions about the MSCD at laura@hopewellnesscenter.com.

Using ION* Gut Health To Protect Yourself Against Glyphosate and Other Dangerous Toxins

Since 1974, when it was first introduced, the synthetic chemical glyphosate has posed one of the world's most significant health threats, not only to humans, but also to animals and the crop soil in which our food supply is grown. Developed by Monsanto (now owned by Bayer), glyphospate is the active ingredient in RoundUp[R], an herbicide first used by the agricultural industry that is now also widely used by homeowners and municipalities, and sprayed in parks, school grounds, playgrounds, and alongside roads.

Since 2007, glyphosate has been the most widely used herbicide in the US agricultural industry, and its production and distribution now extends far beyond Roundup, which came off patent in 2007. The majority of herbicides in the agriculture and consumer products markets contain glyphosate which is produced in China at a far greater volume for the international marketplace than Bayer/Monsanto's production volume.

Over four billion pounds of glyphosate are annually used worldwid. As a result, water-soluble glyphosate residues are found throughout our food and water systems, including fresh water rivers, deep aquifers, and oceans, and in 75 percent of both our rain water and the air we breathe. Glyphosate exposure is so widespread that residues of this toxin are now increasingly found in breast milk. Escaping exposure to glyphosate is virtually impossible.

Research continues to find that glyphosate exposure at levels well below those allowed by US regulatory agencies such as the Environmental Protection Agency (EPA) can contribute to a wide variety of diseases, including a wide range of cancers. In three separate court cases, glyphosate was found to have caused non-Hodgkin's lymphoma in people who used it, with juries ordering Monsanto to pay well over two billion dollars in combined damages to the plaintiffs. Over 19,000 similar lawsuits against Bayer/Monsanto (Bayer acquired Monsanto in 2018) are pending.

In March 2015, the World Health Organization's (WHO) International Agency for Research on Cancer (IARC) classified glyphosate as a probable carcinogen for humans based on numerous scientific studies linking it to a range of cancers. More recently, a number of municipalities across the US have banned the use of glyphosate-containing products for nonresidential use.

Studies also show that glyphosate can cause kidney and liver disease, and researchers have found that glyphosate in pregnant women can damage the placenta and may contribute to birth defects in as little as 18 hours following exposure to it. Glyphosate has also been shown to disrupt the body's endocrine system, cause cell damage and oxidative stress, disrupt metabolic pathways, and damage the gut microbiome.

Unlike other pesticides and herbicides, which can be rinsed off of foods, at least to some degree, glyphosate cannot be rinsed off because it is absorbed internally by the food crops it is sprayed upon. Eating such foods results in eating glyphosate, as well.

Fortunately, thanks to the discoveries of Zach Bush, MD, and his colleagues, we now know that nature has provided a solution to help protect against glyphosate and other environmental toxins. Dr. Bush is the founder and director of the M Clinic, an integrative medicine center in Charlottesville, Virginia. He is also a triple board certified physician in the fields of endocrinology, metabolism, and internal medicine and end-of-life care.

The following passage from a white paper authored by Dr. Bush and his colleagues further explains how and why glyphosate poses such a grave risk to our health:

"The water-soluble characteristic of glyphosate allows the chemical to move via the root systems of plants with the intracellular water of the primary plant and the resulting fruits or vegetables. In addition, glyphosate can travel in the microecosystem in all phases of the water cycle, contaminating fossil aquifers, ground water runoff, streams, rivers, and oceans, as well as air humidity and rainfall...Glyphosate kills bacteria, fungi, and plants by blocking the Shikimate enzyme pathway in these organisms. The Shikimate pathway is responsible for producing the carbon-ringed essential amino acids, such as tryptophan, that serve as critical building blocks for hormones and other proteins in animals and humans."

Dr. Bush and his team also demonstrated that "glyphosate can directly damage tight junction proteins in both epithelial (intestinal) and endothelial (vascular) cell barriers." As Dr. Bush explains, "The gut lining is a barrier, our first line of defense, working to protect our bloodstream and the rest of our body from toxic substances such as glyphosate, gluten, and other foreign particles. But just as importantly, it functions to allow the passage of beneficial nutrients. Preserving the integrity of this barrier is key to health.

"Tight junctions (the seals between cells) fortify our gut linings. Good health depends entirely on the gut, and a healthy gut depends on tight junction integrity. When tight junctions are exposed to glyphosate and other ubiquitous environmental toxins, they break apart, allowing foreign particles to invade the bloodstream. This compromises your immune system." Compounding this problem, glyphosate also stimulates the production of a protein known as zonulin, which acts as a modulator of the tight junctions. Glyphosate causes zonulin to disrupt tight junction function, resulting in a wide range of GI disorders and other chronic inflammatory and autoimmune diseases.

Dr. Bush has discovered that a unique class of soil-derived carbon molecules act to maintain tight junction integrity, thereby protecting against the harmful effects of glyphosate and other environmental toxins, antibiotics, and other harmful substances, including gluten. These carbon molecules, which collectively are known as Terrahydrate(R), are produced by soil bacteria and are rich in trace minerals, amino acids, and other substances that have a positive effect on the gut.

Further research into these unique carbon molecules led Dr. Bush and his team to create a liquid Terrahydrate supplement known as ION* Gut Health (formerly Restore™). Since its development, clinical studies have established that ION* Gut Health, when used regularly, not only improves and maintains tight junction integrity, but also helps promote healthy diversification of microbiome bacteria.

In one double-blind, placebo controlled study conducted by Dr. Bush and others, ION* Gut Health (then known as Restore) decreased baseline levels of glyphosate in the bodies of test subjects by 23 percent after only two weeks, while also decreasing zonulin, and TNFa and IL-6, two significant markers for chronic inflammation. "The mechanism by which this complex family of microbial metabolites that serve as the active ingredient in ION*Gut Health has begun to be elucidated in the same clinical study with analysis of urine amino acid and neuropeptide levels," Dr. Bush says. "Of significance, the essential amino acid lysine was markedly increased in the urine by two weeks. This increased availability of this amino acid that is produced uniquely by the microbiome, rather than in the human gut or other organ systems, is noteworthy because lysine an essential constituent of tens of thousands of proteins throughout all of the organ systems, and also uniquely serves broader functions that can impact all protein production in the body. Lysine stabilizes protein synthesis and protein folding and regulates epigenetic response to environmental insult."

As a result of such studies, an increasing number of ACIM and other integrative physicians and health practitioners now recommend ION* Gut Health to their patients as a first line of defense against glyphosate and other toxins.

"Instead of feeding your microbiome with various bacterial strains, ION* Gut Health works via redox signaling to maintain tight junction integrity in the epithelial layer of the gut lining," Dr. Bush explains. "This not only shields your system from toxins, it creates a stable environment where the microbiome can thrive, helping to promote diversification and immune system function.

"We use ION* Gut Health as a foundation of health for a broad spectrum of patients. ION* Gut Health does not treat any disease. Instead, it promotes strong membrane integrity through its direct and indirect effects on the tight junctions of the bowel wall and vascular systems of the body, and restoration of the bowel ecology with the unique bacterial communication attribute of the supplement. Microbiome balance and tight junction integrity are widely recognized to constitute a major portion of the human immune system, and directly affect DNA transcription of human cells to promote optimal health. The well-proven biology of ION* Gut Health demonstrates its role as a foundational resource in your pursuit for optimal health."

ION* Gut Health supplements are available for both humans and pets. The original ION* Gut Health supplement is recommended to be taken three times a day, ideally 30 minutes before each meal, at a dose of one teaspoon. A similar product developed especially for children, known as ION* Gut Health for Kids, is also available, as is ION* Sinus, a nasal spray that was developed to both support the microbiome and soothe and hydrate the delicate membranes lining the nasal passages, protecting them from dust, pollen, and other environmental irritants.

Since cats, dogs, and other animals are also exposed to glyphosate and other toxins in much the same way humans are, Dr. Bush and his team have also developed a formula for pets known as ION* Gut Health for Pets.

All ION* products can be ordered online at www.IONBiome. com, where you will also find more research demonstrating ION* Gut Health's proven health benefits.

Other Gut Health-Enhancing Strategies

Other steps you can take to improve and maintain the health of your gut and microbiome include time restricted eating, fasting, eating fruits and vegetable "right off the vine", regularly spending time outdoors, and regularly exposing yourself to different natural environments.

Time restricted eating, or TRE, means consuming all of the foods you eat each day within an eight to 12-hour period. By doing so, you allow your body 12 to 16 hours to rest and repair itself through a process known as autophagy.

Autophagy is a natural process of cellular cleansing in which the body essentially "eats" parts of itself by breaking down and then eliminating old, worn down proteins, cell membranes, and other parts of cells which can no longer be sustained by the body's energy. This enables the body to replace these cellular components with new, healthier versions, thereby helping the body to maintain itself.

Autophagy can only occur during times of fasting, which TRE mimics to some extent. TRE is not the same thing as dieting or calorie restriction. You can eat as you normally do as long as you limit the window of time each day in which you do so.

You can increase the benefits autophagy provides by periodically fasting. A 24-hour water fast done weekly or every other week is safe for most people to undergo. In addition to enabling cell cleansing, fasting has also been shown to stimulate the body's production of growth hormones, which typically decline as we age. You may also wish to explore periodic longer fasts of three to five days, although these should initially be undertaken under the supervision of a doctor or other health practitioner familiar with fasting's therapeutic benefits.

Dr. Bush recommends eating organic fruits and vegetables as soon as they are picked if you have access to a garden or farmers in your area. Fresh-picked fruits and vegetables contain the microbiome of their external environment on their skin, Dr. Bush points out. By eating these foods off the vine you introduce the elements of that microbiome into your own GI environment, resulting in greater diversity of gut bacteria. If you don't have access to a garden, consider growing one, or planting one or more vegetables in pots inside your home.

Dr. Bush also recommends spending at least ten minutes of the day outdoors, ideally barefoot in the grass or dirt. Doing so will also help to strengthen your microbiome, as will regularly spending time outdoors in diverse natural environments, especially state and National parks, which for the most part are free of glyphosate and other environmental toxins. Since he is based in Virginia, Dr. Bush tells his patients to spend time at the shores of Virginia Beach, and in the mountains, by waterfalls, and even the swamps in the southern part of the state. All natural settings contain their own microbiomes that mix with our own as we breathe because of how our nasal passages are designed to capture bacteria in the air. The more varied the nature settings that you can spend time within, the more diverse will be the bacteria you inhale, further strengthening your own microbiome and overall gut health.

By adopting at least some of the above strategies, and following the healthy eating guidelines in Chapter 2, you will go a long way in improving the health of your gut and microbiome, and your overall health.

CHAPTER 4

The Fourth Key: The Wise Use Of Nutritional Supplements

I N CHAPTER 2, you learned about the importance a healthy diet can play in keeping you healthy and promoting longevity. Unfortunately, the level of nutrients in a healthy diet, even one that is rich in organically grown foods, is no longer sufficient by itself to ensure excellent health.

Because of how devitalized crop soil in the U.S. has become due to commercial farming methods, even organically-farmed foods today contain far less minerals than they did before such farming methods became so dominant in the early- to mid-20th century. As a result, food crops are less nutrient dense than they were 100 years ago. This problem is made worse by the rampant use of glyphosate and other pesticides, herbicides, and other nutrient-sapping chemicals. The heavy metals and many other toxins that we are all exposed to in our environment also increase our need for nutrients in order for us to stay healthy, as do the stresses of daily life.

The wise use of certain nutritional supplements can help rectify these problems. However, as with diet, when it comes to nutritional supplements, there is no such thing as a "one-size-fits-all" recommendation for everyone. Determining your nutritional needs may require blood tests or other types of diagnostic methods, such as those discussed in Chapter 1. Overall, though, most people will obtain benefit from nutritional supplementation.

In this chapter you will learn about the nutrients that are most essential for supplementing a healthy diet, starting with four vital nutrients that most doctors ignore.

Dr. Sinatra's "Awesome Foursome"

Stephen Sinatra, MD, is a world-renowned cardiologist with over 40 years of clinical experience, and a pioneer in the field of metabolic cardiology. Metabolic cardiology focuses on the prevention, management and treatment of cardiovascular disease through nutritional and bioenergetic interventions that have been shown to improve energy metabolism in heart cells.

"A metabolic cardiologist views prevention and treatment of cardiovascular disease through the eyes of both a cellular biochemist and a physician," Dr. Sinatra explains. "In doing so, she or he can complement, and perhaps prevent, pharmaceutical and surgical interventions through targeted nutritional support. As conventional therapies often result in unpleasant side effects due to nutrient depletion, metabolic cardiology is the most ethical and logical approach for prevention and treatment of cardiovascular disease.

"Metabolic cardiology has been a game changer for compromised patients. I've had probably over three dozen patients over the years—pediatric, young adults, seniors, it didn't matter—who were waiting for heart transplants, who absolutely did not go for a heart transplant once a heart was found. This is the essence of metabolic cardiology."

According to Dr. Sinatra, a primary aim of metabolic cardiology is to improve and maintain levels of adenosine triphosate, or ATP, in the body, and most especially in the heart. Produced by mitochondria, the "energy factories" in the cells, "ATP provides the energy of life for virtually all the body's processes," Dr. Sinatra says. "Its role in health maintenance, especially with regard to heart health, cannot be overestimated. The human heart needs a minimum of 6,000 grams of ATP per day to function. As the universal cellular energy currency, ATP is constantly spent and re-made within the body.

"It's important to remember that the heart has the largest number of mitochondria which make ATP. A third of the weight of the heart is mitochondria. The heart is endowed with more mitochondria per cell than any other organ in the body, including the brain.

"How much ATP the body needs, as well as how efficiently it produces ATP, depends on the availability of oxygen and various nutrients in the blood, as well as the heart's ability to continually circulate blood. Maintaining a healthy cardiovascular system through a heart-healthy diet, inhaling enough oxygen, and obtaining appropriate nutrients through the diet and nutraceutical supplementation are essential means of staying energetic and maintaining wellness."

A quartet of nutrients that Dr. Sinatra has dubbed "the awesome foursome" make up the foundation of the nutraceutical supplementation aspect of metabolic cardiology. They are coenzyme Q10 (CoQ10), L-carnitine, magnesium, and D-ribose.

"While we cannot take an ATP pill, we can do the next best thing by supporting our bodies in producing it," Dr. Sinatra says. "As we can fertilize a garden so that it blooms, we can enrich our mitochondria with essential nutrients that facilitate ATP production and protect mitochondrial structures. I strongly suggest doing so with the awesome foursome. This dream team of metabolic cardiology features individual benefits which best work synergistically. As transporters of vital substances like electrons and fatty acids, CoQ10 and L-carnitine are responsible for several facets of the ATP production process. Additionally, CoQ10 acts as an important antioxidant to protect mitochondrial membranes from free-radical damage. D-ribose supports CoQ10 and carnitine's abilities by maintaining a healthy pool of energy substrates. By partnering in over 300 enzymatic reactions in the body, including ATP production and muscle relaxation, magnesium helps improve metabolic efficiency.

"Supplementing with the awesome foursome becomes especially important when our energy demands start to exceed our natural production of ATP. Increasing age, illness, a lack of oxygen (ischemia), and nutritional deficiencies can all contribute to ATP imbalance in the body. Supplementing with, and consuming through food, the awesome foursome, as well as essential fatty acids and low-glycemic, vitamin-filled sources of glucose, can help us boost ATP production, and therefore help prevent and treat degenerative diseases like cardiovascular disease."

The first of the awesome foursome nutrients that Dr. Sinatra researched was CoQ10, beginning in the early 1980s. His interest in this nutrient stemmed from the experience of one of his patients at that time. "I saw a young woman who was waiting for a heart transplant," he recounts. "She already had a two-year-old and had given birth to a second child. After her delivery, she went into heart failure. We call it postpartum cardiomyopathy. It's really a nightmare for a cardiologist because you're dealing with a young woman who had a normal heart and then all of a sudden, following delivery, basically the baby gets everything, all the nutrients out of the mother's body. It's a very rare condition in which a mother is susceptible to the baby draining her of energy and nutrients and she develops heart failure.

"This woman was so short of breath that she could not even walk up a flight of stairs. She was dying of heart failure and had gone from doctor to doctor, then was told about what I was doing with some of my patients through some of her friends. By the time she came to see me, she was waiting for a heart transplant from the Medical College of Virginia. They had typed and crossed her and taken tissue samples, and she was waiting for a donor heart while being treated with the usual medications for heart failure. I put her on CoQ10. I was only using low doses then, typically 10 milligrams three times a day.

"I saw her a week later and she said to me, I don't know, doctor, but I think I feel a little better. So I doubled the medication to 20 milligrams three times a day. A week later I saw her again and she said, I feel a little better. I'm not coughing as much. I have a little more strength. So I doubled her dose of CoQ10 again to 40 milligrams, three times a day. I never used doses that high before because back then the use of CoQ10 clinically was in the larval stage. One week after that I saw her again, and she said to me, This is unbelievable, but I feel good."

Because of the improvement in her health she achieved using

CoQ10, the woman no longer needed a new heart. "She was like a messenger to me," Dr. Sinatra says, "because her turnaround was so dramatic after only three weeks. Now I know it makes sense because of what I learned about the nature of CoQ10 in the years that followed. It takes about three weeks to build up a sufficient blood level."

Following that remarkable outcome Dr. Sinatra became very involved with the International Coenzyme Q10 Association (http://icqaproject.org). "I presented papers at their international conferences and I was one of the first doctors to strongly suggest that when it comes to CoQ10, you need five to seven times the normal blood level to make a difference. I realized that CoQ10 was almost like pharmaceutical drugs, such as ACE inhibitors or digitalis, where we would use low doses and then increase the dose slowly. So it made sense that, even though the body produces it, when you have an inexorable drain of CoQ10 from tissues that are starving for it, you need to give a lot of it.

"After that particular case, I reported on three cases in the medical literature about refractory heart failure that improved dramatically after blood levels of five to seven times of CoQ10 were obtained. The normal blood level for CoQ10 is about 0.5 to 0.6 ug/mL. For really severe heart failure, I would get the level to 2.5 ug/mL or even higher. I've had patients with blood levels of 3.5 where they developed a dramatic therapeutic response. In patients who are very sick, it's very important to tailor the CoQ10 blood level and get it up to where it will make a difference.

"There have been over 60 double-blind, placebo-controlled clinical trials of CoQ10, and only in four trials CoQ 10 made no difference. But in these four trials the blood levels of CoQ10 were insignificant to even obtain a bio-sensitive result. In other words, the researchers said that CoQ10 made no difference in heart failure, that it failed, but the patients in the trials never obtained the level of 2.5 to 3.5 ug/mL. So none of those patients had a chance. You've got to realize that the human body is really a high energy output machine, and if you use low doses or inadequate doses of CoQ10— and the same thing is true of pharmaceuticals—you are not going to achieve the blood level that the body needs. Over the years, as I published these cases in the medical literature and discussed them at international conferences on CoQ10, it became clear that, when it comes to CoQ10 failures, the first thing to look at is whether or not there was a bio- sensitive result. Was there a respectable blood level?"

Following the success he achieved with his patients using CoQ10, Dr. Sinatra continued to investigate other nutrients and soon added L-carnitine and magnesium to his protocol. Doing so led to another extraordinary patient outcome. "I've had so many patients needing heart transplantation over the years," he says. "Probably the most profound was a young boy named Ryan. I'll never forget him. He was this nine-year-old boy and his parents were sobbing in my office because they couldn't find a heart transplant to treat him. He'd already had palliative surgery. He had a very rare congenital disorder called singlet outlet ventricle, a condition you cannot really survive unless you have palliative surgeries. But really heart transplantation is the only recourse if palliative surgery is done because people won't live with this condition.

"I put Ryan on my program, which back then was CoQ10, L-carnitine, and magnesium, because I hadn't learned about D-ribose yet. And like my other patients I was treating, he began improving. He went from dying of heart failure to an acceptable quality of life. It was recommended that he received heart transplantation and he refused three times. Today, Ryan is in his early thirties and now he's on D-ribose in addition to the other three nutrients."

Though he was having great success treating most of his heart patients with CoQ10, carnitine, and magnesium, Dr. Sinatra remained puzzled as to why a small percentage of them did not respond. "I would have nine out of ten patients thrive, but the one failure would keep me up at night," he says. "I was always questioning why my protocol didn't work in this one particular patient? It really bothered me."

The answer Dr. Sinatra was searching for came about when he heard a lecture given by fellow cardiologist Dr. Jim Roberts in 2004. "I'm sitting in the audience and Jim's lecturing about the physiology and the pharmacology of D-ribose," Dr. Sinatra recounts. "And all of a sudden, I got it. Jim had just delivered the missing link that I'd spent years looking for. I started to use D-ribose in my patients who were not recovering and they started to thrive." As a result of that lecture, Dr. Sinatra invited Dr. Roberts to collaborate with him on two books, *The Sinatra Solution: Metabolic Cardiology*, for which Dr. Roberts wrote the Introduction, and *Reverse Heart Disease Now*, which they co-wrote.

In 2009, another answer as to why Dr. Sinatra was having such great success with Ryan and his other patients using his awesome foursome was revealed when he read a scientific paper published by Scandinavian researchers in the journal *Science*. "What these researchers suggested was that, because of the release of the radioactive isotope carbon 14 into the atmosphere during the atomic bomb testing that took place in the 1940s and 50s, carbon 14 testing could be used to determine the age of cells, including the cells of the heart," Dr. Sinatra explains. "And they determined that the heart could actually regenerate itself by as much as 40 percent over several years. Now, that's huge because they had established that the heart is capable of regeneration. We know that new blood cells are formed every 120 days, and the epithelial cells in the GI tract are replaced after a few days. Our body is constantly regenerating new cells, but nobody believed that the heart could be regenerated until this paper came out.

"When I read the article, I had this great joy because I realized that Ryan was regenerating his cardiac cells, forming new heart cells, and that was the reason why he didn't need heart transplantation. Then I thought about my other patients who had been spared the need for heart transplants after being told transplantation was their only hope and this just made a lot of sense. I had this incredible Aha realization that metabolic cardiology was working in the direction of supporting ATP, but there was a missing link, so to speak. I used to just think that CoQ10, carnitine, ribose, and magnesium did something unusual to the heart to resurrect it to the point where patients felt so much better that they refused transplantation. Reading this article, I realized that the hearts of my patients were literally regenerating themselves.

"Someday somebody is going to discover the missing link between metabolic cardiology and the re-emergence of stem cell repair or stem cell rejuvenation in the cardiac cells. Is it exosomes? Is it cytokines? Is it chemical messengers? Is it proteins? I don't know. But what I do know is that when you bring metabolic cardiology to the table and you drive ATP in a preferential direction miracles happen."

To maintain your cardiovascular health, Dr. Sinatra recommends the following daily doses.

CoQ10: 100-150 mg to maintain health; therapeutic doses of 200-300 mg to restore health. "The highest doses I have given have been 500 milligrams to up to a gram," Dr. Sinatra says. "People can usually tolerate high doses of CoQ10 in the form of a high quality ubiquinone product. The story about ubiquinol versus ubiquinone [the two forms of CoQ10] is, I believe, exaggerated advertising because we've shown with blood level testing that a highly bioavailable ubiquinone is as good as ubiquinol."

L-carnitine: "Usually 1000 mg a day is sufficient for most people," Dr. Sinatra says. "Higher doses can sometimes cause diminished thyroid function."

D-ribose: 5,000 milligrams once to three times a day, depending on a person's symptoms. "For therapeutic purposes, you must give D-ribose at least three times a day for people with moderate to severe heart failure," Dr. Sinatra notes. "For people with mild heart failure once or twice a day is sufficient."

Magnesium: "Most people are deficient in magnesium," Dr. Sinatra points out. "I think everybody should be taking magnesium because it's not in the soil anymore, and vegetables don't carry it like they used to. For most people I recommend a minimum of 400 milligrams of magnesium per day, usually at bedtime. For metabolic cardiology, sometimes I might give more, but I usually start with 400 milligrams and most of these people do well."

Dr. Sinatra has developed a broad-spectrum magnesium formula based on the body's Krebs cycle. It provides four forms of bioavailable magnesium—citrate, glycinate, taurinate, and orotate. "Australian researchers have shown that magnesium orotate drives ATP even more than other forms of magnesium," he says. "The product I developed combines orotate with the other three components, and that's the magnesium I use with my patients because I find it to be most effective."

Dr. Sinatra's Magnesium Broad-Spectrum Complex product and all of the other nutritional products he's developed based on his decades-long experience as a leading metabolic cardiologist are available at DrSinatra.com. You can also find a wealth of health and nutritional information he provides at his companion website www. HeartMDInstitute.com, where you can also sign up to receive his free health updates via email.

Other Nutrients You Should Consider

Dr. Sinatra's awesome foursome are far from the only nutritional supplements that can enhance your health, of course. Other helpful nutrients fall into three main categories—vitamins, minerals, and essential fatty acids. What follow are the most important nutrients in each group that you should consider.

Vitamins

Most people are not obtaining enough of the vitamins below from their food. When they begin to supplement with them, their health typically improves.

Vitamin A/Beta carotene: Vitamin A is required for good health of the eyes, skin, and mucosal surfaces in the gut and respiratory tract. In addition, vitamin A plays a key role in bone growth, cell differentiation, and tissue repair. It is also a potent antioxidant and important for proper immune function and protection against infectious disease.

Both stress and disease can diminish vitamin A stores, as can alcohol consumption. Signs of vitamin A deficiency include night blindness, impaired bone and teeth health, impaired immunity, and inflammation of the eyes.

One of the best ways to supplement with vitamin A is in the form of beta-carotene, which your body can convert to vitamin A in the liver. Beta-carotene is abundant in many colored and green, leafy vegetables, but since studies have found that nearly one-third of the American public consumes less than 65 percent of the recommended daily allowance (RDA) for vitamin A, supplementing with 5,000-10,000 IU of beta-carotene once a day can be helpful. Emulsified vitamin A is a better form to use to temporarily boost the immune system and combat respiratory infections.

B Complex vitamins: B complex vitamins are essential for helping your body convert food into energy. In addition, B vitamins, especially vitamins B6, B12, and folate, are vital for proper methylation, a biochemical process that converts homocysteine into the amino acids S-adenosyl-methionine, methionine, and cysteine. Unconverted homocysteine is a marker for heart disease and overall inflammation in the body. Methylation is therefore important for maintaining overall cardiovascular health, but also for protecting the brain, mental functioning, the body's nervous system, and nerve cell function, all of which can be impaired by chronic inflammation.

B vitamins also play an important role in regulating gene expression, maintaining proper energy metabolism, and assisting the body's immune system, and are necessary to protect against the ravages of chronic stress. Because B vitamins are water-soluble, they cannot be stored in the body and therefore must be replenished on a daily basis.

Coenzymated B complex vitamins are the best bioavailable form of B vitamins, and include all of the individual B vitamins your body needs. You can find a good coenzymated B complex formula at your local health food store. Look for a brand that includes active forms of the essential B vitamins: B1 (thiamine), B2 (riboflavin), B3 (niacin), B5 (pantothenic acid), B6, B12 (as methylcobalamin), biotin, choline, inositol and methyl folate, the biologically active form of folic acid, for optimal methylation. A typical recommended dosage is one capsule one to three times per day taken with meals.

Vitamin C: Vitamin C, also known as ascorbic acid or ascorbate, is one of the most important nutrients that your body requires because of the many functions it plays a key role in. Besides being a potent antioxidant, vitamin is essential for proper immune function and supports the health of bones, blood vessels, capillary walls, cartilage, joint linings, ligaments, skin, teeth, and vertebrae. It also is needed for proper wound healing, plays an important role in your body's detoxification processes, and can enhance calcium absorption.

Vitamin C can neither be manufactured nor stored by your body. Therefore, it is crucial that you receive adequate vitamin C intake each and every day.

Signs of vitamin C deficiency are numerous. They include anemia, bleeding gums, increased tendency toward bruising, lowered resistance to infections, mouth ulcers, and slow wound healing. Currently, the recommend daily allowance (RDA) for vitamin C is only 60 mg, an amount that is extremely low. A higher dose of between 1,000-3,000 mg of vitamin C per day is recommended. 3,000 mg of vitamin C can be divided into three doses of 1,000 mg each spread throughout the day. You can safely increase this dose during times of illnesses such as colds and flu.

Vitamin D: Vitamin D is produced by the body as a result of sunlight exposure. Daily sun light exposure is the preferred method for ensuring your body receives the vitamin D it requires, followed by vitamin D-rich foods. Ideally, try to expose at least one-third of your body (arms, face, and hands) to sunlight for 20 to 30 minutes each day. Good food sources of vitamin D include butter, cod liver oil, egg yolk, liver, milk, and oily fish such as herring, mackerel, sardines, and salmon.

During winter months and at other times when you are unable to get out in the sun, short-term vitamin D supplementation, in the form of D3 can be advisable. This is also true during cold and flu season. Overall, though, regular sunlight exposure and consumption of vitamin D-rich foods are the best means for maintaining healthy vitamin D levels.

Vitamin E: Vitamin E is the name given to group of eight fat-soluble compounds consisting of four tocopherols and four tocotrienols, each of which offers distinct health benefits. Together, they act as another important antioxidant that neutralizes free-radical damage, and as a powerful immune enhancer,because of their ability to increase levels of the interferon and interleukin, two biochemicals that are required by the immune system to prevent and fight off infections.

The bioavailability of vitamin E is crucial when you choose a vitamin E supplement. Synthetic versions of vitamin E are poorly absorbed and often lack all eight tocopherols and tocotrienols. For best results, look for a natural version of vitamin E that contains the full range of these compounds. Two such products are Super Vitamin E and Gamma E Mixed Tocopherols & Tocotrienols, both of which are manufactured and sold by the Life Extension Foundation (www.lifeextension.com). You can order them directly from LEF's website. A recommend dose is between 400-800 IU/day.

Vitamin K: Vitamin K is a fat-soluble vitamin that plays an important role in healthy blood clotting. It has also been shown to help maintain healthy heart function, and to support the health of the bones and the body's immune system. Vitamin K also helps prevent calcium from being displaced into the arteries and kidneys. It should always be taken whenever you use a vitamin D supplement.

There are two natural forms of vitamin K: K1 (phylloquinone), which is found in green vegetables, especially leafy greens, and K2 (menaquinone), which is found in fermented foods, such as miso, kimchi, and kefir, and can be formed by certain healthy gut bacteria. As a supplement, the most absorbable, and therefore most effective, form of vitamin K is K2. K2 is also the form of vitamin K that has been shown to offer the best benefits for overall health, and for preventing vitamin D displacement. However,

K1 is the form that best supports healthy blood clotting. For this reason, a supplement that contains both vitamin K1 and K2 is recommended.

Minerals

The following minerals are also important for your health.

Boron: Boron helps your body metabolize and make use of various other nutrients, such as calcium, vitamin D, and magnesium. Boron also contributes to the overall health of the bones, which is where your body stores much of the minerals it uses to buffer and neutralize acid buildup. Recent research suggests that boron helps regulate your body's endocrine system, which is responsible for how your body produces and makes use of hormones, including testosterone in men. It also helps to regulate estrogen levels in both men and women, and prevents them from becoming excessive in men.

Potential signs of boron deficiency include osteoporosis and other bone conditions, and all forms of arthritis. Among older women, boron deficiency can also contribute to problems related to post-menopause.

While boron can be obtained from your diet by eating plentiful amounts of fruits, nuts, and vegetables, boron deficiencies are common among most Americans today. Therefore, supplementing with between one to three mg of boron once a day should be considered. This low dosage range should be enough to ensure your body has enough boron to meet its needs.

Chromium: Chromium is a mineral essential for regulating the production of insulin, which is responsible for stabilizing blood sugar levels and preventing the conversion of blood sugar into fat. Chromium also plays important roles in helping to protect against type II diabetes and unhealthy weight gain and obesity. Although your body requires only small amounts of this important mineral, Americans are more likely to be deficient in chromium than many other micronutrients.

Food sources of chromium include brewer's yeast, wheat germ, beef and chicken, liver, whole grains, potatoes, eggs, apples, bananas, and spinach. However, chromium obtained from food can be quickly depleted by a variety of factors, including a high-carbohydrate diet, infections, air pollution, exposure to radiation, and physical and emotional stress. Regular chromium supplementation is therefore important for maintaining your health.

Chromium is better absorbed in the body when bound in a "transporter" molecule, called a chelate. Chelated minerals are better protected from damage in the digestive system. Glucose tolerance factor chelate (GTF chromium) is a more bioavailable form of chromium than other chromium supplements. Chromium polynicotinate (ChromeMate brand, which is not to be confused with picolinate) is another chelated variety that is chemically bound to niacin, a B-complex vitamin, and is also well absorbed. A typical recommended daily dosage is between 200-600 mcg. depending on the level of one's stress.

Magnesium: Approximately 65 percent of your body's magnesium stores are found in your bones and teeth, followed by high concentrations in your muscles. Magnesium is also contained in the blood and other body fluids, and inside your cells.

Magnesium's numerous health benefits make it easy to understand why Dr. Sinatra has included it in his awesome foursome nutritional protocol. It plays many crucial health-promoting roles in your body, including participating in hundreds of enzymatic reactions and acting as a musculoskeletal relaxant. It is also important for the health of your heart, and for preventing heart attacks because of its ability to relax coronary arteries and for its role in cellular energy production in the form of ATP. As Dr. Sinatra explained, your heart has the highest need of ATP of any organ in your body.

Magnesium also aids in proper cell division, cell maintenance and repair, hormone regulation, proper nerve transmission, protein metabolism, and thyroid function, helps the body assimilate and use calcium and vitamin D, and is necessary for healthy bones and teeth.

As Dr. Sinatra points out, the vast majority of Americans suffer from chronic magnesium deficiencies, though this condition is often undiagnosed. Symptoms of magnesium deficiency include depression, fatigue, gastrointestinal disorders, hypertension, irregular heartbeat, memory problems, mood swings, impaired motor skills, muscle spasms, nausea, and osteoporosis. Some of the best food sources of magnesium are dark green vegetables, apricots, avocado, brown rice, legumes, nuts, seaweed, and seeds.

Because of how easily magnesium can be depleted in the body, a multi-pronged approach for meeting your daily magnesium needs is essential. First, be sure to eat an abundant supply of magnesium-rich foods each day. Then consider using magnesium supplements, especially during times of elevated stress. You can also obtain magnesium from Epsom salt baths. Simply add one to two cups of Epsom salt to a bath of hot water (as hot as you can comfortably tolerate) and soak your body for 30 to 40 minutes at least once a week.

If you don't have a tub to soak in, you can add ¼ cup of Epsom salt to two gallons of very warm water in a five-gallon plastic bucket or other container and soak both feet for 30 minutes. Alternatively, if two hand-towels are soaked in a sink of very warm water containing ¼ cup of Epsom salt, one wet towel can be placed on each bare thigh while sitting for 30 minutes.

MSM: MSM (*methyl sulfonyl methane*) is a sulfur compound that helps build healthy cells and enhances the health and growth of hair, muscles, nails, and skin. It also plays an important role in the manufacture of collagen, the primary component of your body's cartilage and connective tissue.

In recent years, MSM has gained a reputation as a natural means of alleviating pain related to arthritis. Additional research indicates that MSM can increase hair and nail growth and help repair damaged skin. It also enhances the ability of body fluids to more easily pass through tissues, thus improving the delivery of oxygen and nutrients to the cells, and the elimination of cellular waste products.

Though MSM is available in fresh fruits and vegetables, meats, milk, and seafood, most people are deficient in sulfur because of how the body continuously uses and excretes it. This deficiency is made worse by the fact that people often do not eat enough MSM-rich foods. In addition, MSM levels in the body naturally decline with age.

Supplementing with MSM is an effective and inexpensive way to ensure your body abundantly meets its daily sulfur requirements. MSM is an extremely safe and nontoxic substance. Your body will use what it needs and eliminate what it does not. A typical supplement dose ranges between 2,000 to 5,000 mg of MSM daily. For best results, take it with meals, along with vitamin C.

Potassium: Potassium is an essential body salt. Approximately 98 percent of your body's potassium stores are found within the cells. Potassium helps conduct bioelectrical current throughout the body, maintains cellular integrity and fluid balance, helps regulate nerve function, aids in energy production and heart function, and is crucial for proper pH levels.

Potassium deficiency is quite common among most Americans, especially among the elderly and people with chronic illness. One of the main causes of potassium deficiencies, besides poor diet, is the use of diuretics and laxatives, both of which strip potassium from the body. Eating canned and processed foods can also deplete potassium supplies because of their high sodium (salt) content. Symptoms of potassium deficiency include arrhythmia, depression, fatigue, hypertension, hyperglycemia, mood swings, and impaired nerve function.

The best food sources of potassium are fresh fruits and vegetables. Bananas, avocados, sweet potatoes, spinach, apricots and grapefruit, in particular, are rich in potassium. Other good food sources include nuts, seeds, whole grains, and fish such as salmon and sardines. Though there is no established RDA for potassium, most people require between 2,000 to 5,000 mg per day. A variety of potassium supplements are available, in the forms of both tablets and liquid. Either form is well-absorbed, but potassium levels often remain low until magnesium deficiency is corrected .

Selenium This essential trace mineral works well with vitamin E. Together, they enhance each other's beneficial effects in the body, especially with regard to protecting against free radical damage. Selenium is an essential cofactor for glutathione peroxidase (one of the most important antioxidants that the body produces), and for antioxidant enzymes known as *selenoproteins*. Selenium has been shown by research to help reduce the risk of both cancer and heart disease, and also arthritis. Additionally, selenium helps to boost immune function and can increase male fertility.

Selenium-rich foods include Brazil nuts (the highest food source; because of their high selenium content, they should only be eaten a few times per week to avoid selenium toxicity), sardines, yellow fin tuna, shellfish (clams, oysters, shrimp), sunflower seeds, beef, chicken, and pork. As a supplement, the recommend dose is 55-100 mcg (micrograms) daily if not consuming Brazil nuts.

Zinc: Zinc is another mineral that your body needs to ensure its health. In addition to being a cofactor for a potent antioxidant called superoxide dismutase, zinc is necessary for over two hundred enzymatic reactions in the body. It also is important for detoxification, bone repair, maintaining healthy cellular membranes and tissues, ensuring proper immune function, and regulating insulin production. Zinc also helps your body absorb and utilize vitamins A and D and calcium. In men, zinc is essential for the health of the prostate gland.

Zinc deficiencies among Americans are quite common, especially among vegetarians. Lack of zinc can result in dermatitis, fatigue, hair loss, impaired immune function, loss of libido, and osteoporosis, and can also increase risk of prostate problems, including enlargement, infection, and prostate cancer. The RDA for zinc is 15 mg for adults, although many health researchers believe this level is too low. 30 mg per day, especially for men over 40 years of age, may be more appropriate. When supplementing with zinc, it is best to take it in the form of picolinate for optimum absorption. The best food sources of zinc include beef, egg yolk, herring, and shellfish.

Two Minerals You Should Avoid Supplementing With

While maintaining your body's supply of minerals via supplementation is a good idea, there are two minerals that your body needs—calcium and iron—that are best obtained solely from your diet.

Calcium: Calcium is the most abundant mineral in your body. Nearly all of it is stored in bone tissue, where it is used to ensure the health of both bones and teeth. Your body uses the remainder of its calcium supply to help regulate blood clotting and blood pressure levels, cardiovascular function, cell division, and muscle and nerve function. Calcium is also required for healthy skin, and is one of the primary acid-buffering minerals called upon by your body whenever excess tissue acids pose a problem.

It is important to supply your body with adequate amounts of calcium each and every day through your diet. Though most Americans derive calcium from dairy foods, the best food sources of calcium are vegetables (especially broccoli, collard greens, and dark green leafy vegetables), and certain types of fish, such as sardines and salmon. Almonds are another good source. Vegetable sources of calcium do not cause tissue acidity like dairy products can.

Since the 1980s, calcium supplements have been recommended to women by physicians as a means of preventing osteoporosis. Yet, the advisability of calcium supplementation has been called into question by research showing that calcium supplements can increase the risk of calcification of the arteries and, therefore, heart attack and stroke. Calcium obtained from foods does not pose this same health risk. For this reason, it's best to you meet your body's calcium requirements through the calcium-rich foods listed above.

Iron: Iron is required for the production of hemoglobin in red blood cells, and works synergistically with copper in this process. Hemoglobin transports oxygen throughout the body, and gives red blood cells their color. Iron deficiencies can lead to anemia, a condition characterized by fatigue, shortness of breath, and pale skin caused by a lack of tissue oxygen. Iron bound to myoglobin, a protein found in muscle tissue, also helps supply muscles with oxygen so that they can contract and function properly.

But as you learned in Chapter 1, iron can build up in your body, causing iron overload and unbound iron. Research has shown that even mild cases of iron overload can increase the risk for cancer, diabetes and metabolic syndrome, heart attack and heart failure, hypothyroidism, liver disease osteoarthritis, osteoporosis, and in some cases premature death. Iron overload has also been linked to neurodegenerative diseases such as Alzheimer's, Parkinson's, Huntington's, epilepsy and multiple sclerosis. For these reasons, it is not advisable to consume iron as a supplement, whether alone or as an ingredient in multivitamin/mineral formulas.

Foods high in iron include beef, dark-meat poultry, eggs, dark green leafy vegetables, black-eyed peas, chickpeas, other dried beans, beets, raisins, dates and apricots. If you are at risk for iron overload, consume these foods sparingly. In addition, you can reduce excess iron levels by donating blood a few times each year and by exercising regularly.

Essential Fatty Acids

A third class of nutrients that are important for your health are essential fatty acids.

Though excess fat consumption can lead to a variety of health problems, your body requires certain types of fat each day in order to be healthy. These fats, which are not produced by your body, and therefore must be obtained through diet and supplementation, are known as "essential fatty acids" (EFAs) because of the many important roles they play in the body.

EFAs help produce energy, regulate hormone and nerve function, maintain healthy brain function, aid in overall musculoskeletal function and calcium metabolism, and help to reduce inflammation in the body. EFAs make up a part of cell membranes and are particularly concentrated in the adrenal glands, brain cells, the eyes, nerve cells, and the sex glands.

There are two primary forms of essential fatty acids—omega-3 fatty acids and omega-6 fatty acids.

Omega-3 fatty acids occur in three forms, alpha-linoleic acid (ALA), docosahexanoic acid (DHA), and eicosapentaenoic acid (EPA). DHA and EPA are found in various cold-water fish, such as mackerel, salmon, and sardines, or from krill, while ALA, which acts as a precursor to both DHA and EPA, is contained in healthy oils such as fish oil and oils derived from flaxseed, hemp, pumpkin, and walnut. Since your body has to convert ALA into DHA and EPA, Dr. Lee Cowden recommends that people who suffer from illness or weakness obtain omega-3 fatty acids from fish or krill, as this spares the body from having to expend energy in the conversion process. "This is particularly important for people who are chronically ill because the tissue enzyme that makes this conversion, delta-6-desaturase, is often impaired and ineffective in their bodies," Dr. Cowden explains.

The primary forms of omega-6 fatty acids are gamma-linolenic acid (GLA) and linoleic acid. Both forms of found in black currant, borage seed, primrose, safflower, sunflower oils, and fish oils. Almonds and pumpkin seeds also contain them.

The standard U.S. diet has excessive amounts of omega-6s compared to omega-3s, which results in more inflammation in joints, arteries and other tissues. Omega-3 and omega-6 fatty acids in the proper ratio with each other help to reduce the presence of trans-saturated fats (from hydrogenated oils) and other toxins in the arteries, thus helping to prevent atherosclerosis and minimizing the risk of unhealthy blood clots. In addition, they reduce total serum cholesterol, low-density lipoprotein (LDL), and triglyceride levels, all of which are directly associated with heart attack, hypertension, stroke, and atherosclerosis.

Other benefits of EFAs include improved metabolism of fats, more efficient energy production, and better regulation of insulin. Other conditions that have shown improvement when optimal EFA levels are obtained from the diet or through supplementation include alcoholism, arthritis, diabetes, eczema, kidney and liver problems, multiple sclerosis, premenstrual syndrome (PMS), and skin problems. Research also suggests that EFAs may play a role in inhibiting the growth and spread of cancerous tumors.

It is best to obtain all your EFAs from the foods and oils mentioned above, though supplementation may also be advisable. EFA supplements are available in capsule form. If you choose this option, make sure the capsules are fresh. To be certain, break one capsule open and smell it. If you notice a foul odor, do not consume it. An easy way to meet your omega-3 EFA requirements is to take a capsule containing both EPA and DHA once a day at a combined dose of 1,000 mg. To ensure that you are receiving an adequate supply of omega-6 EFAs, you might also take 1,000 mg of evening primrose oil.

Other Important Supplements

The following supplements can also make an important positive difference in your overall health.

Alpha Lipoic Acid: Alpha-lipoic acid is a co-enzyme, meaning that it aids the function of enzymes in the body.

Within the body's cells, alpha-lipoic acid assists in energy production, protects against free radical damage, and combats insulin resistance and insulin spikes associated with type II diabetes and other disease conditions, including cancer, heart disease, stroke, blood clots, kidney and liver disease, and rheumatoid arthritis. Alpha-lipoic acid may also provide relief from the pain, burning, tingling, and numbing caused by peripheral neuropathy. For most people, a recommended daily dosage is 300-600 mg.

Iodine: Iodine is a negatively charged mineral called a halogen. Three other halogens found in our water and food are chlorine, fluoride and bromine. They are toxins and compete for iodine absorption sites in the gut and for iodine binding sites on cells in the body and possibly also on the T4 thyroid hormone, which should have four iodine molecules bound to it. Iodine deficiency is associated with a goiter swelling in the neck, hypothyroidism, slow metabolism, weight gain, polycystic ovaries, uterine fibroids, fibrocystic breast disease, high blood cholesterol and cardiovascular disease. Research suggests that the 150 mcg amount of iodine per day recommended by the U.S. government from studies 80 years ago may be grossly inadequate and that the amount necessary now may be 6,000 to 12,000 mcg daily in order to compete against the other three halogens.

Since iodine is also a powerful antimicrobial, using Lugol's iodine liquid instead of iodine tablets is preferable, since iodine tablets can kill more of the gut flora before getting absorbed. The daily dose of Lugol's 2% iodine for an average sized adult would be 2-4 drops.

PQQ (pyrroloquinoline quinone): PQQ is another vitamin-like compound that offers a number of significant health benefits, most notably helping to create new mitochondria within the cells, supporting overall mitochondrial function. and protecting mitochondrial DNA damage. PQQ has also been shown to protect the brain and enhance brain function, protect against and reduce inflammation and free radical damage, and improve sleep. In addition, PQQ acts to support the many functions and health benefits of CoQ10. A recommended daily dose of PQQ is between 20 to 40 mg taken along with CoQ10.

Quercetin: Quercetin is a flavonoid nutrient. Most flavonoids are water-soluble pigments found in fruits and vegetables that support vitamin function and act as potent antioxidants. Quercetin helps prevent and reduce chronic inflammation, alleviate pain, protect against heart disease, lower unhealthy blood pressure levels, boost healthy immune function, protect against certain types of cancer, manage symptoms of type II diabetes, and protect against and reduce skin irritations.

Quercetin-rich foods include apples, blueberries, broccoli, cherries, cranberries, dates, garlic, grapes, kale, plums, and sweet potatoes. A quercetin supplement can also be taken at a dose of 250-500 mg once or twice a day.

Guidelines For Using Nutritional Supplements

Unless otherwise indicated, take nutritional supplements with meals to aid in their absorption. Fat-soluble nutrients such as vitamins A, D, E and K, and essential fatty acids should be taken with the meal of the day that has the highest fat content, to enhance their absorption and effectiveness. If you are taking high dosages of nutrient supplements, be sure to do so with your physician's full awareness and approval. In such cases, do not take the dosages all at once, but divide them up throughout the day. Doing so will make it easier for your body to make use of them. Here are other guidelines to follow when taking nutritional supplements:

Take mineral supplements away from high-phytate meals, as phytates can interfere with your body's ability to absorb minerals. Beans, legumes, grains, nuts and seeds are high in phytates.

When supplementing with individual B vitamins, also supplement with a complete vitamin B-complex supplement, as B vitamins work most effectively in concert with each other.

Avoid supplements that contain artificial colorings, sweeteners, binders, coatings, fillers, fructose, or preservatives.

If you are also using prescribed medications, be sure to inform your physician about your nutritional supplement use, as certain nutrients can interfere with some pharmaceutical drugs, and possibly cause adverse side-effects.

CHAPTER 5

The Fifth Key: Cleaning Your Engine—How To Thrive In A Toxin-Filled World

L IVING IN AN environment that is free of toxins and pollutants, breathing good quality air, and drinking pure, clean water is vital for good health, yet doing so is becoming an increasingly difficult challenge, given our daily exposure to toxins in our air, water, and food supply.

Protecting yourself from these harmful toxins is a must if you want to stay healthy. This chapter will show you a variety of effective self-care measures you can use to do so.

Types of Toxins and How They Harm Your Health

Your body's detoxification system has two main functions: preventing toxins from entering the body, and neutralizing and eliminating them when they get through this initial line of defense.

It works in tandem with your immune system and is comprised of your GI tract (see Chapter 3), your lymphatic system, your kidneys, liver, lungs, bladder and other components of your urinary tract, the sinuses, and skin, including the sebaceous and sweat glands.

In addition to the heavy metals, pesticides, herbicides, synthetic food additives, plastics, fluoride, chloride, and pharmaceutical drug residues found in our nation's air, food, and water supply, other toxins to which we are regularly exposed include petrochemicals, harmful micro-organisms (bacteria, viruses, fungi), parasites (worms, and protozoa), dust, mold, and pollen. Common household products are another source of environmental toxins due to the chemicals they contain, as are dental amalgam fillings. In recent decades, ionizing and non-ionizing radiation, and harmful electromagnetic fields (EMFs) have also become major environmental health threats.

Most conventional physicians not only neglect to screen their patients for toxins, but are also not trained in how to effectively do so. Nor do they know how to help their patients eliminate toxins. Instead, they may claim that detoxification methods are unnecessary because the human body is designed to handle toxin exposure on its own. This may have been true long ago when our planet was in a pristine state, but it is not true now.

Dr. Cowden has for decades made helping his patients reduce their toxic burden a primary focus of his medical practice. Because of his expertise in this area, physicians from all around the world have for years studied under him so that they can offer their own patients the same treatments that he employs. Using his recommended self-care methods that follow, you will learn how to reduce your exposure to toxins, while eliminating (draining) toxins already present in your body's cells, tissues, and organs, and increasing the inflow of the healing agents you need to stay healthy. First, let's take a look at one of the most overlooked parts of your body's detoxification system.

The Importance of the Lymphatic System

The lymphatic system oversees the flow of lymph, the fluid that fills the spaces between the cells, containing various nutrients to be delivered to the cells, and bacteria, dead cells, and other waste products to be removed. The lymphatic system acts as your body's filtration system, or "master drain." It includes a vast network of capillaries, collectors, ducts, and nodes, concentrated in the neck (cervical nodes), armpits (axillary nodes), groin (inguinal nodes), and the abdomen where 80 percent of your immune system is.

The lymphatic system is responsible for ridding the body of toxins, dead cells and other cellular debris, heavy metals, and harmful microorganisms such as bacteria, fungi, and viruses. In this capacity, the lymphatic system plays a key role in detoxification while also assisting the body's immune system. Often, however, the lymphatic system becomes congested and clogged, causing a toxic buildup of the above substances. Lymph flow depends on muscle contractions, general body activity, and breathing, but can also be assisted by various self-care methods.

When toxic overload in the body causes congestion in the lymphatic system lymph thickens and begins to accumulate in the lymph nodes instead of emptying into the blood where the toxins it contains would normally be disposed of. In addition, the body's cells become incapable of properly utilizing oxygen.

One of the foremost experts on the lymphatic system and the important roles it plays in keeping the body healthy is Dr. Jennifer Gramith, founder and president of Rightway Health and Wellness LLC in Canton, Georgia. Dr. Gramith began her medical career as a nurse of internal medicine working in the fields of cardiology and oncology. "During that time, my father developed lymphoma cancer, which is a cancer of the lymphatic system," she says. "He had tumors the size of grapefruit under his arms and in his abdomen. He received chemotherapy and radiation because I was an oncology nurse and that was all I knew. After a few rounds of treatment his doctors gave him less than two months to live because the chemo and radiation were destroying his heart and they just kind of gave up."

Fortunately for Dr. Gramith and her father, her medical director at the time advised her to see an integrative physician. "I thought his suggestion was crazy but I did what he recommended because we had no other options and the integrative physician saved my father's life," Dr. Gramith continues. "After that, watching my father get well and my patients at the clinic get worse, I went back to school and become a naturopathic doctor. My focus and passion was for cancer patients. I wanted to help them in a way that I couldn't help them as a nurse. Approximately half of them develop lymphedema in the United States as a result of surgery and radiation. And 83 to 90 percent of those patients are women. This kind of forced me into looking at the lymphatic system, which I knew nothing about. I didn't get any real training in nursing school about the lymphatic system and very little as a naturopath. So I continued my education and became a lymphedema specialist, initially, learning how to move lymph through manual massage."

Today, after spending 20 years researching the lymphatic system, Dr. Gramith is certified through the Academy of Lymphatic Studies in Manual Lymph Drainage and Complete Decongestive Therapy and specializes in nutritional counseling, lymphatic decongestive therapy and low level laser detoxification therapy, in addition to being accredited by the American Naturopathic Medical and Accreditation Board, Inc. She is also the founder and president of the Foundation for the Advancement of Energy Medicine Technology (FAEMT), an organization dedicated to research and support of this emerging field, and shares her knowledge with a growing number of health practitioners across the U.S., and from other countries.

"The main issue, and the reason why so many Americans have problems with their lymphatic system and a degree of congestion, is because of their sedentary lives," Dr. Gramith says. "Since your lymphatic system doesn't have an automatic pump, if you're not moving and exercising then it's going to become congested. I find in my practice that most people have significant congestion. And because the lymphatic system is your structure that holds your immune system, if it is congested, you slow down your immune response. People don't connect those two things together."

In addition to a sedentary lifestyle, Dr. Gramith points out that poor breathing is another cause of lymph congestion. "Most Americans are shallow breathers," she says. "Even I catch myself not breathing deeply enough at times, despite knowing this."

Poor diet is another cause of lymph congestion. According to Dr. Cowden, the two biggest dietary offenders are cow's milk and other dairy products, followed by wheat and other gluten-containing grains. "If you eliminate dairy and wheat products from your diet you will have a huge improvement in your lymphatic function and in your ability to detoxify," he says.

Self-Care Methods For Improving Lymphatic Function

To prevent and alleviate lymph congestion, take the following steps.

Eat Healthy and Protect Your Gut: In addition to avoiding dairy, wheat products, and other gluten grains, follow the overall guidelines for healthy eating that you learned in Chapter 2, including eating fermented foods. Also follow the recommendations for achieving and maintaining a healthy gut outlined in Chapter 3. Both Dr. Cowden and Dr. Gramith also recommend consuming fresh-squeezed, organic vegetable juices on a regular basis. If you do not already own one, consider purchasing a high-quality juicer so that you can easily make your own juices.

Train Yourself To Breathe Deeply Throughout the Day: Dr. Gramith advises setting aside one to two minutes every hour to breathe deeply. "I typically teach my clients to take the breath in and then double the time that they exhale," she says. "Not only does this practice help keep lymph moving, it is amazing how it drops anxiety, lowers cortisol levels, and calms things down. Anxiety and stress cause inflammation in your lymphatic system. If you can lower the inflammatory process, lymph will flow and circulate better. People see a difference very quickly if they start implementing breathing in this manner into their lifestyle. But you have to retrain yourself so that it becomes a habit."

Dr. Gramith adds that there are various downloadable smart phone apps that act as hourly reminders, and also offer guided deep breathing sessions. You can also set a timer on your phone to go off every hour.

Don't Be Sedentary: Even if you work at a desk all day, it's important that you make time to exercise or engage in some other form of physical activity. Even a gentle 20-30-minute walk can make a healthy difference. For the greatest benefit, breathe deeply, without forcing your breath, and swing your arms as you walk.

One of the best exercises for stimulating lymph flow is rebounding (bouncing on a mini-trampoline), which is easy to incorporate into your daily lifestyle. All you need is a mini-trampoline. When selecting a rebounder, be sure that it is sturdy (good models will support a 250-300-pound person). Also be sure that the trampoline pad is supported by sturdy springs that are not connected directly to the frame. This will ensure a better and gentler bouncing action. Well-designed models cost between $200 to $300 and are well worth the investment if you can afford one.

Because of how gentle rebounding is, it is a safe exercise for just about anyone, regardless of their age or condition. (Health benefits can even be achieved by bouncing while sitting on the edge of the rebounder.) Some models also come with a support bar that you can hold onto as you bounce. Once you're on it, just start bouncing. Initially, you may want to only do so for a few minutes, but as you get used to it, try to aim for 10 minutes twice per day. "Rebounding ten minutes twice a day is excellent for helping to maintain health lymphatic function," Dr. Gramith says, "And you can always move up from that. When rebounding you don't have to jump. You're just bouncing and your feet never have to leave the mat to benefit."

If you do not have access to a rebounder, you can achieve similar results from lightly bouncing up and down on the balls of your feet, or by jumping rope.

Dr. Cowden also recommends the following exercise to stimulate lymph flow. Lay on your back, either on the floor or in bed. Then raise one leg up and pretend that you're pedaling a one-pedal bicycle. Each time your knee extends, also extend your ankle so that your foot points forward, and when your knee comes back toward your chest, bring your foot back as well. Once your leg begins to tire, repeat the exercise with your other leg, and then continue to alternate between legs. This exercise causes contraction of the muscles in the lower extremities, which in turn puts pressure on the lymphatic vessels, and the pelvis, abdomen, and chest, to keep the lymph flowing.

Skin Brushing: Another method for improving lymph flow and overall lymphatic function is skin brushing. Skin brushing also helps rid the outer layer of skin of accumulated dead skin cells and other debris, while enhancing overall circulation and helping your skin to "breathe" easier.

Skin brushing is performed with a dry skin brush. Starting with your upper arms, then forearms, then hands, brush towards the middle ends of your collar bones in 8 to 10 inch long strokes. Then do the same with your chest, abdomen, thighs, lower legs, and finally your ankles, always brushing upward toward your collar bones. Use light strokes as you brush, and be sure to take full, deep, relaxed breaths. Once you finish brushing, take a shower.

All of the above measures, if performed regularly, will go a long way toward keeping your lymphatic system healthy. From time to time, also consider receiving a manual lymphatic massage from a massage therapist certified in its use.

For cases of significant lymphatic congestion, Dr. Gramith recommends assisted lymphatic therapy (ALT). "ALT is a gentle, light touch, non-invasive technique to stimulate the proper flow and drainage of the lymphatic system," she explains. "It is administered using an inert gas ionization device. The device I use and recommend is called an XP2 and was developed according to my specifications by Sky David, who developed most of the inert gas ionization devices for the lymphatics. It employs a combination of vibrational light, and electrical waves to help stimulate lymph flow much more effectively than manual lymphatic massage is capable of doing.

"Once I began using the XP2, it took my success rate from about 35 percent with stage four cancer patients to a 75 to 85 percent success rate."

Dr. Gramith has trained over 800 other practitioners from around the country in its use. To locate a practitioner in your area, visit her website, www.rightwayhealthandwellness.com.

Supporting Liver and Overall Biliary Tract Function

The primary detoxification organ in your body is your liver, which is part of your body's biliary tract, which also includes your gallbladder and a series of bile ducts. These organs work together to produce, transport, and store bile.

"Healthy bile is like dishwashing soap for the bile ducts," explains Steven Hines, ND, NE. "It is slick and proficient at moving waste products quickly into the small intestine, en route to elimination. But as toxins build up over time, all components of the biliary tract become impaired, and that slick healthy bile becomes a toxic, thick biliary sludge, hardened bile duct stones, and even larger gallstones. Sludge and stones can develop in all parts of the biliary tract, anywhere unhealthy bile is present."

Self-Care Liver Cleansing Tips: Cleansing your liver and improving its overall functioning can go a very long way toward boosting your health and energy. Doing so on your own is not complicated. For example, you can start your day by drinking a glass of pure, filtered water to which you add the juice of a fresh-squeezed, organic lemon. This will aid your liver in eliminating toxins and also help reduce acidity in your body.

Eating liver-cleansing foods on a regular basis is also important. Some of the best liver supporting foods are cruciferous vegetables, such as broccoli, Brussels sprouts, cabbage, cauliflower, kale, and radishes. These foods help boost the production of enzymes in the liver that flush out toxins. As an added and very important bonus, cruciferous vegetables have also been shown to reduce the risk of cancer. Beet roots and dandelion greens are other excellent food choices, as are organic apples, berries, and grapefruit.

Various nutritional supplements, such as vitamin C, alpha lipoic acid, and N-acetyl-cysteine (NAC), can also help, as can various herbs and spices, such as garlic, ginger, turmeric, dandelion root tea, peppermint, burdock root, chicory, and licorice root.

Regularly drinking fresh squeezed, organic vegetable juice supports liver function and overall detoxification, while also supplying an abundance of vitamins, minerals, and enzymes. If you have a juicer at home, try this recipe: Combine one medium-sized, organic carrot, one medium, organic cucumber, two medium-sized, organic beets (including the beet tops), and one whole, peeled, organic clove of garlic. Once you are done juicing these ingredients, drink the juice immediately.

Another self-care technique that can help enhance liver function is to massage the acupuncture point called Liver 3 with your thumb for a few minutes twice a day, massaging in a clockwise motion. This point is located in the groove between your big and second toes, approximately one inch below them. It will feel slightly tender when you find it. According to acupuncture theory, regularly massaging this point helps to reduce liver stagnation. For best results, massage this point on both of your feet.

Liver-Gallbladder Flush: According to Dr. Hines, one of the most effective self-care methods for cleansing the liver and gallbladder and restoring full functioning to the biliary system is a liver-gallbladder flush, a six-day process that can be repeated as needed over time. The flush provides significant benefits because of how it helps improve the many overall biliary tract functions and eliminate gallstones.

"The flush tricks the digestive system into thinking it has consumed an extremely high-fat meal," Dr. Hines explains. "If the body thinks it has to digest that extreme amount of fat, it will pump out the maximum amount of bile possible, thus purging the biliary tract of old, sludgy bile and any hardened stones that have formed."

Dr. Hines has helped numerous patients improve their health by teaching them how to safely conduct the liver-gallbladder flush in the comfort of their own home. You can learn how to do so, as well, by visiting his website, www.hopewellness.com/client-resources. Once there, click on Gallbladder/Liver Cleanse to obtain a free, downloadable PDF of detailed instructions.

Sweating And Sauna Therapy

A growing body of research has established that induced sweating is also effective for physical cleansing and the elimination of toxins. In a study published in the *Archives of Environmental and Contamination Toxicology, for example, researchers noted that toxic metals "appeared to be* preferentially excreted through sweat" rather than through the blood or urine. Their findings were confirmed in a subsequent meta-analysis published in the *Journal of Public and Environmental Health.* In that study, researchers found that sweating was effective for removing the heavy metals arsenic, cadmium, lead, and mercury. Other research has found that sweating is effective for eliminating bisphenol A (BPA) and phthalates from the body.

Exercise (see Chapter 7) can induce sweating, which is one reason why staying physically active is important for optimal health. Physical activity alone, however, is not enough to fully dislodge toxins from your body. A much more effective method is sauna therapy, particularly the use of near- and far-infrared saunas.

One of the main benefits of sauna therapy is its proven ability to mobilize toxins out of the body's fat cells and fat tissues, which is where heavy metals and other toxins are primarily found. As the body heats up during sauna therapy, fat-stored toxins are released and eliminated through sweat. Traditional saunas provide these benefits, though not to the same degree that near- and far-infrared saunas do.

There are a variety of infrared devices you can use. They range from stationary walk-in and portable, tent-like infrared sauna units, to infrared blankets and pads. All of them emit a dry, radiant infrared heat capable of penetrating deep inside the body (as deep as three inches, depending on the device). Compared to traditional saunas, they also increase sweat volume and therefore the release of toxins by as much as 300 percent.

"We know that infrared therapy also stimulates the production of nitric oxide," Dr. Cowden says. "Nitric oxide is a blood vessel dilator. When you dilate the blood vessels next to tissues that are holding toxins, you're bringing fresh, oxygenated blood, fresh nutrients, and fresh fluid in to neutralize the toxins. And you're dilating the veins that carry the toxins away, all at the same time. That's just one mechanism by which infrared sauna therapy helps to improve the detoxification pathways."

To obtain the most benefit from sauna therapy, Dr. Cowden recommends first doing some type of lymphatic massage, such as dry skin brushing or rebounding for a few minutes, and to drink pure, filtered water before, during, or immediately after each sauna session to avoid dehydration. Molecular hydrogen water is particularly helpful to drink after you finish your session.

If you are new to sauna therapy start with a short session of 15 to 20 minutes, and then buildup up to a 45-minute session. Initially, set temperatures inside the sauna between 100 to 110°F. Over time, increase the temperature to 140 to 150°F.

Once you complete your session, immediately take a short, lukewarm shower, washing your body with soap. This is necessary to wash away toxins that remain on your skin. Otherwise they will be reabsorbed into your body.

A growing number of physicians and health spas now offer infrared sessions to their patients and clients. You can also consider purchasing a home infrared unit if that is within your budget. Stationary walk-in units typically cost $2000 or more, while foldable tent-like units and infrared blankets cost $500 or more. Infrared pads prices vary, depending on size, with full-length mats typically priced between $500 to $1500.

As an alternative to purchasing an infrared device, you can achieve some degree of benefit by sitting in your bathroom with the door closed while heating it as high as possible with an electric heater, so that it causes you to sweat.

Sauna therapy sessions once or more times per week can dramatically decrease toxins in your body over time.

Other Self-Care Detoxification Measures

The following preventive measures are also essential for reducing your exposure to toxins and achieving and maintaining optimal health.

Cleaning Your Household Water Supply: Tap water throughout the United States is increasingly becoming a health hazard. Pesticides and other toxic runoff from "factory farms", toxic residues of pharmaceutical drugs, hazardous levels of lead and other heavy metals, radon, gasoline solvents, synthetic chemicals, disinfectant residues, industrial waste byproducts, and disease-causing microorganisms (bacteria, viruses, and water borne parasites) are all commonly found in municipal water supplies today, as are chlorine and fluoride, which are intentionally added to our nation's water supply despite being known carcinogens.

Many municipal water systems also contain *radionuclides*, such as uranium, radium, and radon. A radionuclide is a radioactive decay product, called an isotope, that is naturally-occurring in underground rock beds and various geological formations. Over time, these substances, as they decay, release harmful particles into groundwater which then enter into municipal drinking water supplies.

Another source of polluted tap water can be water lines into your home. Unless your home has new copper water lines, lead and other heavy metals can leach out of the older water pipes and plumbing to get into your water supply.

Given these facts, it's important that you don't drink water straight out of the tap. Nor is drinking bottled water an effective solution. Not only does bottled water contain harmful chemicals leached from plastic containers, many bottled water brands have been shown to contain as many, and sometimes more, of the pollutants found in tap water. In addition, plastic bottles now pose a serious threat to our environment.

A much healthier solution is to invest in a water filtration system. Until recently, the most effective type was a high-quality reverse osmosis, multistage water filtration system installed beneath sinks. Now, there is a comparable available option developed by the company ClearlyFiltered™, which offers an under-the-sink, 3-stage system at a similar price point as reverse osmosis systems, and water pitchers and shower head filters. Independent lab testing has found that the proprietary filtration technology used in both the company's sink system and water pitcher removes over 230 chemicals and contaminants from tap water, including fluoride. For more information, visit www.ClearlyFiltered.com. To learn more about reverse osmosis systems, visit www.MultiPure.com.

To have pure filtered water available to you away from home, invest in a non-disposable, eco-friendly water bottle so that you can take your pure, filtered water from your home with you.

Tap water can also affect you in your bath and shower. In fact, approximately 70 percent of the disease-causing toxins found in tap water enter the body through the skin during bathing and showering. To prevent this, install a quality shower filter inside of your shower head. This is easy to do and can go a long way toward further minimizing your exposure to water-borne toxins.

If you don't have a water filter when showering (especially when traveling and showering in a hotel shower), do a "military shower". Adjust the water to a comfortable temperature before getting in, then step in and quickly wet your wash cloth, your body, and your scalp (if you want to wash your hair). Then turn the water off, lather your washcloth with soap, then scrub your skin all over and finally lather your scalp with shampoo (if you are going to wash your hair). Then turn the water back on to rinse off all the soap, which should take less than one additional minute.

Juicing: Drinking 16 to 32 ounces of fresh-squeezed, organic vegetable juices each day provides many detoxification benefits, and is a delicious, inexpensive way to cleanse your body of toxins. When vegetable juices are consumed hours away from meals, especially the last meal of the day, they automatically stimulate the body's detoxification system. Fresh, organic vegetable juices are also rich in many of the nutrients your body needs to stay healthy. Moreover, because your body doesn't need to expend much energy to digest such juices, the nutrients they contain are quickly absorbed.

The following are some of the best vegetables you can include in your juice drinks, along with some of the benefits they provide: asparagus (aids the kidneys and protects against inflammation), beets (aids the liver and gallbladder in eliminating toxins), broccoli (aids the liver in eliminating toxins), cabbage (aids the liver and lowers

LDL and total cholesterol), carrots (aids the liver and lymphatic system), cucumber (acts as a diuretic and the silica in the cucumber skins boosts collagen production), dandelion greens (strengthen the liver), and kale (helps flush toxins and debris from the kidneys). There are many other organic vegetables you can also use. (**Note:** Because of the natural sugars they contain, beet and carrot juice should be avoided by people suffering from candida because their sugars can feed fungus.)

Sinus Cleansing: Sinus infections and various polluted particulate matter that we inhale also contribute to toxic overload in the body. Many people have some degree of sinus infection though they may seem to be asymptomatic. Therefore, it is a good idea to regularly clean your sinuses to clear up or prevent infection and to flush out toxins before they can move from the sinuses into the bloodstream to attack cells, tissues, and organs.

The easiest way to cleanse your sinuses is to use a 3-ounce rubber bulb syringe with all but about one inch of the tip cut off (or a 100 cc piston syringe with a naso-gastric tip) to perform the nasal irrigation. Start with a saline solution. To make saline solution, combine a quarter teaspoon of salt to a cup of warm (not hot) distilled water (do not use tap water, and you may want to double the amount of both salt and water if you feel that one cup of irrigation is insufficient). Stir the salt until it fully dissolves. Then place the solution into a syringe. Position your head over your sink, face-down with your forehead a little lower than your chin, place the tip of the syringe tightly into your right nostril, take a deep breath, then hold your breath and squeeze the saline solution into the nostril.

When you feel saline getting into the back of your throat, remove the syringe and let the saline from your nose run into the sink. Then repeat the process with your left nostril. Alternate from one nostril to the other until the saline is used up. Some of the solution will drip out of your nostrils for several minutes after you finish irrigating. Blow your nose as often as needed after the irrigation is complete.

If you are not in the habit of already cleansing your sinuses, Dr. Cowden recommends performing nasal irrigation once a day for between one to four weeks, depending on the amount of infection present, and once a month after that on a maintenance basis. After the first week, you can add half a tablespoon of whole leaf, filtered aloe vera to the saline solution. Aloe vera is a potent natural antimicrobial agent that is proven to fight infections. If infections are present, you may experience a burning sensation in your sinuses from the aloe. This will clear as your sinuses become healthier.

If there is infection in the sinuses and you are not allergic to iodine, adding ¼ drop of Lugol's 2% iodine solution per cup of saline can help eradicate it. To make ¼ drop of iodine, put three drops of distilled water or the saline irrigant described above in a spoon, add one drop of Lugol's solution to those three drops, mix together well and place one drop of that diluted iodine in your cup of saline sinus irrigant. You can build up by ¼ drop increments each day until you are using three undiluted drops of Lugol's iodine per cup of saline irrigant.

In addition to nasal irrigation, the use of Ion*Sinus spray, which was developed by Dr. Zach Bush (see Chapter 3) is also recommended. Comprised of the same soil-derived elements in Dr. Zach's Ion*Gut Health formula for the GI tract, this sinus spray is designed to help support the microbiome of the sinuses while cleansing, soothing, and hydrating the sinus membranes. Ion*Sinus spray is also proven to protect against dust, dander, and other airborne irritants. It is available at https://ionbiome.com/products/ion-sinus.

Using Toxin-Binding Supplements: There are a number of supplements that can further assist your body's detoxification processes. They work by binding with heavy metals, radioactive elements, and other toxins, making it easier for the body to eliminate them.

Effective toxin-binding products include chlorella and other algae products, bentonite clay, liposomal glutathione, modified apple and modified citrus pectins, and some low-aluminum zeolite products, all of which are safe to use on an ongoing basis. Their use helps to reduce the body's toxic burden and helps prevent new toxins from gaining a foothold in the body. These toxin-binding products are available at most health food stores and online. For best results, consider taking one or more of them on a daily basis.

Other Helpful Nutritional Supplements: Dr. Norm Shealy advises that everyone take precautions to protect themselves against fluoride and glyphosate. For fluoride protection, especially for preventing fluoride from harming the brain, Dr. Shealy recommends liposomal curcumin. "Liposomal curcumin has been proven to protect the brain from the toxic effect of fluoride," he says. "I'm not certain that it protects the rest of the body but at least your most important organ benefits from this natural anti-fluoride essential."

To protect against glyphosate, Dr. Shealy recommends a combination of the amino acid glycine and organic, unpasteurized apple cider vinegar. "Take one teaspoon of glycine powder twice daily for two weeks and then one-half teaspoon twice a day for life," he says. "Also take one tablespoon of organic, unpasteurized apple cider vinegar daily." You can find the brands of these products that Dr. Shealy recommends at https://normshealy.shop.

Among the most dangerous types of environmental toxins that we may be exposed to is radiation in the form of radioactive elements such as cesium, plutonium, radium, strontium, and uranium, all of which we inhale because they are prevalent in the atmosphere. Fortunately, a number of nutritional products can help protect you from these elements. Among the most effective are certain zeolite products (like Biopure ZeoBind), high-quality, bioavailable vitamin C, chlorella, and spirulina. Iodine, especially liquid iodine in the form of Lugol's solution, is also helpful, particularly for protecting the thyroid gland from radiation. In addition, unlike iodine capsules or tablets, Lugol's solution poses no risk of entering the GI tract, whereas iodine capsules or tablets, as they pass through the GI tract, can damage healthy bacteria.

Dr. Cowden has assisted the Nutramedix company in developing a number of detoxification tinctured supplements. Among them are Burbur-Pinella, Parsley, Algas, and Sealantro (the latter two being very helpful for heavy metal and radioactive element overload).

To purchase or find out more information about them, visit www. nutramedix.com.

Replacing Toxic Personal Care Products: Most commercial personal care products, such as antiperspirants, cosmetics, lip balms and lipstick, shampoos and conditioners, skincare lotions, and toothpaste are common sources of toxins. With the exception of commercial toothpaste, which contains fluoride that enters the body through the mouth, the toxins these other personal care products contain are absorbed through the skin and then enter the bloodstream.

Toxins commonly found in such products are carcinogenic and include aluminum, cadmium, lead, BHT, BHA, parabens, petroleum jelly (petrolatum) and other petroleum products (found in cosmetics, lip balms, lipstick, and skin care lotions) sodium lauryl sulfate (found in shampoos and conditioners), and coal tar (found in skin lotions and shampoos and conditioners).

Nontoxic alternatives to commercial personal care products are now widely available. In addition, in many cases you can make your own healthy versions. For example, coconut oil can be used as a skin moisturizer, a hair conditioner, and a toothpaste. You can also make your own healthy toothpaste by combining a pinch of sea salt with baking soda mixed with water. Baking soda mixed with potato vodka can also be used as natural antiperspirant. Cocoa and shea butters can also be used as lip balms.

Common soaps should also be avoided because they are alkaline in nature and interfere with the skin's microbiome. Healthy skin has a slightly acidic pH, which is necessary for the skin to maintain its healthy bacteria which, in turn, help skin to act as a protective barrier for the body's internal environment. Antibacterial soaps are even worse. "I am opposed to using antibacterial soaps because they typically select out the good skin bacteria, enabling bad skin bacteria to thrive and cause disease," Dr. Cowden says. Moreover, the use of antibacterial soaps is known to increase the growing problem of antibiotic-resistant bacteria.

In place of such soaps, Dr. Cowden recommends glycerin soaps.

Apple cider vinegar with the "mother" tincture is also a very effective skin cleanser.

Oil Pulling: Oil pulling, which has been a traditional healing remedy within the Ayurvedic system of medicine for centuries, is another effective method for eliminating toxins from the body, especially fat soluble toxins.

To perform oil pulling, place one tablespoon of organic, extra virgin coconut or olive oil (sesame seed oil, sunflower oil, and walnut oil can also be used) in your mouth, retaining it for five minutes or more, while vigorously swishing the oil, almost as if you were chewing it. As you do so, your saliva will mix with the oil to begin pulling and binding toxins and harmful bacteria from your teeth, gums, and mouth. Since all of the blood in your body passes through your mouth about once per minute, the mixture of saliva and oil will also bind with toxins in your bloodstream that come through the mouth lining.

Be careful not swallow any of the oil during this process so that you do not reabsorb the toxins it pulls out. After at least five minutes have elapsed, spit the oil into your toilet, rather than your sink. Then rinse your mouth with warm water.

Dental Toxins

There are two types of dental toxins—dental infections and heavy metals found in dental amalgam fillings. Although both types of toxins often require a properly trained dentist in place of self-care to address them, it is important that you know the dangers they pose and what you can do on your own to safeguard against them.

Dental Infections: Untreated buildup of plaque on gums and teeth poses health risks because the bacteria that plaque contains have been linked to chronic inflammation, heart disease, and other illnesses. In addition to plaque, it is quite common for people to have a concentration of other harmful microorganisms. Such concentrations are known as toxic foci. German doctors and US integrative doctors report that eighty percent of toxic foci in the body are located in the head and neck, with the most common infection sites being the sinuses and tonsils. Bone infection and bone-rot near the tip of a root canal tooth and in many wisdom tooth extraction sites, known as dental cavitations, are other high risk toxic foci locations because of a lack of thorough cleaning and sanitization in the cavitations formed by root canal and wisdom tooth removal procedures. (This has been documented at autopsy.) As a result, toxic infectious agents can thrive in these areas, and spread from them into the bloodstream to attack other parts of the body.

If you have had a root canal or had your wisdom teeth removed, unless these procedures were performed by a biological dentist, you may have undetected toxic foci within those dental sites. The field of biological dentistry was pioneered by the late Hal Huggins, DDS, one of the first dentists to teach the dangers of dental infection following root canal surgery and tooth extraction. He trained hundreds of dentists across the US and elsewhere in how to safely perform such procedures without leaving the cavitation sites prone to infection. He also developed biological dentistry methods for eliminating toxic foci and treating autoimmune and other diseases that appeared to be caused as a result of dental procedures. (To find out more about Dr. Huggins and his work, visit www. HugginsAppliedHealing.com.)

Because of the direct relationship between dental and overall health, you must do all you can to keep your teeth, gums, and mouth clean and free of bacterial buildup. This includes brushing your teeth after meals, flossing and/or using a Water Pik at least twice daily, using a nontoxic mouthwash, and receiving regular dental checkups and cleanings every three to six months, ideally by a biological dentist. If you suspect you have toxic foci as a result of a root canal or tooth extraction, a biological dentist can also help you address that problem. You can also help to reduce infection with the daily practice of oil pulling discussed above.

Dental Amalgam Fillings: Although a growing number of dentists across the US are now phasing them out, dental fillings in the United

States are often silver amalgam fillings. Despite their name, such fillings actually contain 50 percent mercury and only 25 percent silver. Dentists who use silver amalgams may not inform their patients that they contain mercury.

Mercury in dental amalgams has been linked to a wide variety of serious health issues, including autoimmune diseases, cancer, and neurological disorders. Recognizing these facts, the governments of Denmark, Sweden, and Norway have all banned the use of silver amalgam fillings, making their use illegal. Other countries, such as Austria and Germany, ban the use of amalgams in children, pregnant women, and people with certain health conditions, while in Japan the use of amalgams is tightly regulated.

Mercury vapor is continuously released from such amalgam fillings and then readily absorbed into the bloodstream. Additionally, after mercury passes from the bloodstream into the body, it can turn into its organic form (methylmercury), a substance that is 100 times more toxic than elemental mercury (the form used in amalgams). Methylmercury is also far more able to penetrate the blood-brain barrier, which is why it is associated with numerous neurodegenerative diseases, including Alzheimer's, MS, and ALS (Lou Gehrig's disease).

Because of the serious health threats posed by amalgam toxicity, ACIM member physicians and other integrative health practitioners routinely advise their patients to have their mercury amalgams replaced. Metallic and porcelain crowns are also sometimes toxic for the patient. Many ACIM physicians work directly with biological dentists to ensure their patients have their amalgams and toxic crowns removed properly. If you have dental silver amalgams or crowns in your mouth, seriously consider having them replaced, if you can afford it (especially the amalgams). Be sure to select a dentist trained in the proper removal of dental amalgams. This procedure is known as the Huggins Protocol, developed by Dr. Huggins.

In addition to Huggins Applied Healing, the following organizations can help you locate a biological dentist near you: the International Academy of Biological Dentistry and Medicine (www.iabdm.org), the International Academy of Oral Medicine and Toxicology (www.iaomt.org), the Holistic Dental Association (www.holisticdental.org), and Mercury Free Dentists (www. mercuryfreedentists.com).

A Word About Electromagnetic Radiation Toxicity

One of the most pervasive, potentially dangerous, yet often ignored sources of toxicity in our modern world is the rapidly increasing proliferation of low-level electromagnetic radiation (EMR), also known as electromagnetic field (EMF) exposure. Unless you are living "off the grid," you are exposed to EMR on a nearly constant basis via your cell phone, laptop or computer tablet, WiFi, smart meters used by water and utility companies, and many other wireless devices, including home appliances, wireless burglar alarm systems, baby monitors, and fitness bands and watches. Since electromagnetic fields are able to penetrate through walls, EMR from outside sources can enter your home and workplace, as well. Even new cars expose you to EMR due to their now standard features of satellite tracking, Bluetooth and other "conveniences" which they include.

Further compounding the EMR problem is "dirty" electricity that is commonly found in houses, apartment complexes, and other buildings. Living in close proximity to power lines, power substations and/or cell phone towers is another danger, as are the blue light emissions from cell phones, computers, TV screens, compact fluorescent light bulbs, and older-model LED light bulbs.

Another type of EMR health threat is microwave/radio-frequency (RF) electromagnetic radiation. Sources of RF exposure include mobile and cordless phones, cell phone antennas and towers, microwave ovens, wireless networks, portable radios, radio and radar transceivers, WiFi, Bluetooth, GPS devices and smart TVs. The coming roll-out of 5G wireless networks is likely to further increase these potential EMR health threats.

Addressing the impact of EMR on health is beyond the scope of this book. However, be aware of the harm EMR can cause so that you can take protective measures to minimize your risks. A good place to start is by reading the book *EMF*D* by Dr. Joseph Mercola. To receive a free 25 page PDF on how to protect yourself from EMF, go to EMF.Mercola.com.

The following organizations and websites can also help you keep you informed:

Americans For Responsible Technology (americansforresponsibletech.org)

BioInitiative 2012 (bioinitiative.org)

Center For Electrosmog Prevention (www. electrosmogprevention.org)

Electromagnetic Health (electromagnetichealth.org)

EMF Consultancy (emfacts.com)

Environmental Health Trust (ehtrust.org)

Lloyd Burrell/Electric Sense (electricsense.com)

Dr. Magda Havas (magdahavas.com)

Physicians For Safe Technology (mdsafetech.org)

Take Back Your Power (takebackyourpower.net)

CHAPTER 6

The Sixth Key: Mastering Stress, Optimizing Your Mindset, and Healing Unresolved Emotions and Beliefs

ACCORDING TO THE Centers for Disease Control and Prevention (CDC), stress is the primary cause of 85 percent of all diseases. Yet, little attention to managing stress is given by most conventional physicians when they consult with their patients.

All of us are daily exposed to stress. Stress can be physical, mental and emotional, or triggered by exposures in our environment. It is often mental and emotional stress, rather than physical stress, that is at the root of disease. A growing body of research demonstrates that our habitual thoughts and beliefs have a powerful influence over whether we remain healthy or get sick.

When stress occurs, a body system known as the hypothalamus-pituitary-adrenal (HPA) axis springs into action, with the hypothalamus signaling the HPA axis to initiate a "flight or fight" response. During "flight or fight" responses, the HPA axis causes the adrenal glands to suppress immune function in order to conserve the body's energy reserves via the adrenal glands' increased production of stress hormones. Stress hormones are so effective at suppressing immune function that the stress hormone cortisol in the form of cortisone or prednisone drugs is administered to patients who receive organ transplants to prevent their immune systems from rejecting the organs.

The "flight or fight" response was essential for keeping our ancestors alive in the face of such dangers as attacking animals and natural occurrences such as earthquakes, floods, and volcanic eruptions, but actual physical danger is not necessary to trigger the "flight or fight" response. It can also be triggered by your limiting and negative thoughts and beliefs. This results in chronic production of stress hormones and a corresponding suppression of immune function, making stress a major risk factor for cancer, heart disease, and many other conditions related to immune dysfunction. Gastrointestinal disorders, skin problems, and neurological and emotional disorders have also been linked to stress.

Therefore, one of the most important steps you can take to ensure your health is to deal with stress effectively. To do so, you first must become better aware of the types of stress to which you are most commonly exposed. Start by using the stress and depression assessment questionnaires in Chapter 1. Go through them now if you haven't already done so.

Also consider sources of physical (illness and chronic infection) and environmental (environmental toxins and exposures to electromagnetic radiation, or EMR) stress that may be affecting you. Solutions to such problems are presented elsewhere in this book, yet what you learn in this chapter can help you better manage the mental and emotional stress exacerbated by such problems.

Cultivating Stress-Reducing Habits

The amount of stress you experience and how well you cope with it is largely due to your lifestyle choices. What follow are simple, effective lifestyle tips you can use to reduce stress in your life and manage it better.

- Be sure to get enough sleep and try to go to bed at the same time each night. (See Chapter 8.)

- Be sure the foods you eat are healthy for you. (See Chapter 2)
- Get regular exercise. (See Chapter 7.)
- Schedule your day so that you have free time to relax and spend with your loved ones.
- Find a hobby you enjoy and commit to pursuing it on a regular basis.
- Know what's most essential and important in your life and commit yourself to that instead of wasting time on matters that are unimportant.
- Set up your daily schedule so that you have plenty of time to devote to your daily tasks, instead of having to hurry to meet your responsibilities.
- Once you decide to do something, act on it as soon as possible. Hesitations about taking action can increase your stress levels.
- Cultivate laughter in your daily life and make a conscious effort to find the humor in things.
- Make a commitment to yourself and those you care about to be more loving.
- Avoid long periods of isolation, especially if you live alone. Seek out and enjoy your friends and loved ones.
- Regularly engage in relaxation exercises and/or meditation.
- Avoid the use of alcohol, caffeine, and comfort foods when you do feel stress. They are unhealthy for you and serve only to mask or numb your problems, not resolve them.
- Don't be afraid to discuss stressful situations with your family or friends, and to ask for help if you need it.

Stress-Reducing Self-Care Methods

As with your overall health, when it comes to stress you need to be proactive. Rather than allowing stress to build up and become chronic, when you find yourself experiencing stress in any form take a moment to identify what is triggering it and then do your best to resolve it. The self-care techniques that follow can help you do so.

Take A Walk: Besides being one of the most effective ways to exercise, walking can also be relaxing. Try to walk every day, ideally, in a nature setting.

Smile: The simple act of smiling can improve your mood and relieve stress even if you do not feel happy or optimistic in the moment. This was proven by a study conducted by researchers at Echnische Universität in Munich, Germany. Using functional magnetic resonance imaging (fMRI), the researchers found that when we smile the brain's "happiness circuitry" is immediately activated, regardless of our present mood. These brain circuits, in turn, stimulate the production of the "feel-good" hormones dopamine, serotonin, and oxytocin.

Another study, conducted by researchers in Sweden, found that smiling can change how we react to negative external stimuli. In that study, test subjects were instructed to either smile or frown while they were shown pictures of positive and negative images. Regardless of the pictures they were shown, "participants experienced the stimuli as more pleasant during smiling as compared to when frowning."

Research has also found that the degree of a person's smile can be an accurate predictor of how long they will live. A study conducted by researchers at Wayne State University in Detroit, Michigan examined baseball card photographs of 230 professional baseball players taken in 1952, analyzing the degree to which the players smiled. 42 percent of the players were not smiling in their photographs, 43 percent had a partial smile, and 15 percent exhibited what is known as a full Duchenne smile, which is characterized by a genuine, full-faced expression of happiness that is measured by the degree that the muscles surrounding one's eyes contract or crinkle. Of the 230 athletes, 150 had died by 2009. What the researchers discovered was that the players' smiles predicted how long they lived. On average, those who had not smiled only lived to age 72. The partially smiling players lived for an average of 75 years, while the players with full Duchenne smiles lived for an average of 80 years.

Other research has shown that people who habitually exhibit full Duchenne smiles in college experience greater overall happiness and well-being throughout the rest of their adult lives, are found to be more inspiring by others, and have more fulfilling marriages.

Studies have found that healthy children tend to smile up to 400 times a day, in stark contrast to how infrequently most adults smile (only 30 percent smile over 20 times a day). Getting in the habit of genuinely smiling more often can have a significant positive impact on both your mood and overall health.

Meditate: Since the 1960s, research has confirmed that meditation, when practiced once or twice a day provides numerous physical and psychological health benefits, including reducing many physiological and biochemical markers associated with stress, such as decreased heart and respiration rates, and improved regulation of stress hormones such as cortisol. In addition, meditation has been shown to increase brain waves associated with relaxation.

A simple, yet effective way to meditate is to close your eyes as you bring your attention to your belly. Then begin breathing in and out in a relaxed manner through your diaphragm. Keep your attention focused on your breathing. Each time you notice that your mind has "wandered off" simply return your focus to back to your breath, letting your thoughts flow by. Instead of becoming absorbed by your thoughts, increasingly you will find yourself witnessing them from a calm state of detachment.

The following exercise, which can be practiced each day for four minutes before meals and before bedtime, is also effective for relieving stress.

Find a quiet place where you will not be disturbed and sit comfortably in a chair. Keep your spine straight and relax your shoulders.

Close your eyes and breathe deeply, inhaling through your nose and exhaling through your mouth, while imagining yourself in a peaceful place in nature. Envision that place with all of your senses— sight, sound, taste, smell and touch. "You can imagine yourself there conversing with God, if you wish," Dr. Cowden says, "but not with another person, because your mind may wander to unpleasant emotional memories that you have had with that person. After visualizing with all of your senses and breathing deeply for four minutes, and saying a prayer of thanks for the food and/or for the events of the day, you then can eat the meal or, if at bedtime, fall off to sleep."

Dr. Cowden reports that his patients find that this four-minute technique works better than meditating for 15 to 20 minutes once per day because stress is additive and cumulative. "Commit to practicing this technique four times daily before mealtimes and bedtime for at least four weeks, and notice any changes in how you feel and act as a result," he advises. "Most people who do this find that they can sleep 30 minutes less per night and still feel well-rested."

Laugh: Studies have shown that genuine laughter reduces stress and the production of stress-related hormones while simultaneously boosting immune function. Laughter also provides what psychologists call "cognitive control," improving one's ability to positively respond to external events. Although the events themselves may be beyond your control, you do have a choice as to how you respond to them. Laughter enables you to shift the perspective from which you perceive such events so that they become less stressful and even humorous. As the great comedienne Carol Burnett has said, "Comedy is tragedy plus time."

Learning to find humor in, and laugh about, the situations you experience each day can be a powerful antidote to stress. Your sense of humor provides you with the ability to find delight, experience joy and happiness, and release tension. Additionally, being able to laugh at a situation, problem, and even yourself, can be very empowering. People who laugh each day tend to have more positive and hopeful attitudes and are less likely to succumb to depression and worry, compared to people who don't laugh a lot.

Breathe Stress Away: The next time you notice that you are stressed or feeling tension in your body, close your eyes for a few moments and take ten deep breaths. Don't force them. Breathe in through your nose, expanding your belly. Inhale as fully as you comfortably can, then let the exhale naturally follow. Learning to do this on a regular basis throughout the day can pay big dividends and keep stress at bay.

A breathing exercise known as box breathing is particularly effective for managing stress, which is why it is used by Navy SEAL teams to control their physiology when faced with threatening situations. With regular practice, box breathing can become a powerful tool you can use to stay calm and maintain your mental/emotional equilibrium. You simply inhale for four seconds, hold your breath for four seconds, exhale for four seconds, and then hold your breath once more for another four seconds, and repeat this sequence for a few minutes.

Take A Stretch Break and Soothe Your Eyes: The following recommendations are particularly useful for people who sit at a desk during most of their working day. Once an hour, step away from your desk and take a stretch break. Exaggerate a yawn and stretch fully and comfortably. If you can, duck outside for a breath of fresh air as well. This simple routine can increase your energy and make you more productive.

Another useful technique to help reduce eyestrain is to cup both eyes with the palms of your hands periodically each day. Take a few deep breaths and focus on the soothing energy of your hands moving into your eyes and down through your body.

Spend Time With Loved Ones: One of the most enjoyable ways for reducing and managing stress is spending time with people whose company you enjoy. Research consistently shows that people who have strong relationships with friends and family are far less prone to stress and illness compared to people who primarily live lives of solitude. People with strong social connections also tend to live longer than people who are loners, and to cope better with whatever challenges life may bring their way.

The next time you find yourself struggling with stress reach out to loved ones, either in person or through a phone call. Share what's on your mind and let them do the same.

All of the above methods and recommendations can help you manage stress and experience positive, health-enhancing thoughts, emotions, and beliefs more consistently. However, often, the causes of stress and negative thoughts and emotions we experience are not based in the present, but are triggered by the effects of past events and the unhealed emotions and beliefs we formed about them. Scientists have discovered that these events and their effects are stored within our cells as *cellular memories.*

Just as your brain records what happens to you each moment, so do the cells of your body absorb the effects of everything you experience, and how you interpret each experience when it occurs. Everything that you have ever perceived and experienced, and how you interpreted each experience, is stored in your cellular memory, generating internal chemical reactions that, unless the cellular memories are healed, can recur for the rest of your life any time that the cellular memories are triggered. This triggering process occurs automatically without our conscious awareness.

Your cells not only record all of the stimuli, events, conversations, suspicions, and criticisms that you experience during your life, they also record your *reactions* to these events, absorbing them as facts regardless of how distorted or out of proportion they may be. Every perceived slight, failure, fright, and feeling of inadequacy you've suffered is embedded in your body's cells, giving rise to anger, frustration, fear, pain, and other feelings whenever something activates your cellular memories. This is why you may still find yourself mentally replaying unpleasant events from your past, or repeatedly rehashing old grudges. Even if decades have passed and you tell yourself you no longer care about such things, you will relive the same harmful emotions until you eliminate what causes them— the cellular memories themselves.

A variety of energy-based techniques are proving to be effective for healing unresolved cellular memories. Most of these techniques and therapies fall within an entirely new field of energy medicine known as energy psychology. They include therapies such as the emotional freedom technique (EFT), Tapas acupressure technique (TAT), Callahan Thought Field Therapy, or TFT (developed by Roger Callahan, who pioneered the development of the energy psychology field), and EMDR (Eye Movement Desensitization and Reprocessing).

All therapies within this field are initially best learned by working with a professional trained in their use, yet most of them can also be used as self-care methods. If you are interested in learning more about them, you can do so online via various websites and instructional videos. They can be quite helpful for resolving stored cellular memories that are causing you stress and negatively impacting your mental and emotional health.

The following methods are also well-worth exploring.

Autogenic Training and Dr. Norm Shealy's Biogenics Method

Autogenic training is a technique that was developed in the early 1930s by Johannes Schultz, a German psychiatrist. It involves the daily practice of 10 to 15 minute sessions during which a specific set of statements and visualizations are repeated that induce a state of relaxation. Autogenic training has for decades been an integral part of Dr. C. Norman Shealy's medical practice at the Shealy-Sorin Wellness Institute in Fair Grove, Missouri, and is also used by many other physicians around the world to help their patients relieve stress and stress-induced disorders. It works by restoring the balance between the activity of the sympathetic ("flight or fight" response) and the parasympathetic ("rest, repair, and assimilate" response) branches of the autonomic nervous system.

Practicing autogenic training on a regular basis can help improve digestion and elimination, lower blood pressure, slow your heart rate, and enhance immune function. Autogenic training is also an effective sleep aid.

To perform autogenic training, sit comfortably in a chair or lie down. Close your eyes and mentally scan your body, noticing any areas of tension. Then mentally repeat to yourself the following suggestions three times, starting on the inhalation of each breath and finishing on the exhale, breathing in a relaxed, unforced manner. As you repeat each phrase, visualize and feel the sensations you are stating for each area of your body.

My arms and legs are heavy and warm.
My heartbeat is calm and regular.
My solar plexus is warm.
My forehead is cool.
My neck and shoulders are heavy.
I am at peace.

Now count to ten, breathing deeply and easily, then open your eyes when you are ready. Try to take at least 10 minutes to perform the above exercise. Spend a few moments with each suggestion, feeling it occurring in your body. For best results, repeat this exercise three times a day, once before lunch, once before the last meal of the day, and once at bedtime.

You can also record the above suggestions and listen to them rather than having to remember each of the suggestions and their proper sequence. However, memorizing the sequence of suggestions is recommended so that you can practice autogenic training any time that you may need to banish stress.

Dr. Shealy has developed a variation of autogenic training called Biogenics, which forms the foundation of his 90 Days To Self-Health Program. "*Biogenics* is a word meaning origin of life, and is a system of mental exercises designed to help you learn to regulate your own body functioning at will," Dr. Shealy explains. You can learn how to practice it by downloading Dr. Shealy's 90 Days To Self-Health ebook at www.realholisticdoc.com. You can also receive a downloadable audio MP3 file called Autogenic Focus by signing up to receive Dr. Shealy's emails. The ebook, MP3 file, and the emails are free and available at realholisticdoc.com/free-offers-autogenic-focus. "Autogenic Focus is an essential self-regulation tool and is a key component in the foundation of the Biogenics system, Dr. Shealy states. "This audio program is combined with Samvit Sound™

technology that directs the brain to the optimal state of consciousness for the training to have maximum impact."

Dr. Shealy, along with Dr. Sergey Sorin, medical director of the Shealy-Sorin Wellness Institute, has also created over 50 other downloadable audio recordings that incorporate guided Biogenic visualizations with Samvit Sound technology to address specific health and lifestyle issues. "Our Biogenics audio products are delivered digitally in convenient MP3 format playable on any mobile device, along with headphones or earbuds," Dr. Sorin explains. "They are designed to support the brain wave states conducive to healing, recovery, focus, concentration, relaxation, sleep and much more. Combined with one's intention, these audios are inexpensive tools anyone can use to enhance their life."

Dr. Shealy's Bliss Oils

Among the many important health discoveries Dr. Shealy has made over the course of his medical career was his discovery of what he has named the five Sacred Rings. "Over a ten-year period I discovered five energetic acupuncture circuits which help balance our elemental energies," he explains. These elemental energies are fire, air, water, earth, and crystal.

Dr. Shealy's discovery of the Sacred Rings began when he started to research the hormone DHEA (dehydroepiandrosterone), seeking optimum ways to safely increase it. As Dr. Shealy explains in his book, *Living Bliss*, "Optimal health requires optimal levels of DHEA, but these levels in the body begin to decrease naturally after age 30." However, taking DHEA as an oral supplement is not a wise choice because doing so may activate dormant cancer cells in the breasts, prostate gland, ovaries, and uterus.

Dr. Shealy has found that most people over 40 have DHEA levels that are less than half of what he considers to be ideal (750 to 1200 ng/dL in men and 500 to 980 ng/dL in women). "I had an insight that natural progesterone should increase DHEA, and indeed it did, but only by an average of 60 percent. Yet, if you start at a level of 200 ng/dL, even a 100 percent increase does not get you to the ideal.

I pondered what else would raise DHEA. Since DHEA is essentially the chemical battery of fire energy, I knew that if I stimulated the points that connect the kidneys, the gonads, the adrenals, the thyroid and the pituitary through a window of the sky point—there are 22 windows of the sky points in acupuncture—it could enhance fire energy. There is no pituitary point in Chinese cosmology, so I had to intuit that one also."

The five points that Dr. Shealy worked with corresponding to the kidneys, gonads, and adrenal, thyroid, and pituitary glands became the first Sacred Ring, the ring of fire. He later discovered the rings of air, earth, water, and crystal.

Originally, Dr. Shealy researched these Sacred Rings by stimulating them with a specific TENS (Transcutaneous Electrical Nerve Stimulation) device he invented called the Shealy Pain Pro. Using that approach, he proved that the circuits of the Sacred Rings provide specific biochemical and bioenergetic benefits that can improve overall health, including mood. Achieving these benefits with electrical stimulation required an average of 18 minutes of treatment per day for each ring. Feedback from his patients indicated this was too much effort for most people.

This feedback left Dr. Shealy determined to seek a faster and easier way to achieve the same type of results. He discovered that he could instead use specific mixtures of essential oils applied topically over the circuit points of the Sacred Rings. Today, these oils are known as Bliss Oils. "When you learn the positions of each circuit point, it takes literally 30 seconds to activate each Sacred Ring using the Bliss Oils," Dr. Shealy says. "They are applied with an applicator roll-on."

"Years ago, I had a sudden intuitive hit that the Ring of Air would raise oxytocin and I have now proven that this is true. Even more remarkably, I have discovered an essential oil blend I call Air Bliss, when placed on the circuit points of the Ring of Air, is significantly helpful in relieving depression and anxiety. Oxytocin is the key to relieving anxiety and depression."

Dr. Shealy reports that daily use of Air Bliss can enhance mental creativity and intuition, stimulate insights and feelings of integration and non-separatism with all of Life, and assist with hearing issues such as tinnitus. Early reports also show its use can result in improvements in cases of autism and Asperger's syndrome.

Among the other important benefits Dr. Shealy has documented that his Bliss Oils provide are improved overall emotional balance, regulation of the entire endocrine system, improved thyroid function, elevation of DHEA, reduction of free radicals in the body, and increased levels of calcitonin. "Calcitonin not only maintains the strength of the skeleton, it is also the strongest pain reliever the body produces, 40 to 60 times as powerful as morphine," Dr. Shealy says.

"Perhaps the greatest benefit of all that we have found is that when you use the Bliss Oils for fire, earth, and crystal daily for over a year, this regenerates telomeres by an average of 3.5 percent. Telomeres ordinarily shrink an average of one percent for every year of life. If you have good health habits, I have now demonstrated over a period of many years that by stimulating the circuits of those three Sacred Rings, which only takes a minute and a half a day to do, you are going to regenerate telomeres. We've regenerated telomeres by as much as 10 percent in some people, and only one percent in others, but the average is 3.5 percent a year. What that means, theoretically, when you do that, is that you are going to live longer and healthier."

Dr. Shealy's Bliss Oils are available at normshealy.shop/collections/essentials-oils. For more information about the Sacred Rings, their corresponding circuit points and how to use the Bliss Oils, visit realholisticdoc.com.

HeartMath®

Your heart is directly involved in all of the emotions you experience. Emotions such as anxiety, fright, and stress can increase your heart rate. A "pounding" heart rate almost always occurs during times of strong emotions. But scientists have found that even the slightest change in emotion can immediately change heart rhythm (the rate your heart beats).

Contrary to popular belief, a healthy heart does not beat at the same steady rate throughout the day. Heart beat rates vary, even during sleep. This change in heart beat rhythm is now recognized by scientists as a communication tool that signals messages to and from the heart, brain, and body.

Much of the recent research in heart beat rhythms and their relation to stress has been conducted by scientists at the Institute of HeartMath®, in Boulder Creek, California. There, researchers have explored the heart's "intelligence," and developed a variety of techniques, including the one below, for using that intelligence to reduce stress. These techniques have been clinically proven to turn off the stress response and lower the release of cortisol, improve mood and cognitive performance, and reduce high blood pressure and the risk of dying from heart disease.

The research conducted at the Institute of HeartMath proves that when people learn how to modulate their heart rate variability, they can quickly reduce negative reactions to stress and improve their overall health.

One of the most popular HeartMath techniques is known as the Freeze-Frame. It helps stop stress responses to difficult situations by replacing negative perceptions with positive feelings, such as appreciation, enjoyment, and love. Research shows that these positive emotions restore calm and control to the heart rate.

The Freeze-Frame technique is practiced as follows:

1. As soon as you recognize a stressful feeling, take a "time out" and "freeze" it.

2. Make a sincere effort to shift your focus away from whatever racing thoughts or upset emotions you may have, placing your focus instead on the area around your heart. Imagine that you are literally breathing through your heart to help focus your energy in this area. Do this for at least ten seconds.

3. Now recall a positive, enjoyable feeling or memory that you've had in your life and allow yourself to re-experience it.

4. As your renewed experience of the positive feeling that you've selected takes hold of you, mentally ask your heart: What would be the best response to the situation I am in,

that would take away my stress and minimize the return of stress in my future?

5. "Listen" to the response your heart provides and act on it.

This deceptively simple process can quickly rein in your reactive mind and emotions to help you find the most effective and appropriate response to your situation. Practicing the Freeze-Frame technique regularly will help you become aware of your heart's intelligence, and deepen your connection to heart-centered emotions such as calm, peace, love, and happiness.

A growing number of forward-thinking physicians now share various HeartMath tools and techniques with their patients, and encourage them to make use of them on their own. One of them is Angelique Hart, MD, who practices integrative medicine in Albuquerque, New Mexico.

"A lot of patients are not aware how their emotional state affects their heart, blood pressure, and overall health in a major way," Dr. Hart says. "The HeartMath tools and techniques provide them with tangible means of knowing what is happening in their bodies, showing them how they're breathing, how calm they are or if they're able to calm themselves, and, most importantly, how practicing the techniques helps them improve their blood pressure and their heart rate, leading to better health and less stress. That is the most important thing.

"In my clinic, we provide our patients with training in some of the HeartMath techniques, using the programs from the Institute, such the Inner Balance program, which teaches them how to let go of emotional stress and create a state of emotional balance and coherence. Usually within two or three sessions, they're able to stay mostly in a balanced state. Then we recommend that they buy a phone app from the HeartMath company so that they can monitor themselves throughout the day. If they get into a situation where they feel flustered, angry, or they feel off, they can sit down, grab their smart phone and take care of themselves in a very quick way. Eventually, they're able to do it without the app. They start to know what to do and they start to track themselves better.

"One of the problems I think that we have in general in relation to our health is that we are not able to look inside and say, Hey, wait, where am I today? Am I in my body? That's a very important question. HeartMath helps to bring you back and get the sensation of grounding coming into the body and lock it in. I often have my patients do that first, and then I proceed to treat them. When you're not conscious of where you are how are you going to help yourself? Part of yourself is not there to have that experience to keep it there. Centering and grounding with HeartMath helps with all of that because it's a teaching tool. It helps people become more conscious of what they are doing, how it's affecting them, and what they can do to fix that." To find out more about the Institute of HeartMath and the tools and techniques it offers visit www.HeartMath.org.

The Emotion Code™

The Emotion Code™ is a potent self-care method you can use to discover and release trapped emotional energies or emotional "baggage" stored in your body and energy field due to past experiences. It was developed by Dr. Bradley Nelson and is easily learned.

Dr. Nelson, who has a background as both a chiropractor and a computer programmer, credits God with the discovery of the Emotion Code. His recognition of the power of the divine began when he was only seven years old.

"I was really sick with the measles," he recounts, "and I'd overheard my parents discussing their plan to admit me to the hospital the next day to be placed in an oxygen tent, which I didn't understand. My mother asked my father if he would pray for me so I'd be able to get well, and my parents knelt down by the side of the couch where they had made a bed for me. In the midst of my father's heartfelt prayer, I suddenly felt something that started at the top of my head and passed through my body to the soles of my feet, and I was instantly made well. I was only seven years old, but I remember every moment of that event. That unforgettable experience taught me that there's an unseen higher power that we can draw upon for help."

When Dr. Nelson was 14, he developed a life-threatening form of kidney disease. "There was nothing that Western medicine had to offer me, so my parents took me to see some holistic osteopathic doctors. They began working on me, realigning my spine and more, and in short order the crippling pain was gone. Subsequent tests at the hospital proved that I was completely healed. That's when I decided what I wanted to do with my life, I wanted to become a healer."

After first training in computers, Dr. Nelson became a chiropractor. "Since it was a profound answer to prayer that guided me into the healing arts, I believed that I could get help from that higher power for my patients," he explains. "During all the years that I was in practice I had this private, personal habit where I would take a moment before I'd work on each patient to make a connection with that higher power and ask for help. Sometimes, in answer to those short, silent prayers on behalf of my patients, the answer would come back as a flood of information and understanding that would pour into my mind like an avalanche of data.

"Dramatic answers like that are rare. I've found that when we ask the higher power for help, answers most often come in the form of thoughts or ideas or impressions that are so subtle we often overlook them. During those years, one of the most important things that I learned was that the subconscious mind is an incredibly powerful computer that remembers everything you've ever done and experienced. The entire history of your health or disease is all stored in your subconscious mind. Through a simple form of biofeedback known as muscle-testing, anyone can tap into that internal computer and get relevant and powerful answers. The physical, mental, and emotional symptoms that we suffer from are simply the body's way of communicating to us that something needs attention. While Western medicine focuses on alleviating our symptoms, our symptoms need to be the beginning of a conversation with the inner mind, which can easily reveal those symptoms' true underlying causes. The causes of our difficulties are many, but can all be organized into six different categories.

"The number one type of imbalance that I found in all my patients, no matter how young or old they were, or what kind of symptoms they were suffering from, was their emotional baggage. All things are ultimately made of energy, and the emotions we feel are energy as well. Every emotion has a unique vibrational frequency. At the quantum level your body feels emotion as an energetic vibration or frequency. If the emotion is intense, the energy of that emotion can sometimes become overwhelming to the body and that emotional energy may become trapped in the body. Trapped emotions consist of balls of energy between the size of a baseball and a softball that distort the normal energy field of the body and interfere with its functioning. This causes the chemical reactions taking place in that area of tissue, as well as the flow of energy in the meridians in that area, to be interfered with to some degree. When we remove these trapped emotions we remove the distorting effect that they have on the body, often resulting in an immediate reduction in physical symptoms, as well as improvement in mental and emotional distress."

The Emotion Code has proven to be highly effective for achieving these types of results. It is used by physicians and certified Emotion Code practitioners in nearly 80 countries around the world. From the onset of its development, however, Dr. Nelson has always intended it to primarily be a self-care treatment. He wrote the book *The Emotion Code* to empower anyone to begin using the Emotion Code on their own.

The Emotion Code incorporates a simple process of using muscle-testing to narrow down and identify trapped emotions. This is done by the use of the Emotion Code Chart™, which consists of six rows and two columns. The rows correspond to specific organs and the columns correspond to a range of emotions associated with the organs. Using one of the various muscle-testing techniques that *The Emotion Code* book provides instruction for, readers determine which column and row contains the trapped emotion that needs to be released. Once this information is determined, the trapped emotion is quickly released by passing any type of household magnet (or your hand) over any portion of the body's governing meridian, which runs from the nose, up the center of the forehead, over the top midline of the head, and down the spine to the tailbone This is done three times, with intention.

"Finding a trapped emotion is a very rapid," Dr. Nelson says. "When you're trained how to do this and become used to it, you can usually find a trapped emotion and release it within 60 seconds. We use magnets because trapped emotions are an energy and to deal with them effectively we need to use some other form of energy. In testing all strengths and all varieties and polarities of magnets, we have found that any kind of magnet will work. But if you don't have a magnet, you can swipe your fingers or your hand over the governing meridian and that's enough magnetic energy to release the trapped emotion because your body has a biomagnetic charge."

To fully explain how to apply the Emotion Code is beyond the scope of this chapter, which is why I recommend that you read *The Emotion Code* book.

Though the Emotion Code is not intended to diagnose or treat disease, many people who have experienced it report that their health problems rapidlyly resolved once their trapped emotions were identified and released. "For example," Dr. Nelson says, "a man came to me with severe low back pain that he'd been suffering from for weeks. When I tested him using the Emotion Code, I found that he had a trapped emotion of anger that had become trapped in his body 20 years before. He immediately remembered what had happened. It involved a situation at work where he had become very upset over being unjustly treated. I released the trapped emotion. When I did, to his astonishment ,his pain disappeared instantaneously."

A few days later, the man returned to see Dr. Nelson. He said "My back pain is still gone and has not come back, which is just incredible, and I'm very grateful for that. But I need to tell you something. When I first came in here, I had another issue that I didn't tell you about. For as long as I can remember, I've been what you would call a rage-aholic. I'm always yelling at my wife and kids, I have to be careful about road rage, and I've gone to anger management classes several times, but it hasn't really helped me. I'm always on edge, and little things can make me really upset, really fast. But ever since you released that trapped emotion of anger from me, I don't feel angry anymore. I feel relaxed and peaceful, and like a different person."

Dr. Nelson explains, "When you have a trapped emotion, the body's tissues in that vicinity are literally feeling that emotion's vibration or frequency 24 hours a day. This man had a 'ball of anger' that had been distorting the energy field in his low back to the point that it was causing him severe physical pain. But there was something else going on as well. Whenever a situation arose in his life where he might tend to feel the emotion of anger, he would feel that anger much more readily than he otherwise would have, because his low back was already feeling that emotion 24/7.

"When we remove these trapped emotions and people get rid of their emotional baggage, it changes how they feel. It often changes who they are, and always for the better. It's almost like stepping out of this old suit that you've been walking around in for your entire life. You release the emotional baggage, and step into this new state of being that is much closer to who you are really supposed to be. It's very exciting."

In addition to the Emotion Code, Dr. Nelson has also developed the Body Code, which encompasses the Emotion Code. "The Body Code is a patented energy balancing system that's intended to help people uncover the root causes of discomfort, sickness, and suffering in body and spirit," Dr. Nelson says. "Our goal is to help you identify the underlying causes of your physical or emotional concerns, then release them in minutes so you can start feeling like yourself again."

Besides the energetic imbalances caused by trapped emotions and internalized trauma, Dr. Nelson identified five other primary areas of imbalance: pathogens (bacteria, viruses, fungi, parasites, mold); structural (misalignments in bones, muscles, nerves, and connective tissues); dietary and nutritional imbalances and deficiencies; toxicity (heavy metals and other environmental pollutants, free radicals, harmful electromagnetic frequencies); and systems and circuitry (organs, glands, muscles, body systems, and the connections between them).

"The Body Code is a mind mapping system that I developed during the years that I was in practice when I was asking patients' subconscious minds what was wrong with them or what their imbalances were that needed to be released," Dr. Nelson adds. "By regaining or maintaining our state of balance in these six areas, we're able to regain or maintain our health. The Body Code, which is a self-study course, enables anyone to open up the subconscious mind like a book and rapidly get answers about what their imbalances truly are. The Body Code has changed the practices of many doctors and healing practitioners around the world because it enables anyone to plug into the incredibly powerful computer we call the subconscious mind, and simply ask for the underlying reasons why they're manifesting any symptom they may be experiencing. The subconscious mind, via muscle-testing, will walk you to the underlying cause or causes of that problem."

The following example illustrates how remarkably effective the Body Code can be.

Years ago, a woman who had been hospitalized for five days with severe pain in her abdomen came to see Dr. Nelson. While hospitalized she underwent numerous medical tests to try to determine what was wrong with her, but all the tests were negative.

"After five days the medical staff decided they couldn't really help her so they released her," Dr. Nelson says. "That was on a Friday. On Monday morning, she came to see me, still in terrible pain. I started using the Body Code and I corrected some imbalances but it didn't really change how she was feeling. One of the imbalances that I found was that she needed a chromium supplement. I thought this was an incidental finding, so I told her she needed to take chromium, but I didn't put much emphasis on my recommendation, believing it to be unrelated to her severe pain.

"The next day, she returned and her condition was even worse. Her pain level was ten out of ten, and I was afraid for her health, thinking that the tests run at the hospital must certainly have missed something. I again started going through the Body Code and immediately, out of nearly 1,000 different possibilities, I was guided by her subconscious mind through muscle-testing right back to chromium. I remembered that chromium had shown up the day before and I hadn't thought much of it. But since it was showing up again, I told her that I thought her body was trying to tell us she needed it. I sent her down the street to the health food store to buy some. Twenty minutes later, she returned and was literally jumping up and down in my waiting room exclaiming, 'I'm fixed! That fixed it! The pain is gone!' The moment she took the chromium, the pain disappeared. She asked, 'How did that work?' I told her I had no idea.

"I still have no idea what the connection was between her pain and her apparent chromium deficiency. But the beauty of it is that what we're doing with the Body Code, and with the Emotion Code as well, is giving the body a voice. Finally, we're able to open the subconscious mind and ask questions and get answers. You can trust the subconscious mind to take you where it needs to take you."

To learn more about both the Emotion Code and the Body Code, visit https://discoverhealing.com, where you can download a free Emotion Code Kit that includes an ebook version of the first two chapters of *The Emotion Code* book, printable versions of the Emotion Code flowcharts, and eight video trainings of Dr. Nelson explaining how and why energy healing works. The same website also provides self-study and certification courses for both the Emotion Code and the Body Code, and articles, other videos, and a directory of certified practitioners in the U.S. and throughout the world.

CHAPTER 7

The Seventh Key: Generating More Energy And Exercising More Effectively

THE SEVENTH KEY to achieving and maintaining optimal health is to become aware of yourself as a "bioenergetic being", and to exercise on a regular basis, ideally every day. This chapter will show you how to most effectively and efficiently do so.

Your Bioenergetic Nature

One of the most exciting developments in the field of healthcare in the last few decades is the rise of what is known as energy medicine, which has become an important component of integrative medicine and is employed by many ACIM physicians as a primary means of diagnosing and treating their patients. A basic tenet of energy medicine is that our bodies are first and foremost bioenergy systems. From this perspective, ACIM physicians recognize that health and disease are primarily outcomes of energy flow or disruption.

"Allopathic medicine totally ignores the system of bioenergy," explains James Lemire, MD, who, with his wife, Nuris Lemire, an occupational therapist, acupuncturist, and certified nutritionist,

oversees the Lemire Clinic in Ocala, Florida (www.LemireClinic.
com). "Conventional physicians are not taught anything about it. Yet,
patients understand energy. We do brainwave analysis procedures,
we do nerve conduction studies to look for neuropathy, we do an
EKG, which shows us our heart. It's an energy wave that we are
examining in these methods of diagnosis, but for many doctors it's
mechanistic and they don't understand the energy of it."

Dr. Lemire admits to once being the same way as a result of
his original conventional medical training. "That changed when
I met Nuris and started exploring Chinese medicine with her and
began understanding Qi and energy as such," he says. "Now, in my
examination room, I have acupuncture charts on the wall and I
explain to patients that we are marvelous, energetic beings. I explain
a little bit about Tai Chi and Qigong and how energy fits into it, and
that because we're energetic beings, we can't ignore that. Because if
you have a short circuit in the battery of your car, what's going to
happen? It's not going to start. And if you have mitochondria that
are not working, it's like you're trying and start an SUV in Michigan
in the middle of the winter, but you're using a Volkswagen four volt
battery. It's not going to work. Patients understand that and they
really understand what we're trying to do with energy and how it
fits in with what we're doing. You can't separate that anymore from
our practice. And because Nuris is an occupational therapist and an
acupuncturist who works with them more directly, patients seem to
really take to that. They seem to be very receptive to all the types of
energy medicine we do.

"If a new patient comes to us and all they are looking for is a
doctor who will prescribe pills and not require much of them, that's
not a good match for our practice. Those people don't usually stay
around because they're not willing to invest in themselves. Investing
in themselves means they have to understand what their personal
energy is.

"The number one reason that people walk through our door
is fatigue. And when we show them the acupuncture charts and
explain the importance of bioenergy as it fits into their health they
tend to understand that. Health and healing also have an emotional

or psychological component. Physicians have to understand the emotional component, and energy really ties right into that."

- Dr. Lemire and other ACIM physicians teach their patients about four ways they can significantly maintain and improve your energy levels, each of which is easy to implement.Keep yourself properly hydrated (with mineralized water).

- Regularly expose yourself to sunlight and fresh outdoors.

- Ground to the earth.

- Regularly engage in physical activity and exercise, which recharges your body's "battery".

Proper Hydration

"Proper hydration is essential," Dr. Lemire says, "because water is what drives the electricity of our cells. Without proper hydration, patients aren't going to get better. Dehydration is rampant. We recommend that everyone drink adequate amounts of a good source of water, with a pinch of Himalayan salt or electrolytes to balance it. Energetically, this helps the cells stay healthy. You have to drink the right amount of water and the right quality of water to have the right energy. Nuris and I recommend starting each day with a glass of lemon water."

Dr. Lemire's point is well supported by science. Research has also established that water is especially important for healthy brain function, since the brain depends on an adequate water supply to operate. In addition, water acts as a bonding agent that enables your cells to maintain their proper structure. Without enough water, cell structure cannot be properly maintained, leading to a loss of structural integrity and, eventually, disease.

Water also helps to prevent your body's DNA from being damaged and aids in its ability to repair itself. Damaged DNA can cause cells to behave abnormally, leading to cancer and various other disease conditions.

Water's numerous health benefits were documented by the late Dr. Fereydoon Batmanghelidj, a recognized authority on the relationship between water and health, and dehydration and disease. Based on his many years of researching the health benefits of water, he recommended drinking one-half ounce of water for every pound of body weight each day, along with a pinch of sea salt in each glass to help the body maintain an adequate supply of minerals.

"That's a good benchmark ," Dr. Lemire says. "However, there are some people who can't handle that. Just as there is not one diet that is optimal for everyone, there is no one prescription for daily water intake that is right for everyone. But giving them a benchmark like that is a good place to start."

"If I have a senior that does not want to drink water late in the day because they don't want to get up at night to go pee," Nuris Lemire adds, "then I cannot tell them that they have to drink that much water. I need to start from where they are. If they are only drinking one glass of water now, I ask them to see if they can drink two glasses daily over the next few days and then let's see where we can go from there. I like meeting patients where they are. Let's go slowly from there to what they feel that they can do."

The Importance Of Daily Sunlight Exposure

In recent decades we have been taught to fear the sun because of claims that sunlight exposure can cause skin cancer. While we should do all we can to avoid skin cancer, failing to obtain the many health benefits regular direct sunlight exposure provides is not the way to go about it. Additionally, research has found that indoor workers who receive little regular exposure to sunlight have a greater risk for developing malignant melanoma (the most dangerous type of skin cancer) compared to outdoor workers.

As with most things in life, moderation is the key. You want to be sure that you *do* get out in the sun each day, but you don't want to overdo it by developing sunburn. Sunburn is the real culprit that links sunlight to skin cancer because, especially when it is severe, causes skin cells to mutate, and that's what cancer is—a mutation of healthy cells.

But don't use synthetic sunscreens to avoid sunburn because

the harmful chemicals they contain are absorbed into the skin to enter the bloodstream. In addition, synthetic sunscreens block 95 percent of ultraviolet B (UVB) rays from the sun. UVB rays are what your body needs in order to produce vitamin D. Regular exposure to sunlight, preferably in a swimsuit or shorts and a short-sleeved shirt without sunscreen, is the best way to ensure that your body maintains its vitamin D supply, which is crucial for maintaining your health.

Vitamin D produced by sunlight exposure is superior to taking vitamin D supplements, which in some cases can displace calcium in the body, resulting in excess calcium in the bloodstream. This can cause kidney problems, including kidney stones, and even kidney failure, and can also cause calcium buildup in the arteries, leading to atherosclerosis and heart disease. None of these problems occur with sunlight exposure. In addition, vitamin D production from the sun lasts two to three times longer in the body than vitamin D obtained from food or supplements

Regular sunlight exposure also helps maintain brain health. The sun's UV rays not only enter your body through your skin, but also through your eyes via the pupil and retina. Once absorbed into your eyes, they enhance production of dopamine, melatonin, and serotonin, all of which are important for healthy brain function.

The following guidelines can help ensure that you get all the sunshine you need.

Make it a point to try and get outdoors every day. The best window of time to expose yourself to the sun is between 10 am to 3 pm. UVA radiation from the sun, which can be harmful and cause skin wrinkling and skin damage, is more pronounced before and after this timeframe as a percentage of all ultraviolet wavelengths.

People with light color skin may only require 15 minutes of sunlight exposure per day. Other may need to stay in the sun for longer periods. If you fall into the latter category you can break up your sunlight exposure times, such as spending 15-20 minutes in the sun during the late morning, and another 15-20 minutes during the afternoon before 3 pm.

For sunlight exposure to be effective, you need to be outside. Glass filters out most of the UVB rays that produce vitamin D in the body. If you wear glasses or contacts, take them off during sunshine exposure.

For best results, expose as much of your body as you can to sunlight in order to maximize vitamin D production. This means not only your head, but also at least your arms. In warm weather, you can also expose your legs.

While getting out in the sun between 10 am and 3 pm is not practical for many people, try to find a way to do so at least a few times a week, such as during a lunch break. Combining sunlight exposure with deep breathing while you are outdoors is even more beneficial.

Grounding For Greater Energy

If you have walked barefoot and slept on the ground, with no barrier between you and the earth, most likely you felt a sense of renewed energy and increased well-being. Now scientists have discovered why.

Research in recent years confirms that walking barefoot and sleeping on the ground outdoors creates a conductive current between the earth and our bodies that allows the earth's healing energies to merge with our own physical energy system.

Today, this process is known as grounding or "earthing". Thanks largely to the efforts of Clint Ober and Dr. Stephen Sinatra, an entire body of science has arisen to investigate its health benefits. Grounding provides many other significant health benefits, as well. Research conducted by Dr. Sinatra and others demonstrated that grounding:

- Improves energy levels.
- Boosts immune function.
- Normalizes the body's rhythms, including circadian rhythm.
- Promotes deeper, healthier sleep, followed by more energy upon awaking.
- Reduces, even eliminates, back, joint, and muscle pain and stiffness.

- Reduces arthritis symptoms.

- Improves blood pressure levels and enhances blood flow.

- Improves metabolic function.

Research also shows that time spent walking or standing barefoot on grass, soil, or sand at the beach can dramatically reduce inflammation levels in the body, and do so to a greater degree than anti-inflammatory nutrients such as fish oil and other vitamins and minerals. The significance of this discovery cannot be overstated.

Martin Zucker, who co-wrote the book *Earthing* with Clint Ober and Dr. Sinatra, explains how and why grounding to the earth's natural healing energies is one of the simplest yet most powerful self-care health approaches you can make on a regular basis.

"We all live and function electrically on an electrical planet," he states. "We are each of us a collection of dynamic electrical circuits. In the living matrix of our complex bodies, trillions of cells constantly transmit and receive energy in the course of their programmed biochemical reactions. The movement of nutrients and water into the cells is regulated by electric fields, and each type of cell has a frequency range in which it operates. Your heart, brain, nervous system, muscles, and immune system are prime examples of electrical subsystems operating within your 'bioelectrical' body. The fact is, all of your movements, behaviors, and actions are energized by electricity...In electricity, all electrical systems are 'grounded'; that is, stabilized by the electrical energy of the Earth's surface. Without a ground, appliances or sophisticated medical devices would not work properly. Similarly, when connected to the Earth, the body receives an electric signal that normalizes and stabilizes its many biological systems and mechanisms. This signal also appears to be the source of negatively charged free electrons, present in unlimited quantity on the surface of the Earth.

"The hypothesis put forward by scientists involved in [grounding] research is that the transfer of electrons into the body quenches or neutralizes positively charged, electron-seeking free radicals that drive chronic inflammation activity at the core of many common diseases. We suggest that the mightiest anti-inflammatory on the planet may be the very planet itself! We further suggest that destructive chronic inflammation may be the result of an electron deficiency that is remedied by contact with the Earth's infinite reservoir of free electrons. Just as sunlight provides us with vitamin D, the Earth provides us with another essential ingredient. Call it vitamin G: G for ground."

Researchers have also found that standing barefoot on concrete surfaces provides the same degree of grounding benefits because concrete does not interfere with the conductivity of the body and its ability to draw energy from the earth. If you live in a home with a basement with a concrete floor, you can stand barefoot upon it during inclement weather.

Dr. Sinatra's Discoveries About Grounding And Harmful Electromagnetic Radiation (EMR): It's long been known that thick blood is a major risk factor for high blood pressure, and therefore heart attack, stroke, and other types of heart disease. Thick blood can also sap your energy levels. Research by Dr. Sinatra shows that certain types of electromagnetic radiation (EMR), such as from cell and portable phones, laptops and computers, smart meters, and WiFi, are major causes of thick blood.

"I think hyper-coagulable blood, blood in which the blood cells stick together and the blood resembles red ketchup, is really the major risk factor of the 21st century," Dr. Sinatra says. "I say that because of electro-hypersensitivity and the wireless soup of electromagnetic contamination or radiation that we now live in. Living in this electromagnetic field or this electromagnetic soup absolutely makes the blood thicken. I did the original research on this. I had a group of 18 people and we were doing a blood analysis with live cell microscopy. We were checking for blood viscosity and everybody but one person had red ketchup blood, including me. I said, that's impossible. I couldn't have this because I take omega 3, I take CoQ10, I eat a healthy diet, I did everything right. The one person out of the 18 of us that had thin, healthy blood, what I call red wine blood, was Clint Ober.

"Why did Clint have red wine blood under the microscope? It was because he was walking out of the room every 15 to 20 minutes to stand barefoot on the grass. He would go outside to ground himself for a few minutes and then come back inside. I wondered how he could have healthy thin blood and the rest of us didn't. Then we found that the room we were in had a cordless phone with a cordless phone base behind a curtain, and I realized that it was poisoning everybody in the room with invisible electromagnetic radiation. I immediately called my main researcher, Dr. Gaetan Chevalier, and told him we needed to study this."

Dr. Chevalier agreed and he, Dr. Sinatra, James Oschman, a leading researcher in the field of energy and vibrational medicine, and Richard Delany, MD, another board-certified cardiologist, conducted a study at the University of San Diego. Study participants were divided into two groups. "One group was ungrounded and the other group was grounded with conductive patches on the soles of their feet and palms of their hands," Dr. Sinatra recounts. "Wires connected the patches to a stainless-steel rod inserted in the earth outdoors." Both groups were then exposed to electromagnetics for two hours and their blood was studied to measure the zeta potential, or electrical charge, on their red blood cells, as well as the effects the exposure had on the extent of red blood cell clumping.

"We found that the grounded group had thinner blood," Dr. Sinatra says. "There was something about grounding that took in the Schumann resonance—we call it 7.83 hertz—to have a positive effect on red blood cells. The grounded subjects had 2.73 times the thinning of the blood compared to the ungrounded subjects. This is the zeta potential, where the red blood cells repel one another instead of sticking or clumping together. It was absolutely amazing that grounding improved the zeta potential and caused thinning of the blood. I thought this was the greatest research I had done in my entire life, and that it could change the landscape of cardiovascular medicine.

"There have been so many patients who had normal coronary arteries but they still had a heart attack. For a long time we couldn't understand why. But now, with all of the electromagnetic radiation we are all being exposed to, I predict that we're going to see more and more stasis, or stagnation, of blood, which is caused when red blood cells clump together and, as a result, are deprived of oxygen and vital nutrients. I think we're going to see more and more stasis situations where the blood clots, where the blood vessel is not diseased with arthrosclerosis, but it clots in the strategic location of the heart or the brain, and you have a stroke or a heart attack. As a heart specialist, I know that thin blood is what you want. You don't want thick, red ketchup blood because that sets the stage for so many diseases."

Dr. Sinatra makes sure to ground multiple times during the day, and recommends that everyone else do the same because of how effective grounding is for restoring energy and counteracting the harmful effects of EMR.

Clint Ober has developed indoor grounding mats, sleeping pads, and other grounding products, that can provide similar health benefits. You can use the mats to ground while reading, watching TV, or while engaged in other indoor activities at the same time, and use the sleeping pads while you sleep. They are available at www.earthing.com.

For more information about grounding, visit earthinginstitute.net. I also recommend the book *Earthing*.

Note: It is not recommended that you ground on lawns sprayed with pesticides and herbicides, since those toxins can pass through the skin of your feet to be absorbed into your body. You should also not ground on land beneath which electrical power lines run, due to the dirty electricity you can be exposed to by doing so.

In addition, since grounding causes spontaneous detoxification in your body, if you are very toxic and start grounding for an hour or more on your first day, you might overload your detoxification organs. It is best to start with only 15 to 30 minutes of grounding on your first day, while drinking plenty of pure water to detoxify. Then gradually increase how long you ground over time.

Exercising For Greater Energy

Regular exercise is also an absolute necessity for maintaining your health and having more energy.

"Pharmaceutical companies would like us to believe that every health ill that ails us requires a trip to the pharmacy," Dr. Sinatra says. "But the fact is one of the best health boosters out there—exercise—doesn't cost you a penny, and doesn't have any side-effects. Just moving for 30 to 60 minutes three to five times a week boosts your health in seven powerful ways. Every time you exercise you lower your stroke risk, protect against osteoporosis, increase your metabolic rate so that you burn more calories, prevent and even reverse high blood pressure, alleviate depression, reduce your risk of developing breast cancer, and lower your blood sugar by improving your use of insulin and preventing insulin resistance and diabetes."

Other important benefits that regular exercise can provide include:

- Increased longevity
- Prevention of heart disease, cancer, and other serious, degenerative diseases
- Prevention of and relief from tension
- Decreased "fight or flight" response, and therefore less stress
- Increased muscle to fat ratio
- Increased muscle strength
- Increased flexibility
- Improved balance
- Improved sleep
- Improved mental function
- Increased stamina and energy
- Increased aerobic capacity
- Improved self-esteem and greater confidence

- Increased incidence of positive attitudes and emotions, including joy.

Regular exercise also aids digestion, increases circulation, and stimulates the lymphatic system (your body's filtration and purification system that you learned about in Chapter 5).

Note: "Proper screening with a graded exercise test should be done for anyone over the age of forty prior to embarking in any exercise program," Dr. Sinatra cautions, "and especially a high intensity interval training program, where cardiovascular risk may be present yet unsuspected in certain individuals."

Given the daily time constraints most people face, it makes good sense to choose an exercise routine that will allow you to most quickly and efficiently maximize your results. What follow are innovative approaches that can provide the best results without a major time commitment.

Nuris Lemire's Energizing Stretching and Meridian Activation Routine

Stretching exercises are an excellent way to start your day. They do not take long and set a positive tone for the rest of your daily activities.

The following energizing stretch routine developed by Nuris Lemire is ideal for this purpose. To perform it, start by standing comfortably, with your feet shoulder width apart. Interlock your hands, then lift your arms above your head as you inhale deeply, stretching upwards. Then exhale deeply. Keeping your arms raised and your hands interlocked, continue breathing fully as you stretch downward along the right side of your body. Then stretch upward again, before stretching downward along your left side. Stretch upward once more, then stretch down towards your right foot at a 45 degree angle, holding your arms and interlaced hands in front of your head as you exhale. Then inhale deeply and stretch upward. Then exhale, stretching downward towards your left foot, again at a 45 degree angle, with your arms once more in front of your head.

Now come upward, inhaling deeply, stretching your arms above your head. As you exhale, bend forward and down towards the floor, going as low as you comfortably can. Continue breathing as you hold this position for a few seconds, relaxing your head, neck, and shoulders. Then, still bending down, reach for your right foot and hold that position for a bit, still keeping your head, neck and torso relaxed. Then, still continuing to breathe easily and fully, twist towards your left foot in the same way. After a few seconds, return to the center and, keeping your eyes even with your hands in front of you, inhale and stretch upward and then backwards as far as is comfortable for you. Then return to an upward position and release your arms, arcing them back down to your sides as you exhale. Shake your arms. As you do so, lift up your right leg a few inches above the ground and shake it as well, then do the same with your left leg. Next, both feet on the ground, shake your whole body for a few more seconds. Then close your eyes for a few moments and feel energy moving through your body as you continue breathing.

"This exercise helps to open up the energetic pathways in the body and is a good way to start your morning," Nuris explains. "In addition to being a form of stretching exercise, it activates all of the meridians. When you stretch all the way up and then go forward, you're activating the gallbladder meridian and the bladder meridian that's in the back. When you stretch sideways, you're activating your kidneys and spleen."

Aerobic Exercise With HIIT

Walking is perhaps the best form of exercise, but in order to get significant benefit from walking, most people need to walk for at least 30 to 60 minutes per day.

Fortunately, there is a way for you to get all of the benefits of walking in only 10 to 15 minutes a day through what is known as high intensity interval training, or HIIT. Its benefits have been shown by researchers to be far superior to what most people achieve from walking an hour or more each day.

HIIT is a type of aerobic exercise that is performed at intense intervals. Unlike normal exercise, in which the greatest expenditure of energy and burning of calories occurs during the exercise routine itself and then stops, when you perform HIIT exercises your body will continue to burn calories for hours after you perform them. Studies show that HIIT exercises burn calories at rates up to nine times higher than regular aerobic exercise. HIIT exercises are also one of the most effective ways to eliminate belly fat. Regular walking is ineffective at eliminating belly fat.

Another major benefit of HIIT exercise is the superior intake of oxygen that it provides, compared to regular walking. Increased oxygen intake results in improved and sustained energy levels and improved metabolism, and has been linked to a reduced risk of heart disease, cancer, and other debilitating conditions. HIIT also activates fast-twitch muscle fibers and triggers the release of human growth hormone, helping to build and maintain muscle strength.

Here's how to turn your daily walks into your own HIIT program.

Wearing appropriate walking shoes or sneakers, begin by walking at your regular pace for one minute. Then walk as fast as you can for 30 seconds. Then return to your slower, regular pace of walking for another minute, and then walk as fast as you can for 30 more seconds. Keep alternating between these two paces for a total of five to six cycles (each cycle consists of one regular and then one accelerated walking pace).

Initially, walk along a flat pathway. Then, as your endurance and ability to walk using HIIT increases, seek out pathways that have inclines to get an even better work out.

If you find that performing six cycles of HIIT is too much for you initially, reduce the amount of HIIT walking you do to one or two cycles, and then slowly increase the amount until you reach six full cycles. Once you finish your HIIT walking routine, replenish your body with fluids by drinking pure, filtered water.

You can also incorporate HIIT with rebounding if you own a rebounder (mini-trampoline) to achieve even greater results. Dr. Jennifer Gramith explained the benefits of rebounding in Chapter 5.

Getting a full HIIT workout with rebounding is similar to incorporating HIIT with walking. Start by bouncing comfortably on the rebounder for one minute. Then run in place on the rebounder for 30 seconds, exerting yourself as much as you can without overdoing it. Then bounce again for one minute. Repeat this cycle five or six times.

Dr. Zach Bush's 4-Minute Nitric Oxide Release Routine

One of the most innovative and effective exercise routines was developed by Dr. Zach Bush, a triple-certified MD in the fields of endocrinology and metabolism, internal medicine, and hospice/palliative care. In addition to being the developer of the ION Gut Health formulas, Dr. Bush is the medical director of the M Clinic in Charlottesville, Virginia and the creator of the Intrinsic Health Series and the Biology Base Camp, which empower participants to develop and integrate health practices in their lives to create a foundation for physical, mental, and spiritual wellness. An important element in those programs is what has become known as Dr. Bush's nitric oxide release routine that, on average, takes only four minutes to perform, and which exercises 16 major muscle groups.

This workout routine employs some of the same principles as HIIT and is easy to perform, making it an excellent exercise that anyone can perform without risk of injury. According to Dr. Bush, its benefits are due to how quickly performing it releases nitric oxide (NO) into the cells.

"Nitric oxide is a molecule your body produces that feeds your muscles," Dr. Bush explains. "When you run out of oxygen during exercise, your muscles start to ache. This triggers a release of nitric oxide to make up for it. As NO moves through your bloodstream, your blood vessels dilate to deliver more oxygen and nutrients, and that's how your muscles develop.

"Our blood vessels actually only store about 90 seconds' worth of nitric oxide before they need to manufacture more, so working each major muscle group out for 90 seconds gives you the most efficient workout to tone and build muscles. The body has the ability to regenerate nitric oxide every couple of hours, giving you the opportunity to release it multiple times a day. The most effective way to increase your muscle function is to work out very briefly every few hours."

Based on his research, and because the exercise routine only takes about four minutes to cycle through and works the largest muscles groups in your body, Dr. Bush says that it is one of the best ways to start toning your body's systems, while also improving aerobic capacity and building and maintaining muscle strength. Because it can conveniently be performed wherever you are, it is an ideal way to quickly achieve a complete workout multiple times per day. For best results, Dr. Bush recommends performing it three times a day, allowing at least two hours between each session.

The entire routine involves three sets of 10 to 20 reps each of squats, arm raises, circular arm raises (similar to those performed while doing jumping jacks, without the jumping), and shoulder presses. The entire sequence is performed without a break between sets while breathing in and out through the nose.

Squats: "A good squat is your butt going back and looking like it's going to sit in a chair. It's not just a simple knee bend," Dr. Bush says. As you squat, he advises holding your arms out in front of you to better maintain your balance.

To begin, place your feet shoulder width apart, with the toes of your feet pointing forward and your weight evenly distributed between your heels and the ball of each foot. Once you are ready, perform 10 squats in rapid sequence, keeping your quadricep muscles engaged the entire time. At first, you may find that you cannot squat too far down. That's okay, as your speed in performing the squats is more important than how far down you can go.

Arm Raises: The second element of the 4-Minute Workout involves arm raises that work both the triceps in the arms, and the deltoid muscles that run along the upper arms and the top of your shoulders. During this sequence, begin by standing straight, with your arms at your sides. Then swing your arms up in front of you, starting from your waist and ending at shoulder level, with your elbows nearly fully extended throughout the entire movement. Start with your right arm and alternate between it and your left arm, swiftly raising and dropping each arm without pausing. Repeat for a total of ten times with each arm. "As you perform this part of the exercise keep your form tight rather than just flapping your arms up and down," Dr. Bush says.

Circular Arm Raises: The third part of the exercise involves rapidly raising and lowering both arms at the same time, starting from your sides and going completely above your head, then back down again in a circular motion, with your elbows fairly fully extended throughout the entire movement. Begin by standing straight and make your hands into loose fists. As you come over your head, let your fists lightly hit each other. Repeat for a total of ten arm raises. This part of the exercise works both the trapezoid muscles and latissimus dorsi (lats) muscles of your upper back.

Shoulder Presses: The final element of the 4-Minute Workout is to raise both of your arms straight up above your head and then down again, pumping them rapidly up and down ten times. Start with your elbows flexed and both fists close to your shoulders, then push both arms straight up while fully extending your elbows. This works the muscles of your neck, upper arms, and shoulders. As you perform this sequence, keep your arms even with your outer shoulders.

Once you complete the shoulder presses, cycle back into performing two more complete sets of ten counts each for all four elements of the 4-Minute Workout. Once you finish all three sets, "Resting with your hands at your sides, close your eyes and experience the sensation in your extremities," Dr. Bush advises. "You may feel tingling or sense increased blood flow as all your blood vessels dilate, delivering oxygen and fuel for optimal health. Relax, shake it out and feel your fingertips. You'll feel a little tingling and a little puffy over the next 20 seconds. That's the nitric oxide effect. You're dilating all those blood vessels, oxygenating everything from your brain to your kidneys and everything else in your body, and you're building muscle for the next couple of hours."

When you first begin the 4-Minute Workout it is important that you focus on your form first. Once you are sure of your form, focus on your speed. When you can comfortably perform the three sets of 10 reps for each of its four elements, gradually increase the number of reps until you reach 20 reps. Over time, you can use light hand weights as you perform this exercise to achieve even greater gains.

To learn more about the 4-Minute Workout, visit www.nitricoxidedump.com, where you can also watch an instruction video by Dr. Bush.

To learn more about Dr. Bush's Intrinsic Health Series and the Biology Base Camp program, visit https://intrinsichealthseries.com.

Live02 and Exercise With Oxygen Therapy (EWOT)

An exciting development in the field of medicine is the combination of exercise and the use of oxygen, which a growing body of physicians, sports trainers, and other exercise specialists now recommend.

The roots of exercise with oxygen therapy (EWOT) originated with research conducted by Manfred von Ardenne (January 20, 1907–May, 26 1997), who developed oxygen multistep therapy during the 1960s. Von Ardenne was a researcher and inventor who made important contributions in a wide range of fields, including medical technology, applied and plasma physics, microscopy (he invented the scanning electron microscope), nuclear technology, and technologies in the fields of both radio and television. His book *Oxygen Multistep Therapy: Physiological and Technical Foundations* extensively documents the many ways that the therapy can improve health and prevent and reverse diseases caused by oxygen deficiencies in the body, including heart disease, cancer, circulatory disorders, and mental illness.

"Lack of oxygen leads to swelling of the cells that form the lining of the blood vessels," explains ACIM physician Angelique Hart, MD. "This causes a reduction of blood flow which, if not addressed, can lead to occlusion, or blockage, in the blood vessels beyond the point of no return. Sufficiently high oxygen levels are able to reverse the swelling, open up the blood vessels, and enhance blood flow, creating an upward spiral effect that improves health."

EWOT is a method of breathing higher levels of oxygen during exercise in order to increase the amount of oxygen in blood plasma, and thus the body's cells, tissues, and organs. The exercise is usually performed on a stationary exercise bike or a treadmill while wearing an oxygen non-rebreather mask through which oxygen is delivered from a large oxygen reservoir bag. One of the main advantages of EWOT is that can produce many desired health benefits when performed as little as two to three times a week.

According to von Ardenne's research, gaining the therapeutic benefits of traditional EWOT requires a minimum of nine hours of EWOT exercise. In addition, Dr. Hart says, "The initial adaptation to Dr. Von Ardenne's clinic-based protocol was the invention of a large 600 liter oxygen reservoir. This use of only oxygen-rich air has a good, but limited, effect for ultimate performance in athletes. Because of the high saturation of oxygen, the heart doesn't get the incentive to increase to the maximum rate needed for maximum benefit."

Researchers, looking for a solution to this limitation, discovered it by investigating the health benefits enjoyed by athletes who engage in high altitude training. "High altitude training enables the body to adapt to low oxygen levels, which improves oxygen transport and utilization efficiency," Dr. Hart explains.

Recognizing these limitations of traditional EWOT, inventor Mark Squibb developed the LiveO2™ and LiveO2 Adaptive Contrast™ systems, both of which deliver oxygen flow rates that meet or exceed the researched levels required to provide traditional EWOT benefits, and both of which do so in only 15 minutes. These are the systems that Dr. Hart and a growing number of other physicians use with their patients.

Dr. Hart particularly likes the LiveO2 Adaptive Contrast system, which mimics the altitude contrast training used by many elite athletes. "Altitude contrast training is used to switch high oxygen air to high altitude air, which equals low oxygen. The LiveO2 Adaptive Contrast system does this, as well. This allows people with different exercise capabilities to experience an increase in respiratory challenge that creates benefits beyond what was previously seen with rich oxygen-only exercise," she says. "LiveO2 Adaptive Contrast

Therapy enables rapid transitions from rich, or high, oxygen to poor, or low, oxygen via an oxygen reservoir bag with two compartments, a large one containing high oxygen content, and a small one with low oxygen. The bag compartments are supplied oxygen from a modified oxygen generator.

"By receiving this therapy people are able to restore and maximize oxygen delivery and oxygen use in their bodies, causing lasting changes in capillary blood vessels and at the cellular level, which in turn leads to hyper-oxygenation of the tissues. The healthy oxygen levels create healthy bioenergy levels, resulting in optimal function because the body's cells are now able to produce the highest amount of energy possible. This allows the cells to dump toxins and excess fluids, better absorb and utilize nutrients from food, and most efficiently produce hormones and other substances that the body needs, among many other improvements to cell function."

EWOT, and especially LiveO2 therapies, have been shown to reduce inflammation and pain, boost metabolism, enhance detoxification, improve immune function, and improve overall brain and cardiac function. It also significantly enhances the overall benefits of other types of exercise by preventing lactic acid buildup. Dr. Hart calls this, "gains without pain."

Dr. Hart reports that it also enhances the effectiveness of other healing therapies. In addition, because of how safe and easy it is to implement, "EWOT enables the very sick and sedentary to start exercising without exhaustion or an increase in pain, which allows for the possibility for them to finally undergo a substantial healing process," she says.

One of the areas in which Dr. Hart has found rapid and significant improvements is with patients suffering from brain dysfunction and post-traumatic brain disease. "At our clinic, we've seen several patients that were barely functional when they first came to us. They didn't have a good memory, were unable to go out by themselves without getting lost, had trouble remembering words and language issues, or were prone to tripping and falling because of clumsiness caused by impaired brain function. Once they started exercising with oxygen training, after five to six sessions, they started to show a real improvement in thinking and overall brain functioning, with less brain fog, and after ten or more sessions they achieved consistent steady progress of improved functioning and life skills.

"I had one patient who was able to regain her native language. She had been in a coma and had to relearn how to talk and walk, and her rehabilitation was conducted in English. She was originally from Chile and her mother tongue was Spanish and she had forgotten her Spanish. She was able to start using her Spanish again after about a dozen treatments. We were able to bring it back."

Dr. Hart has also had great success treating patients with serious cases of heart disease using LiveO2 therapy. "We've seen a lot of patients that had active angina or who already had open heart surgery, and who were reclotting and basically out of options," she says. "I see cardiac patients that are told go get your affairs in order. I use LiveO2 as part of an integrated cardiac rehab program, and find that it really helps.

"Before we started this approach, the manufacturer had never worked with sick patients. Their focus was on athletes. So that first year we put the cardiac patients on EKGs with continuous blood pressure monitoring, and a pulse oximeter showing their oxygen levels in real time. These were very sick patients and what we did was like a stress test, but with full monitoring, and these patients never got into trouble because we are giving them all the oxygen the heart needs in moments of trouble. They were able to improve so much faster than they would have with regular cardiac rehab because of how the oxygen they received reduced the capillary swelling. You improve endothelial function immediately, which was proven by Von Ardenne. In his book, he shows microscope pictures of the capillaries and how the swelling goes away after just one treatment. So for cardiac rehab, to me, this is a no brainer. Every cardiac rehab center should have this equipment and they should allow patients to exercise with oxygen for 15 minutes for an amazing added benefit."

Dr. Hart recommends some form of EWOT for everyone. "In this toxic world, it's great for anyone that wants to do something to detoxify, and to improve their stamina and their conditioning for exercise. Anything that we can use at home to do this is going to be beneficial. If people can afford it, I recommend they purchase their own EWOT system because the entire family can do it, even children, and it is an ideal way to keep toxins from accumulating to the point where they start causing inflammation and disease. And it only takes 15 minutes two to three times a week."

If people cannot afford a LiveO2 or another EWOT system, as a less expensive alternative Dr. Hart suggests they consider purchasing a refurbished oxygen concentrator and an oxygen mask that can be attached to it via a cannula (tube). "This won't provide the same degree of benefit as an actual EWOT system, but it's an option that is the most affordable that people can use and still get some benefit with oxygen, enabling them to train a little harder and reduce more inflammation. I always ask my patients what they can do for themselves at home that is within their budget and to work with that. Any form of exercise is great. If you can combine it with oxygen, all the better."

To watch a video presentation of Dr. Hart explaining the benefits of EWOT and LiveO2, visit https://liveo2.com/5-years-of-md-experience.

CHAPTER 8

The Eighth Key:
Deep, Restorative Sleep

Accoding to the Centers for Disease Control and Prevention (CDC), a third of all Americans are chronically sleep deprived, sleeping less than seven hours a night, and another third, despite sleeping for seven hours or more, fail to obtain enough deep, non-REM (rapid eye movement) sleep. In addition, a study by the Rand Corporation found that insufficient sleep costs the U.S. economy over $410 billion a year. That same study also found that the U.S. "loses the equivalent of 1.23 million working days due to insufficient sleep".

These statistics help to explain why persistent fatigue continues to rank among the top health complaints reported by patients to their doctors, and also why Americans are on track to spend over $50 billion per year on sleep remedies and products, many of which do not work and some of which, such as pharmaceutical sleeping pills, are dangerous.

This chapter explains what you must do to ensure you obtain the best sleep of your life while avoiding such pitfalls.

Why Sleep Is So Important

During sleep your body produces extra protein molecules that help repair your body at a cellular level. This includes repairing damage caused by stress, pollutants, infection, too much sun exposure, and free radical damage caused by poor diet and other factors.

Sleep helps keep your heart healthy: Sleep helps to reduce stress and inflammation levels in your body. High levels of inflammatory markers are linked to heart attacks, heart disease and strokes. Sleep also helps blood pressure and cholesterol levels stay within healthy levels.

Sleep reduces stress: A good night's sleep lowers blood pressure and counteracts elevated levels of stress hormones that increase aging and degeneration of organs, cells, and other body parts.

Sleep improves immune function: During deep sleep your body releases potent substances, including growth hormone, that strengthen your immune system function and aid in the growth and repair of the body. Lack of sleep impairs proper immune function, increasing susceptibility to infection and other diseases.

Sleep improves memory and mood: As you sleep your brain processes, organizes, and correlates memories and new experiences gained during the day. In addition, sleep leads to greater mental alertness and concentration, making it easier to acquire new skills and knowledge. Healthy sleep also help protect against moodiness, irritability, and other unhealthy emotions that affect brain function.

Sleep helps to maintain healthy weight: Sleep helps regulate the hormones that affect and control your appetite. When your body is deprived of sleep, these normal hormone balances are interrupted and your appetite increases, especially for high calorie foods such as fats and carbohydrates. Insulin resistance and elevated blood sugar levels also commonly result from lack of sleep. One study, for example, found that just two days of poor sleep increased insulin resistance in young men of normal weight by nearly 40 percent.

Sleep is essential to maintaining the health of DNA and cleansing the brain: Two of the most important benefits deep sleep provides were only recently discovered. Thanks to these discoveries, scientists now know that deep, non-REM (dream) sleep is essential for repairing DNA damage that occurs daily simply as a consequence of being awake. Scientists also discovered that deep sleep is necessary to efficiently remove wastes and toxic proteins in the brain, including tau proteins and beta amyloid, which are associated with Alzheimer's disease and dementia.

DNA damage can be caused by a variety of factors, all of which are most pronounced while we are awake. Though the DNA within each of our cells contain innate repair systems to counteract this damage, during wakefulness the ability of these repair systems to do their job is low and inefficient. As a result, DNA damage during the day can build up and, if not repaired, trigger disease. Deep, healthy sleep has been found to repair and normalize this DNA damage.

Research also found that the reduced brain activity that occurs during deep non-REM sleep is necessary for the optimal functioning of the brain's glymphatic system, which is responsible for removing waste and toxins from the brain. According to Maiken Nedergaard, M.D., D.M.Sc., co-director of the Center for Translational Neuromedicine at the University of Rochester Medical Center (URMC) and lead author of one of the studies demonstrating this fact, "Sleep is critical to the function of the brain's waste removal system...the deeper the sleep the better. These findings also add to the increasingly clear evidence that quality of sleep or sleep deprivation can predict the onset of Alzheimer's and dementia."

Dr. Nedergaard and her colleagues first discovered the glymphatic system and the roles it plays in the brain in 2012. Their research "revealed a system of plumbing which piggybacks on blood vessels and pumps cerebral spinal fluid (CSF) through brain tissue to wash away waste." Studies since that time show that it is CFS acting within the glymphatic system that clears metabolic waste products from the brain, and that this system primarily works while we are sleeping.

The Multiple Effects of Poor Sleep: "During the day, the brain does a lot of work using a lot of neurochemicals," says Dr. Sergey Sorin. "There are other processes that are also happening inside the brain, the central nervous system, and with the CSF fluid when we are awake. Sleep is when detoxification of the brain happens. If you don't sleep well for at least seven to eight hours a day, you are a person who will actually function like a slightly intoxicated individual. This has been proven by scientific studies. People who don't sleep well generally don't recover. If you can't recover, basically you're going on to complete exhaustion. And then there's a breakdown."

This breakdown is due to a multitude of unhealthy effects of sleep deprivation, beginning with diminished immune function and elevated inflammation levels. Because of its negative effects on immune function, poor sleep can increase the risk for certain types of cancer, including breast, gastrointestinal, ovarian, and prostate cancers. Poor sleep is also associated with diminished decision making skills and overall performance at work, leading to behaviors such as next-day procrastination. Poor sleep can also impair self-control and lead to a diminished ability to focus and pay attention.

In addition, poor sleep has a negative impact on the gut microbiome, a primary determining factor of your overall health, including the health of your brain. Studies show that poor sleep, along with other factors that disrupt the body's natural circadian rhythm discussed below, causes imbalances between the healthy and harmful bacteria and other microorganisms within the GI tract. When this disruption occurs it can lead to a vicious cycle because studies also show that gut dybiosis can upset the body's circadian rhythm.

Common Factors That Can Interfere With A Good Night's Sleep

The most common causes of poor sleep include poor diet and poor eating habits such as eating too close to bedtime, lack of regular exercise, stress, and poor lifestyle choices, such as going to bed too late or consciously attempting to get by on less sleep than you need.

Other factors that negatively impact sleep are psychological in nature. They include unresolved anxiety, depression, despair, fear, and grief. Even positive emotions such as excitement and euphoria can interfere with your ability to get a good night's sleep. Pharmaceutical drugs, both prescription and over-the-counter, can also impair your ability to get a good night's sleep. Ironically, these include sleeping pills, as well as beta- blockers, cold and cough medicines (they contain caffeine and synthetic stimulants such as ephedrine), oral contraceptives, synthetic hormones, and thyroid medicines. In addition, all drugs over time create a toxic burden on the liver and can impair other organ systems as well, further worsening sleep problems.

Another common sleep-impairing factor is structural imbalance, such as muscle tension and/or a misaligned spine. These imbalances impede the flow of nerve signals to and from the brain, and can keep you awake at night due to the pain they cause in the muscles and joints. To help resolve structural imbalances, consider adding a few minutes of gentle stretching exercises to your daily routine, such as Nuris Lemire's stretching routine that you learned about in Chapter 7. (Since this routine is energizing in nature, practice it in the morning as opposed to before bedtime.) For structural problems that you cannot resolve on your own, consider working with a massage therapist, body worker, chiropractor, or osteopathic physician.

Optimize Your Bedroom For Better Sleep

Your bedroom may be another overlooked, yet significant, factor that contributes to unhealthy sleep. To ensure your bedroom is conducive to healthy sleep do the following:

1. Keep your bedroom clean and free of dust. This means cleaning your bedroom at least once a week and frequently washing blankets, sheets, and pillow cases. An unclean bedroom not only interferes with restful sleep, it also makes

you more susceptible to infectious microorganisms and impacts your respiratory system as you breathe in dust while you are sleeping. To further prevent dust build up consider use an air purifier in your home, and also be sure that the filters on your heat and air conditioning ducts are replaced at least every 2-3 months. (For more on how you can create an overall healthy environment in your home, see Chapter 10.)

2. Allow for a flow of fresh air throughout your bedroom as you sleep by keeping at least one window of your bedroom slightly open as you sleep. Breathing fresh, oxygen-rich air will not only enhance the benefits of sleep itself but also make it easier for you to fall asleep.

3. Sleep on a comfortable mattress. What makes a mattress comfortable is a subjective experience. You will know what type of mattress is most comfortable for you when you experience it. If your current mattress is uncomfortable you will find the cost of a new mattress that meets your specific needs is well worth it.

4. Choose cotton or wool blankets, cotton sheets, and feather pillows, which are healthier choices than the same items made from synthetic materials.

5. Protect yourself from dust mites. To avoid house dust mites in your pillow (to which you could become allergic), put your new pillow into a plastic trash bag and put two pillow cases over that bag and wash the pillow cases at least once per week. You can also buy a plastic mattress cover to put over your new mattress. Then, over the plastic mattress cover, put a cotton mattress cover and a fitted cotton sheet that you wash at least once per week.

6. Keep the temperature in your bedroom at a comfortable level. Most people experience better sleep when their bedroom temperature is on the cool side.

7. Make your bedroom a place of sleep, not a place to watch television or work on a computer. If you have a TV in your bedroom, move it to another room. Also keep your bedroom free of other electrical devices (stereos, cell phones, computer, radios, etc.). Such devices interfere with healthy, restorative sleep because of the electromagnetic frequencies they emit, even when they are not in use. In addition, to further reduce the effects of EMR while you sleep, unplug your router device if you have WiFi before you go to bed.

8. Sleep in the dark. This means not only turning off your bedroom lights when you go to bed, but also making sure that curtains and shades are fully drawn to prevent outdoor light from entering your bedroom. Sleeping in complete darkness helps your body to produce the hormone melatonin, which is essential for healthy sleep.

Improve Your Sleep By Understanding Your Body's Circadian Rhythms

Healthy sleep depends on your body's internal "body clock," which is influenced by what is known as circadian rhythm. Circadian rhythm tends to follow the same cycles and patterns of the sun during a 24-hour period. It influences the times of day when you feel most awake and alert, and those times when you feel tired or sleepy. This internal clock also regulates other important functions in your body, including body temperature, blood pressure, and the production of digestive enzymes and various hormones. Disruptions of your circadian rhythm not only interfere with your ability to achieve a good night's sleep but can also impair these other functions.

People with healthy circadian rhythm have little trouble rising early in the day with lots of energy, and also tend to easily fall and remain asleep at night, usually retiring well before midnight. This was the normal waking and sleeping pattern of our ancestors. Due to many factors of the modern world, especially the amount of time we spend inside under artificial light, natural circadian rhythms are easily disrupted. When this happens, achieving healthy sleep becomes more difficult and various other physical and psychological health disturbances are apt to occur.

Assist Your Circadian Rhythm By Going To Bed Early: A growing body of research indicates that the best quality of sleep occurs for most people when they go to bed no later than 10 o'clock and get up by 6 AM or earlier. The reason for this is that the human body is designed to begin the repair mechanisms that occur during sleep at between 9 and 10 PM. Going to sleep later than that interferes with the start of these repairs, making them less efficient.

In addition, research shows that going to sleep earlier in the night results in longer sleep cycles of non-REM sleep, while going to sleep later results in more time spent in REM sleep (dream) cycles. Most of the body and brain's restorative processes only occur during deep non-REM sleep. Maximizing the amount of non-REM sleep you obtain each night improves overall health.

If you are not already doing so, try going to bed at 9 or 10 PM and getting up at 6 AM. Scheduling your meals at the same time each day (ideally finishing dinner no later than 7 PM), will further enhance the quality of your sleep.

The Negative Impact Of Blue Light On Sleep

One of the biggest disruptors of the body's circadian rhythm is our increasing exposure to blue light. This exposure is nearly impossible to escape given our increasing reliance on personal computers, tablets, and cell phones. Compact fluorescent light (CFL) bulbs, LED light bulbs and other LED devices, and new model televisions are other prevalent sources of blue light emissions. Studies show that blue light exposure after dusk disrupts circadian rhythm and suppresses the body's production of melatonin, resulting in poor sleep, insomnia, and other sleep conditions.

How To Protect Yourself From Blue Light: To minimize the harmful effects of blue light do the following:

1. Avoid using your cell phone, TV, computer, laptop, tablet screens, and other electronic devices at least two hours before bedtime.

2. If you must use electronic devices after sunset, wear blue light-blocking glasses and install apps on your devices that filter out blue and green wavelength light during nighttime, such as f.lux (www.justgetflux.com), CareUEyes (https://care-eyes.com), or Iris (https://iristech.co). Most of these programs are free to download and work by filtering out blue light emitted from computer and tablet screens.

3. If you work at night, you should also wear blue light-blocking glasses during your shift.

4. Use red lights for night lights. Red light does not disrupt circadian rhythm and suppress melatonin the way that blue light and, to a lesser extent, green light wavelengths do.

5. As much as possible, expose yourself to outdoor sunlight during the day. Doing so counteracts the effects of blue light exposure. (For more information about the benefits of daily sunlight exposure, see Chapter 7.)

Dr. Sorin's Prescriptions For Better Sleep

When discussing how to achieve restorative sleep with his patients, Dr. Sorin focuses on first explaining what does not work. "Conventional medicine is based on two main things, drugs and surgery," he says. "You can't do surgery for sleep, so that leaves sleeping pills, a common approach. Benzodiazepine medications and other classes of medications can help a person fall asleep. But these drugs do not provide deep, or delta, sleep, which is characterized by the delta brainwave state as measured by an electroencephalogram (EEG). If you don't have that deep sleep, you don't recover. I've seen patients who sleep for eight or nine hours, even up to 10 to 12 hours, yet they're not refreshed because they are not reaching the deeper sleep stages. So how do you get into the deeper stages?

"First, you need to have a balanced lifestyle, with a healthy diet, regular exercise and physical activity, and so forth. Lifestyle choices are very important. For example, there are some people who suffer from sleep apnea because they are overweight and are unable to sleep without wearing a CPAP device. They have two options. Either they use the C-PAP for the rest of their lives, or they adopt a healthier lifestyle, which in this case means losing weight and taking more overall responsibility for their health.

"Second, if possible, to go to bed at the same time, preferably early in the evening. It's also best to get up at the same time each morning, so you have a schedule that becomes a rhythm your body recognizes and begins to automatically program itself for sleep."

Dr. Sorin also points out the importance of the neurochemical serotonin and its conversion into melatonin. "Serotonin gets converted to melatonin in the evening and that's what allows you to get sleep," he explains. To improve melatonin production, he recommends getting as least 30 minutes of exercise each day while getting some sun exposure. "30 to 60 minutes a day of exercise really helps a lot, and of course exercise provides many other benefits on its own," he says.

If necessary, taking a melatonin supplement can also be helpful, he adds. "Melatonin is available over the counter from one milligram to 10 milligrams. If you choose to use it, I recommend taking it about half an hour to an hour before bedtime.

"But there are other factors to consider, as well, to ensure that enough melatonin is being produced at night. One of the most important is managing stress and releasing tension before going to bed. This is where autogenic training and the Biogenics system developed by Dr. Norm Shealy can be very helpful, or an equivalent exercise to a clear and to calm the mind. You can also do meditation. All of these approaches allow you to fall and stay asleep more easily." (See Chapter 6 for more information about Biogenics.)

Dr. Sorin reports that a number of the Biogenic audios that he and Dr. Shealy have developed are very effective in helping people reduce stress and experience better sleep. These recordings are available as downloadable audio files and playable on computers and mobile devices. They incorporate Samvit Sound™, a clinically proven audio guidance technology of binaural beat patterns that entrain the brain to create desired brainwaves through a process called the frequency following response.

"The desired brainwave patterns for deep stage two and stage three sleep are theta and delta, with delta offering the deepest levels of restoration," Dr. Sorin says. "Sleep is a cyclical process. As you sleep, your brain goes through stages. They used to be called four stages, but now it's recognized that there are actually only three stages, with stage three being the delta stage. Studies confirm that we benefit both mentally and physically from regular delta experiences while sleeping. Delta is also involved in global communications of the cortical brain and has a multitude of other functions."

Recognizing this fact, Dr. Sorin and Dr. Shealy developed a non-verbal, eight-hour long Biogenics Sleep Support audio in the pure delta brainwave frequency. "Clinically, we have found that listening to this audio during bedtime is very helpful for supporting stage two and three, deep sleep," Dr. Sorin says. "It sounds basically like a pink noise. Many people have told us they are surprised by how easily they fall and stay asleep by listening to it. But it's really not surprising at all because of how it keeps the brain supported through delta brain activity throughout the night." (For more information and to order this product, go to normshealy.shop/products/shealy-sorin-biogenics-sleep-support.)

Dr. Sorin also recommends supplementing with the mineral lithium orotate and the amino acid taurine, especially for people who have difficulty staying asleep, or who wake up during the night due to anxiety or stress. "Lithium orotate is a mineral involved in the production of melatonin and can help maintain melatonin levels during the night for better sleep," he says. "It has been shown to support brain and nervous system health, enhance memory and cognitive function, and promote a healthy mood. A typical dose is

5 mg. Taurine helps to calm down the central nervous system. An overexcited nervous system can keep a person from sleeping well. A typical dose is from 500 to 2,000 mg, depending on the person's situation."

Dr. Shealy's Bliss Oils that you learned about in Chapter 6 are also effective sleep aids, according to Dr. Sorin. "Air Bliss is especially useful for this purpose," he says. "It helps produce the neurotransmitter neurotensin, which helps to prevent and reduce chronic inflammation in the body, and oxytocin, the feel good hormone. Because of these properties, Air Bliss helps the brain and the mind relax, promoting better sleep."

Dr. Sorin points that most babies without any sleep or other health problems. "They sleep really well and they generally don't have many medical problems," he notes. "As children, we get into some trouble, but for the most part we're still pretty healthy. But by the time people reach adulthood, and even in their teenage years, sleep and other health problems start to emerge, including mental problems, because by then stress and *dis-ease* start to become more prevalent, and unhealthy habits and lifestyle choice begin to be adopted. It all ties together. The question is, how do you move away from this state of *dis-ease* to move back into ease. How do you bring back the balance, physically, mentally, emotionally, and spiritually? That's what self-care is all about. Addressing and improving your sleep using these self-care methods is fundamental to restoring that balance, and therefore your overall health."

Improve Your Sleep By Grounding

"Grounding is one of the best things you can do to achieve healthy sleep," says Dr. Stephen Sinatra, a world renowned metabolic cardiologist and leading expert on the science of grounding (also known as "earthing") that you learned about in Chapter 7.

After Dr. Sinatra first met with Clint Ober, the person most responsible for discovering the benefits of grounding, he obtained a prototype of the grounding mattress pad that Ober developed. In the book *Earthing* that he co-wrote with Ober and Martin Zucker, Dr.

Sinatra described the difference it made in the quality of his and his wife's sleep as "profound." Today, whenever he travels he brings a portable grounding mattress pad with him. "I always sleep grounded," he says. "I walk barefoot in the afternoon whenever I can, and I walk in leather shoes because leather shoes will conduct the energy of the earth. I ground whenever I can. Even when I'm on computers, I'll put a grounded mat under my feet."

A number of studies on the effects of sleeping on a grounding mat to determine sleep quality have been conducted. The initial one was devised by Ober with the assistance of a nurse. It involved 60 men and women, all of whom suffered from sleep problems, and joint or muscle pain. They were divided into two groups, with one group given grounding pads to sleep on, and the other group given sham grounding pads. Over the course of 30 days, the nurse interacted with all of the people in the study, collecting data from both groups. The data revealed 85 percent of the grounding group participants went to sleep faster, 93 percent experienced better sleep throughout the night, 82 percent experienced a significant reduction in muscle stiffness, and chronic back and joint pain was either entirely eliminated or reduced in 74 percent of the participants. In addition, 78 percent of the grounding group reported improvements in their overall health, including improvements in respiratory conditions, rheumatoid arthritis, hypertension, sleep apnea, PMS, and hot flashes, and 100 percent said they were more rested when they woke up. No similar degrees of benefit were reported by the control group.

Another study revealed that sleeping on a grounding pad at night "resynchronizes cortisol secretion more in alignment with its normal, natural rhythm—highest at 8 a.m. and lowest at midnight". This means that sleeping while grounded normalizes and restores the body's circadian rhythm. The same study found that sleeping while grounded can increase melatonin production by as much as 16 percent in some cases, although not all people will experience any level of increase.

As a result of these and subsequent studies, in *Earthing*, Ober and Dr. Sinatra state, "From our research, we believe that not only light conditions but Earth's energy as well coordinates the various biological clocks regulating hormone flow in the body. The slow and gentle rhythms of the Earth's energy field are essential for maintaining these clocks...Our overall hypothesis is that grounding leads to a much greater physiological stability because the diverse bodily rhythms are coordinated not only with the light/dark cycle, but with all the natural rhythms of the environment."

Based on his ongoing research, Clint Ober has developed indoor grounding mats, sleeping pads, and other grounding products that can improve sleep and provide other health benefits. You can find them at www.earthing.com.

For more information about grounding, visit earthinginstitute. net.

Using PEMF To Improve Your Sleep And Reduce Pain

Another effective method for achieving and maintaining deep, restorative sleep, and for effectively dealing with pain that may be keeping you awake, is the use of a PEMF device.

PEMF stands for pulsed electromagnetic field therapy. One of the world's foremost researchers on the positive effects of PEMF is Bob Dennis, PhD, Associate Professor of Biomedical Engineering at the University of North Carolina at Chapel Hill. Both a medical scientist and tissue engineer, Dr. Dennis has worked in the aerospace and defense industries, the medical device industry, and has been a consultant for NASA and many private corporations. During the 1990s, while under contract with NASA, Dr. Dennis began to research the potential health benefits of PEMF, which resulted in him developing the original NASA PEMF systems.

NASA patents confirm that Dr. Dennis is the inventor of those systems, and four additional patents verify the subsequent advances he has made since his original work at NASA, leading to his development of ICES® DigiCeutical® technology. He is also the founder of Micro-Pulse, LLC, which oversees the development of ICES-based safe, low power, science-based, affordable PEMF technology for the control of chronic pain, inflammation, and to accelerate tissue recovery from injury. In addition, with Dr. Mark Tommerdahl, Dr. Dennis co-developed the Brain Gauge, which you learned about in Chapter 1.

Micro-Pulse Advanced ICES DigiCeutical Technology is embedded inside many of the most popular and effective PEMF products on the market today. As Dr. Dennis points out, this fact is often unacknowledged by the manufacturers of these products, which are often priced far higher than he says they need to be.

Given the many important contributions Dr. Dennis has made to the fields of PEMF research and PEMF devices for health, it's ironic that he was initially skeptical that PEMF had any value. "I had just graduated from the University of Michigan in 1996 when I received a call from a person at NASA who was responding to a correspondence I'd had with a different person offering my help on a different research project that the University of Michigan was doing with NASA," he says.

That call led to NASA hiring Dr. Dennis NASA as an independent consultant. "The person who initially called me connected me with a cell culture technician in a laboratory at Johnson Space Center, where they were trying to find ways to grow cells in space. The technician wanted to try to use PEMF to try to get cells to differentiate and grow in space. I told him I thought that was nonsense. This was somewhat related to my dissertation, so I had a distant familiarity with the scientific literature. I told him there was no way for mammalian cells, or any organelles themselves that I knew of, to pick up a magnetic field. I said he was wasting his time."

The technician insisted that he still wanted to pursue this possibility and persuaded Dr. Dennis to review the published scientific literature about PEMF. He agreed, and although he found most of the studies to be poorly designed, "A dozen or so papers were really quite good," he says. "I started replicating their experiments and proposed to NASA that we do a double blind experiment with cells in culture. We ran the experiment and there was a very strong biological effect."

Still skeptical, Dr. Dennis retested and relabeled all the equipment, then sent it back to NASA. The experiment was repeated with the same results. "If you're going to do science, you're going to have a bias, but you have to follow the data," Dr. Dennis continues. "If the data tells you you're wrong, then guess what? You need to rethink it. So I did because we were getting very consistent biological effects. There were genetic effects and whole classes of genes were up- regulated and whole classes of genes were down-regulated. All the genes related to cell growth and tissue repair were up-regulated, for example."

The PEMF devices Dr. Dennis has created and made available through Micro-Pulse offer particular benefit for people who are unable to achieve restful sleep due to acute or chronic pain. Their development came about in large part due to the many years that Dr. Dennis himself suffered from chronic back pain, a condition that was made much worse after an injury he sustained during a rescue mission he was involved in as a fireman in his local volunteer fire department. "We were going very quickly to a house on fire because we thought there were a woman and two children inside it," he says. "I was putting on my fire gear in the back of an old fire truck, twisting to put my breathing apparatus on, when we hit a train track at about 75 miles an hour and I just could feel it. It just kind of broke me. I was just not functioning right. Chiropractic would give me some relief for a little while, but by the next day I was back in pain again. I wasn't getting better, I was getting worse. I was so miserable. I couldn't sleep. I couldn't lie down, I couldn't sit, and I couldn't stand.

"Meanwhile, by this time I was building PEMF systems as a consultant for biotechnology firms. I had a device about the size of a microwave oven with big coils that I was putting together as instrumentation for my consulting for these companies. One night, I thought, since I had this PEMF system, I might as well put one of these coils behind my lower back. With great effort, I was able to reach around and put it behind me between my lower back and the chair that I was in. And I had the most unbelievable back adjustment, as if I'd gone to a chiropractor. It went up and down the entire length of my spine, crack, crack, and the pain just melted away. I was able to sleep for the first time in a long time without tremendous discomfort. And the next day I was still good.

"In two or three days, the pain started coming back, so I used the PEMF machine again and sure enough, I got another adjustment. It wasn't as profound but I got great pain relief. But the machine cost about $72,000 and wasn't affordable. So decided I needed to make myself something portable. My goal was to make it ultra portable, ultra affordable, very safe, and requiring very low power. And that's what I've since dedicated my whole life to. My ICES devices are very efficient. They're lighter, they take less power and can be powered with just batteries, and they emit virtually no stray energy. Using them, my back pain has reduced to almost nothing. I'm walking around without pain."

Dr. Dennis has developed a number of ICES devices. For people who suffer from pain, he recommends the A9 system. For people who like to experiment, he recommends the M1 system, which incorporates the latest ICES gen 6.0 technology in an ultra-portable, wearable package, and which enables users to choose from 30 different ICES protocol patterns, including theta and delta wave patterns associated with the deepest levels of restorative sleep, and 15 intensity levels. Dr. Dennis states that the ICES-PEMF devices he sells are not FDA approved for any human condition. "But people can buy them for self-experiment, with no medical claims."

For more information and to order, visit www.micro-pulse.com.

William Pawluk, MD, who practices integrative medicine in Baltimore, Maryland, is another well-known authority about PEMF, including its benefits for sleep, and the author of *Power Tools For Health*, a book that compiles his many years of research about PEMF devices. "Research studies support the value of PEMF therapy to enhance sleep, and show that using it before going to sleep or during bedtime can enhance and balance circadian rhythm," Dr. Pawluk says.

In one double-blind study, PEMF therapy administered with a small 0.5 mT (5 gauss) 4 Hz generator was given to a group of people, while a control group received a placebo treatment. Both groups were evaluated before the study began, and again after two and six weeks. The researchers found that PEMF reduced sleep disturbances in 83 percent of those who received it, compared with 57 percent of those in the control group, with the best results occurring after six weeks.

In another study, 100 people were evaluated in a four-week double-blind, placebo-controlled PEMF study. "They were placed into three groups: trouble falling asleep (sleep latency), interrupted sleep, or nightmares," Dr. Pawluk explains. "Evaluations were for how long it took to fall asleep, sleep interruptions, sleepiness after getting up, daytime sleepiness, concentration problems, and daytime headaches."

70 percent of those who received PEMF treatments exhibited significant or even complete relief of their complaints, with an additional 24 percent showing clear improvements. The remaining six percent experienced slight improvement. In the placebo group, only one participant had very clear relief, while 49 percent experienced no change in their sleep symptoms. The remainder showed only slight improvement.

Based on his research, Dr. Pawluk states, "I have found that presenting the brain with one frequency, three Hertz, throughout the night, anchors the brain into lower delta levels. Not only does this result in better and deeper delta, you also get longer periods of delta, and you also then begin to have a deeper theta level of sleep. The thing that wakes people up during the night the most is the fact that when you're aware of your dreaming you are in high levels of theta. That's what wakes people up. When you anchor or tether the brain in delta throughout the entire night using PEMF people get a much longer night's sleep."

The PEMF device that Dr. Pawluk most recommends for better sleep is the Flex Pulse. "The Flex Pulse has one program in it that runs at three Hertz, making it very effective for achieving and maintaining delta sleep," he says. "It a small, portable, battery operated device and the coil is not big and bulky. You can wear it under your neck, under your head, or under the pillow. Some devices recommend placing them under the mattress. I don't advise that because entrainment of the brain takes a certain amount of energy. The stronger the signal, then the better the entrainment because you're trying to entrain the whole brain.

"Another benefit of the Flex Pulse is that, because it's so small and portable, you can take it with you during the day and use it for whatever aches or pains you might have. And it works synergistically with anything else you might be using for sleep, such as melatonin."

For more information about Dr. Pawluk and his research into PEMF and the Flex Pulse and other PEMF systems he recommends, visit www.drpawluk.com.

Other Self-Care Approaches For Better Sleep

Other proven self-care methods you can use to enhance the quality of your sleep include:

Diet and Sleep-Promoting Foods and Beverages: For better sleep follow the dietary recommendations in Chapter 2, focusing on meals that primarily contain alkalizing foods, instead of foods that create acidic residues in your body.

Eating foods rich in tryptophan will also help. Tryptophan is an amino acid that the body uses to make serotonin, the neurotransmitter that slows down nerve signals so that your brain is able to relax. Tryptophan is also a precursor of melatonin.

Tryptophan-rich foods include chicken, chickpeas, eggs, fish, lentils, milk, turkey and yogurt. Certain nuts and seeds, such as almonds, hazelnuts, pumpkin seeds, sesame seeds, and sunflower seeds also contain tryptophan and can therefore boost serotonin levels and enhance sleep when snacked on before bed.

Various herbal teas can also help promote restful sleep. They include chamomile, hops, lemon balm, passionflower, skullcap, and valerian root.

Sleep-Enhancing Nutritional Supplements: Nutrients that can improve and restore sleep include various B vitamins, vitamin E, and magnesium. Raising the brain level of the amino acid GABA (gamma-aminobutyric acid) can also help.

GABA acts as a major neurotransmitter and is widely distributed throughout your body's central nervous system (CNS). It is the most important and widespread inhibitory neurotransmitter in the brain, helping to prevent over-firing of nerve cells in the CNS that causes restlessness, spasmodic movements, irritability and anxiety. GABA is also utilized by the brain to create tranquility and calmness. GABA is best taken in liposomal form before bedtime since non-liposomal forms of GABA do not cross the blood brain barrier. Liposomal GABA can be obtained from https://www.quicksilverscientific.com.

As Dr. Sorin stated, melatonin supplements can also improve sleep. Melatonin is a hormone that is secreted by your brain's pineal gland, with the highest levels of production occurring during sleep. Healthy sleepers produce adequate amounts of melatonin each night, while people who struggle to get a good night's sleep typically do not. Melatonin can increase deep sleep, REM (dream) sleep, and overall sleep efficiency, without producing any of the common "hangover" or stupor side effects that are common with both over-the-counter and prescription sleeping pills.

Melatonin supplements can also help boost immune function, prevent premature aging, and help to reverse a variety of sleep problems, including insomnia, the inability to stay asleep during the night, jet lag, and sleep problems caused by late shift work.

Melatonin supplements are non-toxic and available at most health food stores. Since it can promote sleep in as little as 30 minutes after it is consumed, you should only take melatonin at night, before bedtime. When you begin to use melatonin, your initial dose should be small. Most melatonin supplements come in a dose of between 1-3 mg per tablet.

Once you start to realize the benefits of melatonin, it is advisable that you stop using it for at least two weeks, so that your body doesn't stop producing its own amounts of melatonin. If you still have trouble sleeping, you can start another cycle for another 2-4 weeks.

To boost your body's own production of melatonin sleep in absolute darkness. For best results, consider sleeping with a sleep mask to prevent ambient light from getting into your eyes. Additionally, if you find yourself awaking during the night to use the bathroom, get out of bed without turning on the lights if possible, or use a faint red light to find your way to the bathroom.

Take A Bath for Better Sleep: Bathing 90 minutes before bedtime can both improve the quality of your sleep and help you fall asleep faster. This was confirmed by a meta-analysis of over 5,000 previous sleep studies conducted by researchers at the University of Texas. They found that taking a hot bath 90 minutes before bedtime resulted in falling asleep 10 minutes faster than normal.

The researchers also discovered why a hot bath achieves that result. It has to do with the body's core temperature. During the evening, core body temperature drops slightly, and then rises again just before dawn, signaling the body to wake up. A hot bath raises core body temperature and then triggers a faster cool down once you exit the tub. This rapid cool-down process results in better sleep. However, the researchers also found that taking a hot bath too close to bedtime can have the opposite effect, since it can interfere with the body's circadian rhythm.

Other studies revealed that hot baths at night also increase the production of melatonin due to the reaction of the brain's pineal gland to increased body temperature caused by hot bath, which produces a state of enhanced relaxation that carries over into better and deeper sleep.

An Epsom salt bath can also aid sleep. Pour two cups of Epsom salts into your bath as it fills with hot water. Then soak in the solution for 20 minutes. Epsom salts contain a high amount of magnesium, which has potent relaxant properties. As you soak in the hot water, the magnesium contained in the salts will be absorbed into your body through your skin.

Using the Brain Gauge To Monitor The Quality Of Your Sleep

As you begin to implement the above recommendations, you can monitor how well they are impacting your sleep by using the Brain Gauge, invented by Dr. Mark Tommerdahl and Dr. Bob Dennis. This innovative device is a cognitive assessment tool resembling a computer mouse that uses touch-based sensory testing to measure brain health, and is backed by clinically validated science and patented technology. Unlike sleep tracking devices, the Brain Gauge tests and assesses eight essential components of brain health: speed, focus, fatigue, accuracy, sequencing, timing perception, plasticity, and connectivity, and provides a comprehensive mental fitness score known as the "corticalmetric".

If you are not achieving optimal levels of restorative sleep, your brain will be affected negatively. Using the Brain Gauge, you can quickly and easily determine how fast and accurately your brain reacts to stimulation, how well it is able to concentrate on tasks at hand, and how fast it begins to tire out. All of these factors and the other above-mentioned brain health components are dependent on good sleep. The more that your sleep improves, the better your Brain Gauge scores will be.

In addition, the Brain Gauge can be used to accurately monitor the effects that your diet, nutritional supplements, caffeine, alcohol, and any prescribed medications you may be using, as well as other factors such as indoor and outdoor allergies, toxins, and travel, have on your sleep based on how they are impacting your brain.

The home version of the Brain Gauge is available as an inexpensive (as low as $19/month) subscription or can be purchased outright for $499. For more information and to order it, visit www.cortical metrics.com.

CHAPTER 9

The Ninth Key: Key: Creating A Healthy, Toxin-Free Home Environment

A HEALTHY HOME ENVIRONMENT is essential for good health. Creating a healthy, toxin-free home environment must be done to most effectively eliminate toxins from your body and prevent them from recurring. The healthier your home environment is, the better your health will be.

In addition to tap water, which you learned how to address in chapter 5, other common sources of indoor toxins are indoor air, household cleaning products, carpeting and other flooring, mattresses and other furniture, window coverings, pets and pet supplies, mold, and toxins in the garage.

Indoor Air

According to the Environmental Protection Agency (EPA), indoor air in the United States is often far more polluted than the air outdoors. On its website, the EPA states, "In the last several years, a growing body of scientific evidence has indicated that the air within homes and other buildings can be more seriously polluted than the outdoor air in even the largest and most industrialized cities. Other research indicates that people spend approximately 90 percent of their time indoors. Thus, for many people, the risks to health may be greater due to exposure to air pollution indoors than outdoors...While pollutant levels from individual sources may not pose a significant health risk by themselves, most homes have more than one source that contributes to indoor air pollution. There can be a serious risk from the cumulative effects of these sources."

The quality of the air in your home depends on its freshness and degree of moisture. Dry air, especially if it is cold, is a major factor in respiratory allergies and other respiratory conditions. The healthiest indoor air is not only fresh, but also moist and slightly warm, with an average relative humidity level of between 30 to 50 percent. The EPA warns that when home humidity levels are higher than that, indoor mold is more likely to grow.

You can improve the indoor air in your home with a few simple steps. First, make sure that air circulates freely from room to room so that it doesn't become stagnant and stale. When it is not too cold outside, leave your windows open when you are at home, even when you sleep. This ensures an ongoing supply of fresh indoor air and prevents the buildup of offending odors. During warmer months, you can eliminate airborne toxins from your home by opening two windows on opposite sides of a room, setting a fan in one window so that it blows toxins out the window on one side of the room while bringing in clean outdoor air through the opposite window. Done daily for a few hours, this simple step can reduce the amount of airborne toxins by half.

If your air is too dry, use a humidifier, especially in winter months when you run your furnace more. If you own your home, you should also make sure that the furnace you use is energy efficient and consider having the air ducts of your heating system professionally cleaned. The EPA offers guidelines that can help you decide if air duct cleaning is necessary. See www.epa.gov/indoor-air-quality-iaq/should-you-have-air-ducts-your-home-cleaned.

One of the best methods of cleaning indoor air is to use a negative ion generator. Negative ions improve both physical and mental/emotional health. Optimum negative ion concentrations in the air are between 3,000 to 6,000 ions per cubic centimeter. According to the EPA, the average concentration of negative ions in indoor air is only 200 ions per cubic centimeter.

Negative ion generators are capable of eliminating dust, pollen, mold, dander, spores, and harmful bacteria and viruses from the air. They also help improve the health of the mucous membranes in the sinuses by stimulating the cilia that line them. Cilia are microscopic hairs that act as filters in your nasal passages.

There are a number of high quality negative ion generators available for home use. Most models range in price from less than $100 to $200 or more. Negative ion generator car units are also available.

A high-quality air cleaning device such as a HEPA filter is another option. These devices have fine pores and charcoal that pull most contaminants from indoor air. However, because they emit EMFs that can disrupt your sleep, they are best used during daytime hours to clean the air in your bedroom, and in other rooms during the night when you are asleep. A number of air purification products combine a HEPA filter with a negative ion generator at a similar price point to negative ion generators alone.

To further ensure healthy indoor air quality in your home change your HVAC (heating, ventilation, and air conditioning systems) filters every three to four months. The best HVAC filters contain both charcoal and fiber and are known as activated charcoal filters. Though they are more expensive than standard HVAC filters, they are worth the investment because of their superior performance. If they are not available at your local hardware store, you can purchase them from Amazon.com.

To eliminate microorganisms, including mold spores, from indoor air you can also add aromatic oils to either a diffuser or steam humidifier. As the oils are diffused their antimicrobial properties will go to work removing harmful, airborne microbes. Thieves brand of five aromatic oils is particularly useful for this purpose. Other effective aromatic oils include cinnamon, eucalyptus, lemon, oregano, rosemary, tea-tree oil and thyme. "Because people who are exposed to mold often develop multiple chemical sensitivity, it is best if the diffuser or steam humidifier is plugged into a timer and the people in a mold-contaminated home leave the home while the aromatic oils are being diffused and return at least an hour after the diffusing of oils is completed by the timer," Dr. Lee Cowden says. Choose a high quality brand of aromatic oil free of synthetic ingredients and fillers. Two such brands are Revive (www.revive-eo.com) and Now (www.nowfoods.com/essential-oils).

Another healthy indoor air choice that will also enhance the beauty of your home is to fill your rooms with plants. Houseplants provide a number of benefits, including adding more oxygen to indoor environment and keeping indoor air moist. Certain plants, such as ferns (particularly Boston ferns), ficus, garden mums, ivy, lilies, philodendrons, rubber plant, spider plants, and indoor palm trees, are also effective for removing airborne irritants, including chemicals such as formaldehyde, benzene, hexane, and others. In addition, such plants can enhance your mood. Research has found that plants in the home can reduce blood pressure levels and both physiological and psychological stress due to their beneficial effects on the human autonomic nervous system.

If you have plants, make sure that the containers in which the plants are kept have drainage holes in the bottom of the containers and a separate container beneath each plant container to catch excess water if plants are over-watered. This reduces the chance that mold will grow on the plants or in their containers.

Finally, if your home has a basement, make sure that it stays dry. Damp basements act as breeding grounds for harmful microorganisms, including mold. Also consider having your basement inspected to protect against leaks and water damage.

Household Materials And Products

Many common household materials and products are major sources of harmful chemicals and toxins, including cleaning and other household products, carpets, rugs, and furniture, and certain building materials. All such items, if they are made from synthetic materials, expose you to dangerous chemicals. Building materials made from natural materials such as wood and metals are superior home choices than unnatural products like fiber and particle boards, plastics, and polyester. This is also true of your furniture, your flooring, wiring, and sealants made from synthetic materials.

Many commercial dish-washing soaps, laundry detergents, and cleaning products for tiles and walls also contain synthetic agents. Synthetic air fresheners are another common problem.

A published study conducted by researchers at the University of Washington illustrates the dangers such products can pose to your health. Researchers examined six of the nation's top-selling air fresheners and laundry products. They found that all of the products emitted dozens of chemicals. All told, more than 100 potentially harmful chemicals were found to be emitted by the six products.

More disturbingly, at least one chemical in every product studied is listed as toxic or hazardous under federal laws, and five of the chemicals are classified as carcinogenic "hazardous air pollutants" for which the EPA declares there is no safe exposure level. Yet none of these dangerous chemicals were listed on the product labels. A larger, follow-up study of 25 cleaners, personal care products, air fresheners and laundry products by the same researchers found that many other brands contained similar chemicals. Other studies have shown that approximately 20 percent of all Americans suffer from health problems caused by common air freshener products, and approximately 10 percent of the population has health issues related to common laundry products.

It is easy to find safe and natural alternatives to these and nearly all other types of household products. If you currently have synthetic household products in your home, be sure to check that they are properly sealed and stored out of reach from children and any pets you may have. Once you use them up, switch to natural product brands, starting with laundry detergent, dishwasher soap, and floor, sink, toilet, and other home cleaning products. In place of synthetic air fresheners, a much better choice is the use of an aromatic oil in a diffuser.

Also choose nontoxic building, insulation, and other repair materials, paint, adhesives, laminates, and gardening materials. And if you plan to paint or do remodeling inside your home, use low-VOC or no-VOC paints and adhesives. Regular paints and adhesives outgas solvent chemicals into the air of your home for many months or even years.

Garage Toxins: Toxic chemicals are often also found in products stored in garages. If your garage is attached to your home, the chemicals in such products can outgas and enter your home, where they will be inhaled. They can also enter into your car when it's parked in your garage so that you breathe them every time you get in your car. The best option for storing such products is in a detached shed or storage unit. And when you use them, be sure to wear gloves, eye goggles, and an air mask.

Carpeting And Other Flooring

Most carpets are synthetic and contain formaldehyde, a chemical known to cause asthma, allergies, cancer, and other diseases. The padding beneath carpeting typically contains formaldehyde, as well. Formaldehyde continues to outgas for as long as carpeting and its padding remain in place. Synthetic carpets also contain a variety of other toxic chemicals, including DDT and other pesticides. They also collect dust and are a prime breeding ground for bacteria, fungi, and mold.

Another source of home toxins are adhesives used in certain types of flooring, which can outgas benzene, hexane, toluene, and other toxic solvents. In addition, vacuuming carpeting can discharge dust, microbes, and other toxins into the air to be inhaled.

If you have synthetic carpeting in your home you would be wise to get rid of it, replacing it with hardwood flooring that does not require adhesives, or ceramic tiles with nontoxic grout, if you can afford to do so.

Avoid hardwood flooring coated with polyurethane and other toxic materials unless they have been baked onto the surface of the flooring. Ideally, choose pure wood. You can protect it from scratches and stains by coating it with tung oil. Hardwood flooring does not require the use of adhesives, and in many cases can be snapped together, making installation easy.

Tile is another nontoxic option, but be sure to choose a nontoxic grout, which can also be sealed with tung oil. Periodically, grout needs to be thoroughly cleaned to prevent a buildup of dirt, dust, and other toxins from accumulating on its surface.

Washable, non-synthetic throw rugs can be used to cover flooring so long as they are cleaned regularly in a washing machine.

Mattresses, Furniture, And Window Coverings

Your mattress, along with the furniture in your home, and even your window coverings, could all be sources of hidden toxins. Mattresses, in particular, can be a problem.

Mattresses: Most commercially sold mattresses contain toxic materials, including polyurethane foam, which can emit volatile organic compounds (VOCs) known to cause respiratory and other health problems; carcinogenic flame retardant chemicals that disrupt hormone and immune function; solvent-based glues, which also emit VOCs; and PVC (a form of plastic) or vinyl coverings, which also disrupt hormones and impair reproductive function. Mattresses may also contain unhealthy synthetic fragrances and chemical antimicrobials. A wide variety of organic, non-toxic mattresses are now available as healthy alternatives.

In addition to choosing a healthy mattress, use organic, zippered, dust-proof pillow and mattress covers to protect yourself from dust mites. Choose covers made of organic cotton or other organic, tightly woven fabrics, and wash them along with the rest of your bedding frequently in hot water.

Furniture: In place of solid wood, many furniture manufacturers substitute plywood, particle board, or composite pressboard wood, all of which can require the use of glues that emit formaldehyde and other solvents and chemicals. Upholstered furniture also often contains chemical flame retardants and chemical stain-guard or water repellant treatments. These treatments can contain perfluorinated chemicals (PFCs) that suppress immune function and can cause cancer, birth defects, and other health issues. Furniture cushions need to be considered, as well, because they are often made of polyurethane foam that emit VOCs.

Healthy furniture options include products made of solid wood, organic cotton, and organic, natural latex foam. If solid wood furniture is beyond your budget, you can find particle board, plywood and composite wood furniture products made with glues that are certified as "formaldehyde free."

Window Coverings: Another possible source of indoor toxins are window coverings, particularly curtains because of how they attract dust laden with microbes and chemicals. Every time you move curtains, and especially when you take them down to shake them off before cleaning them, the dust and chemicals they contain gets dislodged to be inhaled. Horizontal blinds also attract dust. Better options are vertical blinds and pull-down shades, both of which attract less dust. Just be sure to clean them regularly.

Mold

Mold is a much more common household toxin than most people realize. It is found in basements, and can also permeate walls, floors, and ceilings, often going undetected until the health risks it causes become severe. While some types of mold are detectable by their color, fuzzy appearance, and/or musty odor, other types are invisible. Harmful mold in homes continuously releases spores and mycotoxins as airborne inhalants. According to mold specialist Ritchie Shoemaker, MD, author of the book *Mold Warriors*, 25 percent of people are unable to detoxify from mold on their own once they are exposed to it, making them more susceptible to mold-triggering allergies, chronic fatigue, and other serious diseases.

A little known fact about mold is that the mycotoxins they produce are more harmful to the human body than human-made toxins except for certain radioactive elements. They are also fat-soluble, making them very difficult to eliminate, and enabling them to accumulate in the body's fat cells and tissues while suppressing the immune system.

You need to regularly inspect your home for mold, especially if your home has been subject to water leaks or other water damage. For visible mold, examine your basement walls and areas around your sinks, bathtub and shower, washing machine, and dishwasher. Touch these areas with your hands, feeling for moisture or cold spots.

You can also order do-it-yourself mold inspection kits, but to get meaningful results, you must be educated on how to use them properly. A more expensive mold-testing kit worth considering is the Environmental Relative Mold Index (ERMI) test kit which uses DNA testing to detect over 36 mold and other fungal species and provide rapid and accurate results. These tests are available from EMSL Analytics, Inc. For more information and to order them, visit www.emsltestkits.com/mold.

If your home tests positive for mold, especially black mold such as the species *Aspergillus niger* and certain strains of molds known as stachybotrys, you need to have it removed. Depending on the severity of infestation, you may be able to remove it on your own.

First, find and seal all water leaks and sources of water damage in your home. After sealing off the mold-damaged room from the rest of your house with sheets of plastic and tape around doors and air-conditioner return ducts, replace damaged drywall, flooring, or ceilings while wearing gloves, goggles, long pants, a long-sleeve shirt, and a protective nose and mouth mask (military-grade respirator). Spray or clean the affected areas with 3% hydrogen peroxide and then, several hours later, when the peroxide is completely dried, spray with full strength white vinegar, then wipe up with paper towels.

The use of a HEPA air purifier can also sometimes be effective for preventing the spread of mold spores and mycotoxins elsewhere in the house, and for eliminating other airborne toxins. The filters in the HEPA air purifier will need to be replaced after several days or a couple of weeks of use in a very contaminated environment but should only be changed outside so that mold spores in the filter don't get scattered into the air of the house. After a HEPA filter has been used for several days, an ozone air purifier can then be used to finish cleaning the air. Ozone air purifiers also kill dust mites, fleas, and ticks. Only use them when you and other people and pets are away from the house because the ozone the purifiers emit is dangerous if inhaled because of the free radical damage they cause. Plants should also be removed from rooms before such devices are used.

If you choose to purchase an ozone air purifier, choose one with a timer so that it turns itself off before you return home, allowing enough time for the ozone that it produces to dissipate. Usie an ozone air purifier or an aromatic oil diffuser periodically after mold issues are resolved to reduce the chance of mold recurrence.

It is also a good idea to periodically treat your car, especially its air conditioning system, which is a prime location for mold spores to grow. Mold can incur in cars due to moisture, both inside and out. Since ozone can damage rubber gaskets, it is best to use an aromatic oil diffuser in your car with the air conditioner blowing.

Severe cases of mold buildup in your home require the services of a professional mold remediation specialist. If such services are necessary, you may need to leave your home because of the toxic chemical fungicides the specialists use. Once you are cleared to return home, using a charcoal HEPA filter is advisable.

Testing Yourself For Mold Toxicity: Dr. Shoemaker developed an inexpensive online test that can help you determine whether or not mold and mycotoxins are affecting your health. It is called the Visual Contrast Sensitivity (VCS) test and is available at www.survivingmold. com/diagnosis/visual-contrast-sensitivity-vcs. You will also find other tests Dr. Shoemaker recommends at SurvivingMold.com, and a directory of certified practitioners nationwide trained in the Shoemaker Protocol. ACIM-member physicians can also help you detoxify from mold toxicity.

Toxins From Pets

Having a pet can be good for your health while also raising your spirits and preventing feelings of loneliness and depression. Still, if you have pets, they can also expose you to toxins or microbes.

Cats can carry leptospirosis, a bacterial infection, and a parasite infection called toxoplasmosis. Both of these infectious agents can be transmitted from cats to humans through kitty litter, causing serious illness that is difficult to treat. They can also be aerosolized into the air each time cats scratch in the litter box. Though such cat-to-human infections are rare, they pose a greater risk to people with a compromised immune system or serious illness.

Set a litter box in a special room away from the rest of your home and wear gloves when cleaning it. Keeping a set of shoes that you can change into before entering the litter box room is also advisable to prevent tracking particles of litter into the rest of your home. Also keep litter boxes away from air and heating return ducts since the toxins from litter and cat waste can be transmitted through the ducts to the rest of your home as inhalants. Close off return ducts and forced-air ducts in the litter box room and, if necessary, place a portable heating unit in the room during cold months.

Dogs can be carriers of parasite eggs and cysts, and other disease organisms. If you or anyone else at home is sick, it is a good idea to restrict how much access your dog has inside your home.

Both dogs and cats can also expose you to fleas and ticks that carry Lyme disease and its related co-infections. To protect the health of your pets be sure that they receive regular checkups with a veterinarian, ideally one trained in integrative pet care.

Lead In Your Home

If you live in a house or apartment complex that was built prior to the last 30 to 40 years, there is likely lead in the paint originally used on your walls. Lead, instead of copper, piping (or lead solder) was also likely used for your water pipes if they were installed before 1986.

If you are unsure as to whether or not there is lead in your home, contact your county health department, which can assist you in finding out for certain, and also advise you on how best to deal with the problem if it exists.

The Land Beneath Your Home

Although the houses people live in may be healthy, the land beneath them may not be. Soil can contain numerous harmful toxins and chemicals that can be outgassed into the home as airborne pollutants. This is especially true in residential areas in which there previously was industrial activity, and on lands that abut lakes, rivers or streams located near industrial or chemical plants. Even after such plants close, the chemicals and other toxins they produced in the past can remain in water and soil for many years. If you have any concerns about the land beneath your property (and any water ways nearby), contact your county health department.

Plastics: A Pervasive Health Risk

Plastic products can pose dangerous, often overlooked health risks because they are composed of synthetic chemicals, two classes of which – bisphenol-A and phthalates – have been shown to mimic various hormones in the human body. As a result, either bisphenol-A or phthalates can cause major disruptions in your body's endocrine (hormone-regulating) system, adversely affecting the reproductive systems of both men and women, and causing other hormone-related health problems, including affecting the normal development of boys and girls exposed to such chemicals.

Avoid plastics and plastic products in your house, including plastic water bottles and canned foods, which are often lined with BPA or other phthalate coating material. Phthalates are also common ingredients in many children's toys.

Take Off Your Shoes When You Enter Your Home

In Japan and other Asian countries, the idea of wearing shoes or other outdoor footwear at home is unthinkable. You would do well to follow this Japanese custom. Footwear attracts dust, dirt, pesticides, and other chemicals whenever you go outside, all of which get tracked into your home if you wear the footwear inside. To avoid this problem, remove your footwear when you come inside, changing into either indoor shoes or slippers. This simple precaution can greatly reduce the risk of outdoor toxins entering your home.

CHAPTER 10

The Master Key: Spiritual Health

I<small>T IS MY</small> opinion, based on my own experiences, that spiritual health, while often the most overlooked aspect of healing, is the most important self-care key. As my friend, Dr. W. Lee Cowden explains, "Health is not merely the absence of disease or symptoms, but rather the ability to withstand a significant insult or trauma without incurring symptoms. Your health is tied to your resilience, meaning your ability to rejoice, persevere, and maintain hope and functionality through difficult situations. Our resilience is directly connected to our spiritual health. Knowing what provides meaning in our lives and connecting with something that is larger than ourselves provides the foundation from which all health flows.

"Physical health and mental/emotional health are important, but spiritual health is even more important because it affects us both in this present physical world and in the eternal world after our physical death. Whatever an individual's spiritual foundation is, it needs to be fulfilling and life-giving, focused on restoration and grace, in order to be healthy."

I agree with Dr. Cowden. Moreover, as he also points out, "It is not possible, in my experience, to be completely and permanently healed physically without addressing the deep emotional (soul wounds) and spiritual components of your life. Cultivating a relationship with God is the highest form of self-care and will provide you with innumerable health benefits. Attuning yourself to God's guidance in all areas of your daily life will help you reduce feelings of stress, anxiety, depression, and fear, and provide you with a greater capacity for loving yourself and others unconditionally.

"Having a spiritual connection with our Creator will also help you reconnect to your special talents and gifts and use them to fulfill your life's purpose. I can attest to this in my own life and in the lives of my patients who have an active spiritual life. Such patients also tend to heal and recover from illness more quickly and deeply than other patients."

What is Spirituality?

Dr. Cowden describes spirituality as the process of seeking to align your sense of self to something which is divine beyond self. "It involves the soul's quest for meaning and when successfully pursued, fulfills you with love, joy, wisdom, peace and service," he says. "It extends far beyond the physical world of matter and connects you to a profoundly powerful and divine force, which Christianity calls the Holy Spirit. By cultivating a conscious relationship with God, we also cultivate the ability to relate to the Divine and allow God to guide us in our daily actions."

In addition to being consciously aware of the role spirituality plays in your life, being spiritually healthy also means being intimately connected to your family, friends, and community, resulting in improved social health, as well. Spiritual and social health are interconnected, since it is through our committed relationships that we find the greatest opportunities for spiritual growth and for learning how to receive and impart unconditional love. It's a scientifically proven fact that people who regularly engage in spiritual practices such as prayer and attending services of worship to deepen their relationship with God, and who also have strong relationships with their family members and friends, typically live longer and healthier lives than others.

"I find this to be true among my patients," Dr. Cowden says. "Those who believe in God and have a strong faith, and who are blessed with a loving network of family and friends, tend to be healthier and recover from illness with more resilience than patients who live lives of isolation and who don't have an active spiritual life."

Deepening our connection to our Creator is, to me, the most important step we all need to take, not only to improve our health, but also to live as God intended us to live—making full use of our God-given talents in service to others while at the same time creating true, lasting fulfillment for ourselves.

"When we heed God's guidance, we gain mastery of our physical selves and act as we should and experience a deeper communion with God. By doing so, our selfless actions improve our health," Dr. Cowden adds.

Think back to a time when you may have been sick or otherwise not feeling well, yet still shared a kind word or smile, or otherwise did something nice for someone else without any thought of getting something in return. Such simple acts inevitably leave us feeling better regardless of our current circumstances. We experience more contentment and joy, and our experience of not being well lessens, at least for a little bit. By acting in this way—living from our hearts—we uplift ourselves as we help uplift others. This is one of the many benefits that come our way when we follow the Golden Rule that Jesus taught when he instructed his apostles and disciples, saying, "Whatever you want men to do to you, do also to them." (Matthew 7:12 NKJV)

This instruction by Jesus goes to the heart of what it means to be spiritual and truly connected to God.

The Hierarchy Of Healing

During the many years of his medical practice, Dr. Cowden found that pain was ultimately what drove most of his patients to seek his help. "As a cardiologist, it often began with pain associated with their heart, diagnosed as heart disease," he explains. "When I first started out in my career, I didn't realize that the diagnosis was actually one of the few that was truly accurate among the myriad of conditions that we seek to treat through Western medicine. While each of the patients

I saw had a physical heart condition that was distinguishable, based upon examination and various diagnostic tests, what wasn't as readily apparent was that many of them also had an 'emotional disease of the heart,' or wounding in their soul. While I could work diligently to resolve their physical complaints and achieve some success, I found that they would return with another health complaint in a relatively short period of time.

"As I patiently worked my way upstream to the root of the disease process, ultimately what was revealed was an unresolved emotional pain that kept them from physically being able to achieve abundant, resilient health. As I sought to provide resources to help them resolve their emotional pain, I quickly learned that most, if not all, required a spiritual framework to work through their soul wounds. The amazing part was watching how quickly patients would heal physically once they were connected to their spiritual framework in a healthy manner, free from the limited beliefs they had about their spiritual, emotional or physical condition.

"When patients came to me with a physical manifestation of disease and I treated them only with physical treatments (diet, supplements, pharmaceuticals, etc), I noted that it took a lot of time, a lot of energy-expenditure, and a lot of money to improve their condition. However, if I could help patients to understand that their mental and emotional status was affecting their physical condition and we worked on the mental and emotional issues, hardly using any physical treatments, their physical conditions often improved faster and less expensively than if I had used only physical treatments.

"For those patients who came with physical health challenges and who were willing to work on the spiritual causation of their disease, I saw the fastest and least expensive recovery from the physical conditions. I refer to this as the hierarchy of healing. I have learned that a patient should work as high up in that hierarchy as they feel comfortable for the best, fastest, and most long-lasting results. If a patient feels comfortable using prayer for their healing, then they definitely should. Then, the other efforts they make—cleaning up their diet, getting good sleep each night, stretching and exercising daily, working on mental/emotional issues—will be far more effective. This way they can be working simultaneously on all levels of their health."

Spiritual Self-Care

It is up to each of us to determine how best to go about maintaining our spiritual health. For most people, the following approaches are most helpful, and a growing body of scientific research supports the fact that they are among the most important practices for deepening and improving spiritual, and thus overall, health.

Prayer

"Prayer is a reverent petition to God, asking Him to guide our daily lives, thanking Him for His blessings, and then 'listening' for answers and directions from Him," Dr. Cowden says. "Sometimes God gives us a 'gut feeling' about what we are to do or not do. Sometimes He sends another person to give us an answer to a prayer request. Sometimes He directs us to a particular passage in the Bible that has the answer. Occasionally, we may actually audibly hear His voice." Prayer has a long history of healing. Its ability to heal disease has also been scientifically confirmed in modern times. Prayer is also the most common spiritual practice performed by most Americans. The majority of people who pray report a greater sense of well-being than those who don't. People who pray also report that through prayer they experience a sense of peace, receive guidance about their life issues, and have even felt divinely inspired or "led by God" to take specific actions that led to improvements in their lives or those of their loved ones. People who pray also typically score highest on ratings of general well-being and satisfaction with their lives.

A great deal of research confirms the beneficial effects of prayer, including better health. Decades ago, for instance, famed Harvard researcher and mind/body medicine expert Herbert Benson, MD, found that regular prayer or the repetition of spiritual phrases such as "The Lord is my shepherd," triggers relaxation, reduces stress, improves immune function, and provides many other physiological and psychological benefits. He also found that the degree of benefit is determined by the degree of faith on the part of the person praying.

Research also shows that praying regularly:

- Decreases the incidence of disease and improves recovery rates and the ability to cope among people who do become ill.

- Leads to sharp decreases in pain.

- Results in higher scores on life-purpose indexes.

There are many effective ways to pray, both for yourself and for others. Many people find great benefit using the prayers from their religious upbringing. Others make prayer a time of personal conversation with God, stating their need or concern and asking for divine intervention. Others find taking a walk in a place of natural beauty to be a form of prayerful worship. Taking the time to reflect on all that you have to be grateful for and giving thanks to God can be effective as well.

Research Studies on Prayer: In a prospective, randomized, double-blind protocol on 393 patients newly admitted to the Coronary Care Unit (CCU) in a San Francisco hospital, 192 patients who received daily intercessory prayers from off-site volunteers had significantly lower severity scores during the hospitalization compared to the 201 patients randomized to the control group (there was no one specifically praying daily for the control patients). The severity score included less congestive heart failure, less diuretic and less antibiotic therapy, fewer cardiac arrests, less pneumonia, and less need for mechanical ventilator support in the prayed-for group.

This 1988 study was replicated in 1999 in a large Kansas City, Missouri hospital. In a randomized, controlled, double-blind, prospective, parallel-group trial of 990 newly-admitted coronary care unit patients, researchers found statistically reduced CCU course scores in the 466 patients who were specifically prayed for by off-site, randomized, Christian volunteers compared to 524 CCU patients who were not specifically prayed for. The CCU course scores were a composite score based on other complicating, medical conditions that developed and life-supporting therapies required by the patients in each group.

When prayer is done the way it is described in these two CCU studies, there is only potential benefit, without the side effects that can occur with other therapies used on CCU patients.

Prayerful Meditation: Prayer allows you to see your own spiritual "heart" and bring it into alignment with God's heart. "It isn't a monologue, but rather a dialogue where God downloads the desires of your heart to you, in order to bring them into reality," Dr. Cowden explains. "Through a consistent prayerful life, we develop a relationship with God that is based upon love and trust."

Prayerful meditation is a type of prayer that can take on many forms. To begin the practice of prayer, choose the form that feels most comfortable for you, then establish a daily prayer routine. You can start with any prayer you recall that you were taught as a child, or you can use a favorite passage from the Bible or other spiritual writings that you find especially meaningful. In addition, you can engage in a practice of personal prayer, talking with God directly. State your need or concern and ask for God's help and guidance.

"I find that prayers of gratitude, thanking God for the blessings you already have in your life, are some of the most beneficial types of prayer," Dr. Cowden says. "A simple way to begin praying in this manner is to thank God before every meal for the food you are about to eat. Thanking God for the blessings of that day before you fall asleep at night often calms the body and the mind and helps falling asleep to occur faster. Try to continually expand the things for which you express gratitude. After a life-time of following this practice, I can attest that it makes me more aware and grateful for all of the blessings the Lord has given me.

"Whichever type of prayer you choose, try to establish a regular routine. I recommend praying before you go to bed each night and soon after you awake each morning in order to get guidance for that day, as well as giving a prayer of thanks before each meal.

Doing so only takes a few minutes out of each day, yet the benefits prayer provides can last for a lifetime. Some people have an ongoing conversation with God throughout their day, thanking Him for every blessing, no matter how small, and seeking His guidance on every challenge, no matter how trivial it might seem to others. In this way, God can become your closest and most trusted friend."

Worship Services

In addition to daily prayer, meeting with other people who have similar spiritual beliefs to pray and praise God together and worship at least once a week can also provide significant health benefits, and provide you with a connection to a community. At such meetings, you may choose to make yourself accountable to other people who show that they care about you. "Such accountability can help us to make changes that might be difficult if we tried to do it alone," Dr. Cowden says. "An example of accountability might be stopping a bad habit, such as cigarette smoking, over-eating, pornography, etc. Meeting together to worship God, encouraging each other, releasing negative emotions by talking to a good listener, and getting prayed for by others can also significantly improve your ability to live longer."

Research shows that those who attend church services or other places of worship at least once a week are also more likely to take good care of themselves, including engaging in health-related self-care practices, than those who do not do so. Regular attendees of church or other religious services tend to not smoke or become better able to quit smoking, drink only in moderation or abstain from alcohol altogether, make exercise a part of their daily routine, and also maintain stable, loving marriages. All of these factors help support a long and healthy life.

Interestingly, many regular attendees of worship services did not engage in such health-promoting activities until after they first began participating in such services. Part of the reason for this is due to the positive social support and friendships that people derive from attending them. Such support and camaraderie has been shown to help make it easier for people to adopt and maintain healthier behaviors.

Among the many health benefits that scientists have found regular churchgoing and similar worship activities confer are:

- A reduced risk of high blood pressure.
- A lower incidence of depression and anxiety.
- A lower incidence of mental illness.
- A reduced need for hospitalization.
- Improved immune function.
- A better ability to maintain a healthy weight.

In addition, according to Dr. William Strawbridge, senior research scientist of the Human Population Laboratory at the Public Health Institute, the California Department of Health Services and the University of California-Berkeley, people who infrequently or never attend religious services have a 66 percent higher risk of dying from respiratory diseases and are twice as likely to die from digestive disease.

Other research demonstrates that regularly attending religious services can significantly improve the likelihood that you will live longer. One such study conducted by Harvard researchers over a period of 20 years tracked over 76,000 female nurses in the United States, most of whom were practicing Christians. By the study's conclusion, it was shown that the women who attended religious services an average of twice a week were 33 percent less likely to die prematurely, compared to those who never attended services. The study also found that even occasional churchgoers have a mortality risk that is 13 percent lower than non-churchgoers.

According to Tyler VanderWeele, professor of epidemiology at the Harvard T.H. Chan School of Public Health, one of the authors of this study, "Service attendance may be a powerful and underappreciated health resource."

Commenting on the study to the *Washington Post*, VanderWeele stated that while other studies suggested a similar link between service attendance and decreased mortality, his study demonstrated that religious service attendance in and of itself is what actually causes the better health outcomes. The Post reported, "Because the nurses answered questionnaires periodically over a long time frame, the researchers were able to look at whether a change in service attendance led to a change in health.

"They found numerous benefits associated with attending services. Women who started going to services then became more likely to quit smoking and less likely to show signs of depression, for instance, even when the researchers controlled for a long list of other variables, from age and exercise habits to income and other non-religious social engagement.

"The effect of religious attendance, they found, was stronger than that of any other form of participation in a social group like a book club or a volunteer organization."

A more recent study, headed by Marino Bruce, a Vanderbilt University professor and the associate director of the school's Center for Research on Men's Health, found that both men and women who regularly attend church or other worship services can reduce their risk of death by 55 percent. This is especially for men and women between the ages of 40 and 65, the specific target group of the study.

In the study, Professor Bruce collected data on over 5,000 people, tracking their church attendance along with such variables as socioeconomic status and health insurance coverage. Using this data, he and his team devised a statistical model to predict risk of mortality. The aim of the study was "to examine the relationship between religiosity (church attendance), allostatic load (AL) (a physiologic measure of stress), and all-cause mortality in middle-aged adults... The primary outcomes were AL and mortality. AL was derived from values for metabolic, cardiovascular, and nutritional/inflammatory clinical/biologic markers."

The study found that non-churchgoers "had significantly higher overall mean AL scores and higher prevalence of high-risk values for 3 of the 10 markers of AL than did churchgoers." In addition, men and women who attended church more than once a week had a 55 percent reduction of death from all causes compared with non-churchgoers.

The researchers wrote, "We found a significant association between church attendance and mortality among middle-aged adults after full adjustments. AL, a measure of stress, only partially explained differences in mortality between church and non-church attendees. These findings suggest a potential independent effect of church attendance on mortality."

Forgiveness

"Anger is an emotion and unforgiveness is its spiritual counterpart," Dr. Cowden says. "At the end of His ministry on earth, Jesus demonstrated the most powerful act of forgiveness when He forgave those who were responsible for his crucifixion as he was hanging on the cross, saying, 'Father, forgive them for they know not what they do.' (Luke 23:34 NKJV)

"In my experience, both personally and professionally, the practice of forgiveness is not only one of the greatest opportunities we have for following Christ's example and putting the Golden Rule that He taught into action, it can also make a big, positive difference in your health."

In Chapter 6, you learned how every cell in your body responds to your thoughts, emotions, and actions, and then crystallizes its response in the form of cellular memories. As you also learned, far too often these cellular memories are false "truths" that can sap your energy, cause disease, and even lead to premature death. This is why it is so important that you replace these false cellular memories with divine ones. "Forgiveness is one of the most powerful ways I know of doing this," Dr. Cowden says.

Being unable or unwilling to forgive others is a great source of stress. Many illnesses, in fact, arise from the stressful conditions caused by unforgiveness. Though practicing forgiveness isn't always easy, it is necessary if you truly want to create a healthy, positive life for yourself.

Ironically, when you are unforgiving towards others you hurt yourself the most. Forgiving those you feel have wronged you releases you from stress and its associated, health-sapping emotions. You also free yourself from the influence of negative people. "Over my career, I have treated many people who had cancer and I have never found a person with cancer who did not have anger and unforgiveness towards others or themselves as a major contributor to that cancer condition," Dr. Cowden states. "Other chronic medical conditions often have anger and unforgiveness as a contributor as well.

"When it comes to forgiveness, I follow the instruction of Jesus in the Lord's Prayer to 'forgive those who trespass against us' so that God will forgive us. This is what Jesus promised, and I find that it translates in everyday life to a release of negative thoughts and energy. This, in turn, neutralizes stress and allows us to achieve our full potential, both in terms of our health and in all other aspects of our existence, as well as leading us closer to eternal salvation."

As you work on practicing forgiveness, you will likely discover that the person you have the most difficulty forgiving is yourself. Don't be alarmed by this. It simply means you're human. Typically, we are the harshest judge of ourselves. No matter what you may feel you cannot forgive yourself for, the truth is that you can. It is only when we start to forgive ourselves that we become truly able to love and accept ourselves. And it is only when we truly love and accept ourselves that we find to do all we can to take good care of ourselves.

Embrace the habit of practicing forgiveness, forgiving others *and* yourself. Set out to forgive all those who have hurt you in the past. Sit down and make a list on paper. Recall what was said or done to you. Or what wasn't. Then let it go, without bitterness. It's all in the past after all, and you are still alive today in the present. (On his website, www.drleecowden.com, Dr. Cowden provides helpful instructions on how to release anger and unforgiveness using what he calls a "visualization/shouting and forgiving exercise". There, he also shares more of his perspectives and teachings about spiritual health.)

Practicing Gratitude

When we take time to appreciate the many things in life we have to be grateful for our spirits lift and our well-being improves.

Unfortunately, it is a human tendency to ignore the blessings in our lives because we are too focused on our perceived challenges and problems. "This is why I encourage my patients to get in the habit of taking time each and every day to note all that there is to be grateful for," Dr. Cowden says.

Although we may tend to take our lives for granted, in actuality they are a gift from God, and every day that we are alive brings with it new blessings and opportunities for further growth. By committing yourself to become more aware of your daily blessings you will strengthen your connection with God. Most likely, you will also become more aware of the divine intelligence that is guiding your life as it unfolds, putting you more in touch with your life's purpose. In addition, when you choose to consciously focus on the blessings in your life and express gratitude for them, you will likely start to attract further positive experiences. By focusing on what you have, instead of what you think you lack, you will start to feel a sense of abundance. Your problems will start to seem less acute and you will be more apt to discover solutions to them.

"Practicing gratitude on a daily basis can produce powerful feelings of joy, contentment, and self-acceptance, while also banishing stress," Dr. Cowden says. "No matter what you may be experiencing in your life at any moment, if you take the time to look for it, you will find something to be grateful for. While it's true that there are times when feeling gratitude can be difficult, such as when you are sick or have experienced a tragedy in your life, if you make the effort to choose the attitude of gratitude during such times, even for a moment, most likely you will experience a lightening of your burden."

Adopting the habit of practicing gratitude each day, like the development of any other habit, requires commitment. Here are two methods that Dr. Cowden recommends as the easiest and most effective ways he has found to practice gratitude.

Morning Reflection: This is a gratitude practice you can do as soon as you wake up each morning. Before getting out of bed, close your eyes and take a moment to focus on one of the many blessings you have received in your life. It could be a person in your life, a personal achievement, or anything else that has made you happy to be alive. "Whatever blessing you choose, reconnect with it in your imagination as if it is happening here and now and fully feel how grateful you are for it," Dr. Cowden instructs. "Continue with this reflection until your entire body is filled with the positive emotions that always accompany gratitude and, as you do so, give thanks for what you have received. Then give thanks for the fact that you are still alive with an entire new day in which more blessings await you. By practicing this gratitude exercise each morning you will soon instill in yourself a sense of enthusiasm and appreciation for the day ahead."

A Gratitude List: Another method of cultivating feelings of gratitude is by writing down a list of each day's blessings in a gratitude journal. "You can perform this exercise at any time of the day, yet I find it most effective to do it before you go to bed so that you can better appreciate and give thanks for the blessings and lessons that you experienced that day," Dr. Cowden says. "Simply mentally review your day, and then write down a list of all the things that happened that day for which you feel grateful. Be sure to include things that may not seem momentous, but still made you feel blessed when they occurred. As the saying goes, 'It's the little things that count,' and when you take the time to note them, you will soon find that they really add up.

"Write down enough detail about the blessings of that day so that if you read that gratitude diary years later when you are going through a challenging time, your soul and spirit will be lifted by what God has already done in your life. That reading can build your faith and combat the unbelief that commonly comes against your faith during life's most difficult times. When you finish writing your list, review it and give thanks to God_for all that you wrote down. By making gratitude a regular part of your daily experience, over time your life will be transformed into an increasingly joyous adventure."

Final Thoughts

In concluding this chapter, I want to emphasize that to get healthy and stay well, you need to honor your relationship with God and with all other humans, including those you consider your enemies. In my experience, you can only truly do so by incorporating spiritual practices into your daily life.

Live your life from faith and hope, and remember that it is in giving that you receive. As the Bible teaches, whatever you sow you will reap, so give joyfully and sow goodness plentifully. Most importantly, realize that the greatest medicine of all is Love. Resolve to live your life in love, knowing that you are a child of God. As you increase your capacity to love—including loving yourself—you significantly improve the likelihood that you will live a long life of lasting health. And to that thought, we can all say, Amen!

Conclusion: Staying On Track

CONGRATULATIONS! HAVING READ this far, you now know the most key and effective preventive solutions you can employ on your own to maintain and improve your health. By applying what you have learned you will be well on your way to taking charge of your health and the health of your loved ones, building a solid foundation for long-term well-being, greater energy, and much less stress. Best of all, you can do so without having to rely on a doctor.

Take Action Now

It's been said that knowledge is power. But knowledge only becomes powerful when it is applied. Take action and put into practice what you've learned starting today. Here are some suggestions to follow as you do so.

Go Slow: You will achieve the best results if you slowly yet steadily progress through your journey to greater levels of health and vitality rather than attempting to reach your goals in fits and starts and becoming overwhelmed. Begin by assessing your current health status using the medical tests discussed in Chapter 1 so that you have a clearer idea about what aspects of your health you need to focus on first.

At the same time, begin adopting a healthier diet and improving your gut health by following the guidelines in Chapters 2 and 3.

Remember that there is no such thing as a diet that is universally healthy for everyone. Experiment with your dietary choices and pay attention to how you react to the foods you eat. This will help you discover the foods most appropriate for your unique needs, while also uncovering foods to which you may be sensitive or allergic and which you should avoid or only eat sparingly.

As your diet and gut health improves, incorporate other essential elements into your self-care routine one at a time, such as adding nutritional supplements and committing to regular exercise activities. Before long, as you continue to experiment with and adopt the self-care methods for each key factor that best suit you, you will find they become easier to include as a regular part of your overall healthy lifestyle.

Be Consistent and Persistent: Accomplishing anything worthwhile takes time. That includes optimizing your health. Ours is a culture that constantly seeks instant "silver bullet" solutions. The truth is that real solutions do not occur overnight. Additionally, the journey to the endpoint of our goals is never a straight line. Like everything else in life, your health journey will have its ups and downs. Therefore, it is important that you proceed at your own pace while staying committed to continually taking the steps that will bring you to where you want to go. At times, you may find yourself wanting to indulge in an old, unhealthy habit. If you do, recognize your "slip up" and then "get back on your path" without judging or criticizing yourself. As your health continues to improve you will find that your desire to engage in such indulgences will diminish on its own because of how good sticking to your self-care routine makes you feel.

Make Your Journey Enjoyable: It is human nature to resist or quit activities that feel like drudgery and chores. Conversely, it is almost effortless to find the energy to continue to do what you enjoy. One of the keys to achieving long-term success is to make your self-care practice fun and enjoyable. For example, if you have a spouse, significant other, and/or children living with you, make meal planning and preparation a fun activity you can all participate it and then enjoy together at the dinner table. If you live alone, invite a friend or family member over to share the delicious meals you prepare. Sharing healthy meals with people whose company you enjoy will help keep you motivated to abide by your healthy diet, while also deepening your social connections, bringing you more joy and satisfaction, and keeping stress at bay.

Team Up With A "Health Buddy": You don't have to travel your healthy journey alone and, in fact, you may find it easier to maintain your commitment if you share your journey with someone else. Research shows that partnering with a family member or friend who is supportive of and shares your health goals improves overall compliance with health routines. For example, one study found that working with a supportive exercise partner increased the amount of exercise people engaged in. This was true even if the exercise partners did not exercise together, but simply encouraged each other.

Having someone in your corner to whom you hold yourself accountable can make a positive difference in all aspects of your self-care routine. Invite people you trust and care for, and who you know care about you, to help keep you on track with your self-care goals as your accountability team. This can be done by interacting with them in person, or by asking them to regularly check in with you by phone or email. Because you care for them you won't want to disappoint them by failing to commit to your daily health goals, making it more likely that you will carry them out. In addition, your own efforts and results will likely inspire them to commit to become healthier, as well, resulting in a social network of health-conscious friends and family supporting you and each other long-term.

Final Thoughts

As the famed Chinese sage Lao Tzu wrote, "The journey of a thousand miles begins with the first step." You took that first step when you chose to read this book, and have taken many more steps since by reading it through to the end. Now it's time to further your journey by daily practicing the self-care methods you've learned about. The more that you do so, the greater the heights of wellness you will scale.

As you notice your own health improving as a result of applying what you've read here, please recommend this book to others and spread the word about the Academy of Comprehensive Integrative Medicine (ACIM) and its mission. In doing so, you will be making that mission your own, helping to improve the health and well-being of everyone you care about and deriving great personal satisfaction as you do so. And consider joining the ACIM yourself so that you can benefit from all that ACIM physicians continue to discover about health.

There are two available health-care paths offered by the ACIM:

The informal path. As a member (free membership is also available), you can select the education courses that interest you from an online catalog of topics. All courses are available as online videos.

The formal path. Those who want to take the next step can enter into the ACIM's integrative medicine fellowship program, which includes 300 hours' worth of integrative medicine educational training, much of which can also be done online. (For more information about the ACIM Fellowship, visit www.acimconnect.com/Certifications.)

There are different levels within the fellowship program, with many courses available for laypeople who aspire to be wellness coaches or who just want to help themselves and their family. The training is online, and you only need to commit to one level of training at a time rather than committing to the entire fellowship, as there are 10 levels of the fellowship, about 30 hours each, for 300 hours of total training.

Were enough laypeople in each community around our great

nation versed in the self-care methods you now know and willing to share them with others, before long the health of the American people would start to significantly and permanently improve and we would all be the better for it.

I leave you with this thought from Dr. C. Norman Shealy: "There is only one purpose in life—to help other people."

May God bless you with long-lasting health!

Resources

The Academy of Comprehensive Integrative Medicine (ACIM)
www.acimconnect.com - info@acimconnect.com
Founded in 2008 by Dr. W. Lee Cowden, the mission of the ACIM is to shift the healthcare paradigm toward wellness by restoring hope, empowering people, training and supporting practitioners, conducting research, implementing therapeutic innovations, and creating a new global wellness care community. The ACIM offers a 10-level Fellowship certification program, Wellness Coaching training, and a directory of ACIM integrative physician nationwide.

No Doctors Required

www.nodoctorsrequired.com
Visit this website to be updated on the topics covered in *No Doctors Required* and the latest developments in the field of integrative medicine, and to receive the free report, ***Little Known Cancer Tests That Can Save Your Life***.

Lab Testing

The following companies offer the lab tests that you can order on your own (restrictions may apply residents of certain states).

Everly Well

www.everlywell.com

Life Extension Foundation for Longer Life (LEF)

www.lef.org/Vitamins-Supplements/Blood-Tests/Blood-Tests

Pixel By LabCorp

www.pixel.labcorp.com

Quest Diagnostics

https://questdirect.questdiagnostics.com

Quest Diagnostics Nichols Institute (for DHEA testing)

Phone: (800) 642-4657

Request A Test

https://requestatest.com

SpectraCell Laboratories

www.spectracell.com
(The innovative and unique micronutrient test, or MNT, SpectraCell offers can only be ordered from a provider in SpectraCell's nationwide network of physician. We include this company because of the superiority of the MNT compared to other nutrient tests.)

The following labs provide genetic DNA testing:

23andMe

www.23andme.com

Nutrition Genome

NutritionGenome.com

Self Decode

SelfDecode.com

Biological Dentists

Biological dentists are trained in the proper removal and replacement of dental amalgams containing mercury. The following organizations can help you locate a biological dentist near you.

Huggins Applied Healing

https://hugginsappliedhealing.com

International Academy of Biological Dentistry and Medicine (IABDM)

www.iabdm.org

International Academy of Oral Medicine and Toxicology (IAOMT)

www.iaomt.org

Holistic Dental Association

www.holisticdental.org

Mercury Free Dentists

www.mercuryfreedentists.com

Websites of the Contributors to No Doctors Required

Zach Bush, MD

ZachBushMD.com
https:/themclinic.com
https://intrinsichealthseries.com
https://ionbiome.com
https://farmersfootprint.us (the website for Farmers Footprint, the organization Dr. Bush founded to support farmers and restore the health of our nation's cropland, freeing it from glyphosate and other herbicides, pesticides, and related harmful toxins)

W. Lee Cowden, MD, MD(H)

www.DrLeeCowden.com

Bob Dennis, PhD

www.micro-pulse.com
www.corticalmetrics.com

Jennifer Gramith, ND

https://rightwayhealthandwellness.com

Angelique Hart, MD

https://drhartmd.com
https://healthcarestartsathome.com. (This site offers telemedicine consultations for only $35.00 per month per household. The program also offers access to a patient education platform where you can receive personalized health, food, and nutrient recommendations based on your lab test results and genetic markers.)

Steven Hines, ND, NE

www.hopewellness.com

Doug Kaufman

https://knowthecause.com

James Lemire, MD and Nuris Lemire, MS, OTR/L, NC

http://www.lemireclinic.com

Brad Nelson, DC

http://www.discoverhealing.com

William Pawluk, MD, MSc

www.drpawluk.com

C. Norman Shealy, MD, PhD

www.realholisticdoc.com
www.normshealy.shop
https://realholisticdoc.com/podcasts
https://realholisticdoc.com/radio-show-archive

Stephen Sinatra.com

www.drsinatra.com
www.healthydirections.com/dr-stephen-sinatra
https://www.healthydirections.com/podcasts (Dr. Sinatra's podcast with Drew Sinatra, ND)
https://vervana.com (Dr. Sinatra's website for high quality, organic, natural, non-GMO olive oils, pastas, sauces, vinegars, and spices that are rich in nutrition and minimally processed)
https://agelesspaws.com (Dr. Sinatra's website for healthy pet food, supplements, and other products)

Sergey Sorin, MD

www.drsergeysorin.com

Mark Tommerdahl, PhD

www.corticalmetrics.com

References

Chapter 1

Holmes, T.H. and Rahe, R.H. The social readjustment rating scale. *Journal of Psychosomatic Research*. 1967;11:213-218.

Michaelson DM. APOE epsilon4: the most prevalent yet understudied risk factor for Alzheimer's disease. *Alzheimers & Dementia*. 2014. 10(6): 861-8.

Shealy, C. Norman. *Blueprint For Holistic Healing*. Virgina Beach: A.R.E. Press, 2016.

Shealy, C. Norman. *Living Bliss*. Carlsbad, CA: Hay House, Inc., 2014.

Zung W. A Self-Rating Depression Scale. *Archives of General Psychiatry*. 1965. Jan;12:63-70.

Chapter 2

Burke, Peter. *Year-Round Indoor Salad Gardening*. White River Junction, VT: Chelsea Green Publishing, 2015.

FASTSTATS—Leading Causes of Death, Centers For Disease Control and Prevention (CDC). https://www.cdc.gov/nchs/fastats/leading-causes-of-death.htm

Kohler O, Krogh J, Mors O, Benros ME. Inflammation in Depression and the Potential for Anti-Inflammatory Treatment. *Curr Neuropharmacol*. 2016; 14(7): 732-42.

Morris AA, Zhao L, Ahmed Y, et al. Association between depression and inflammation-differences by race and sex: the META-Health study. *Psychosom Med*. 2011 Jul-Aug;73(6):462-8.

Pierini, CM. Lectins: Their Damaging Role in Intestinal Health, Rheumatoid Arthritis and Weight Loss. *Vitamin Research News*. 2007;21(1):1-4.

Yang T et al. Effectiveness of Commercial and Homemade Washing Agents in Removing Pesticide Residues on and in Apples. J. Agric. Food Chem. 2017; 65(44): 9744-9752.

Zhang JC, Yao W, Hashimoto K. Brain-derived Neurotrophic Factor (BDNF)-TrkB Signaling in Inflammation-related Depression and Potential Therapeutic Targets. *Curr Neuropharmacol*. 2016; 14(7): 721-31.

Chapter 3

Allen J et al. Exercise Alters Gut Microbiota Composition and Function in Lean and Obese Humans. *Medicine & Science in Sports & Exercise.* April 2018;50(4):747–757.

Bush Z et al. The Effects of Restore Dietary Supplement on Markers of Intestinal Permeability and Immune System Function in Healthy Subjects;A Double-Blind, Placebo-Controlled Clinical Trial. A White Paper, Peer-Review Publication Pending. Available at https://ionbiome.com/white-papers/

California Defeats Monsanto in Court to List Glyphosate as Carcinogen. https://sustainablepulse.com/2018/04/20/california-defeats-monsanto-in-court-to-list-glyphosate-as-probable-carcinogen/#.XT8aC9h7mM8

den Besten G et al. The role of short-chain fatty acids in the interplay between diet, gut microbiota, and host energy metabolism. J Lipid Res. 2013 Sep; 54(9): 2325–2340.

Gallagher, J. "More than half of your body is not you." *The Second Genome,* BBC Radio 4. April 10, 2018.

Gasnier C et al., "Glyphosate-Based Herbicides are Toxic and Endocrine Disruptors in Human Cell Lines," *Toxicology* 262 (2009): 184–91.

Gilles-Éric Séralini et al., "Long-Term Toxicity of a Roundup Herbicide and a Roundup-Tolerant Genetically Modified Maize, *Environmental Sciences Europe,* republished study (2014):14.

"Glyphosate," IARC Monographs–112.

Isolauri E, et al. Probiotics: Effects on immunity. *Am J Clin Nutr* Feb 2001; 73(2 Suppl):444S-450S.

Logan AC, Katzman M. Major depressive disorder: probiotics may be an adjuvant therapy. *Med Hypotheses* 2005;64(3):533-538.Mailing, LJ et al. Exercise and the Gut Microbiome: A Review of the Evidence, Potential Mechanisms, and Implications for Human Health. *Exercise and Sport Sciences Reviews.* April 2019;47(2):75-85.

Marc J, Mulner-Lorillon O, and Bellé R, "Glyphosate-Based Pesticides Affect Cell Cycle Regulation," *Biology of the Cell* 96, no. 3 (April 2004): 245–49.

Reid G. Potential uses of probiotics in clinical practice. *Clin Microbial Rev* 2003:16(4):658-672.

The Nobel Assembly at Karolinska Institutet has today decided to award the 2016 Nobel Prize in Physiology or Medicine to Yoshinori Ohsumi for his discoveries of mechanisms for autophagy. Oct 3, 2016. www.nobelprize.org/prizes/medicine/2016/press-release

Samsel A and Seneff S. "Glyphosate, Pathways to Modern Diseases II: Celiac Sprue and Gluten Intolerance," *Interdisciplinary Toxicology* 6, no. 4 (2013): 159–84.

Samsel and Stephanie Seneff, "Glyphosate, Pathways to Modern Diseases II: Celiac Sprue and Gluten Intoler- ance," *Interdisciplinary Toxicology* 6, no. 4 (2013): 159–84

Samsel A and Seneff S. "Glyphosate's Suppression of Cytochrome P450 Enzymes and Amino Acid Biosynthesis by the Gut Microbiome: Pathways to Modern Diseases," *Entropy* 15, no. 4 (2013): 1416–63.

Smith, A.P., Sutherland, D., and Hewlett, P. *An investigation of the acute effects of oligofructose-enriched inulin on subjective wellbeing, mood and cognitive performance Nutrients, October 28, 2015:7(11);8887-8896.*

Chapter 4

Levy, Thomas. *Death By Calcium* Henderson, NV: Medfox Publishing. 2013.

Sinatra, Stephen. *The Sinatra Solution: Metabolic Cardiology.* Laguna Beach, CA: Basic Health Publications. 2008.

Sinatra, Stephen and Roberts, James C. *Reverse Heart Disease Now.* Hoboken, NJ: John Wiley & Sons. 2008.

Trivieri, Larry Jr. *Turmeric For Your Health.* Garden City Park, NY: Square One Publishing. 2018.

Wood MJ, Skoien R, Powell LW. The global burden of iron overload. *Hepatol Int.* Sept 2009; 3(3):434-44.

Chapter 5

Genuis SJ et al. Blood, urine, and sweat (BUS) study: monitoring and elimination of bio-accumulated toxic elements. *Arch Environ Contam Toxicol.* 2011 Aug;61(2):344-57.

Genuis SJ, Beesoon S et al. Human excretion of bisphenol A: blood, urine, and sweat (BUS) study. *J Environ Public Health.* 2012 ;2012:185731.

Genuis SJ, Beesoon S, RA, Birkholz D. Human elimination of phthalate compounds: blood, urine, and sweat (BUS) study. *Scientific World Journal.* 2012 ;2012:615068.

Sears ME, Kerr KJ, I Bray RI. Arsenic, cadmium, lead and mercury in sweat: a systematic review. *J Environ Public Health.* 2012;2012:184745.

Chapter 6

Abel EL, Kruger ML. Smile Intensity in Photographs Predicts Longevity. *Psychological Science,* Feb 26, 2010; 21:542-544.

Church D, Yount G, Brooks AJ. The effect of emotional freedom techniques on stress biochemistry: a randomized controlled trial. *J Nerv Ment Dis.* Oct 2012;200(10):891-896.

Cuthbert SC, Goodheart GJ: On the reliability and validity of manual muscle testing: a literature review. *Chiropractic and Osteopathy* Mar 2007;15:4.

Harker LA, Keltner D. Expressions of positive emotion in women's college yearbook pictures and their relationship to personality and life outcomes across adulthood. *Journal of Personality and Social Psychology.* Jan 2001; 80(1):112-24.

Hennelotter A, Dresel C, et al. The link between facial feedback and neural activity within central circuitries of emotion-new insights from botulinum toxin-induced denervation of frown muscles. *Cereb Cortex.* Mar 2009; 19(3): 537-42.

Huikuri HV et al. Power-Law Relationship of Heart Rate Variability as a Predictor of Mortality in the Elderly. *Circulation.* May 26, 1998; 97: 2031-2036.

Kok BE, Fredrickson BL. Upward spirals of the heart: Autonomic flexibility, as indexed by vagal tone, reciprocally and prospectively predicts positive emotions and social connectedness. *Biological Psychology*. December 2010; 85(3): 432-436.

Nelson, Bradley. *The Emotion Code*. New York, NY: St. Martins Essentials, 2019.

Shealy, C. Norman. *Living Bliss*. Carlsbad, CA: Hay House, Inc. 2014.

Soderkvist S, Ohlen K, Dimberg U, How the Experience of Emotion is Modulated by Facial Feedback. *J Nonverbal Behavior*. 2018: 42(1): 129-151.

Chapter 7

Abe T, Kearns CF, Sato Y. Muscle size and strength are increased following walk training with restricted venous blood flow from the leg muscle, Kaatsu-walk training. *J Appl Physiol* 2006;100(5):1460–1466.

Benefits of Moderate Sun Exposure. *Harvard Health Publishing*. Jan 20, 2017. https://www.health.harvard.edu/family-health-guide/benefits-of-moderate-sun-exposure

Burr HS. *Blueprint for Immortality*, London, Neville Spearman, 1972.

Chevalier G, Sinatra ST, Oschman JL, Sokal K, Sokal P. Earthing: Health Implications of Reconnecting the Human Body to the Earth's Surface Electrons. *Journal of Environmental and Public Health*. Jan 12, 2012.

Counts BR, Dankel SJ, Barnett BE, et al. Influence of relative blood flow restriction pressure on muscle activation and muscle adaptation. *Muscle Nerve* 2016;53:438–45.

Galitzer Michael and Trivieri Larry. "Your Body Is A Dynamic Energy System". *Outstanding Health*. Beyond Words, 2018.

Godar DE, Landry RJ, Lucas AD. Increased UVA exposures and decreased cutaneous Vitamin D(3) levels may be responsible for the increasing incidence of melanoma. *Med Hypotheses*. Apr 2009; 72(4): 434-43.

Holick MF. Vitamin D and Sunlight: Strategies for Cancer Prevention and Other Health Benefits. *CJASN*. Sept. 2008: 3(5): 1548-1554.

Loenneke JP, Wilson JM, Marín PJ, et al. Low intensity blood flow restriction training: a meta-analysis. *Eur J Appl Physiol* 2012a;112:1849–59.

Martín-Hernández J, Ruiz-Aguado J, Herrero JA, et al. Adaptation of perceptual responses to low load blood flow restriction training. *J Strength Cond Res* 2016:1.

Mead MN. Benefits of Sunlight: A Bright Spot for Human Health. *Environ Health Perspect*. Apr 2008; 116(4): A160-A167.

Shealy, C. Norman. "Energy and Electromagnetism". *Sacred Healing*. Boston, MA: Element Books, Inc. 1999.

Sinatra, Stephen. *7 Reasons Why Exercise Is More Powerful than a Drug*. Dec. 10, 2019. https://www.drsinatra.com/7-reasons-why-exercise-is-more-powerful-than-a-drug

Tiller W. Science and Human Transformation, California, Paviour, 1997.

Yasuda T, Fujita S, Ogasawara R, Sato Y, Abe T (2010) Effects of low-intensity bench press training with restricted arm muscle blood flow on chest muscle hypertrophy: a pilot study. *Clin Physiol Funct Imaging* 30(5):338–343.

Young SN. How to increase serotonin in the human brain without drugs. J Psychiatry Neurosci. Nov 2007; 32(6): 394–399.

Chapter 8

Bar-Ilan University. "Sleep tight! Researchers identify the beneficial role of sleep: Sleep increases chromosome dynamics that clear out DNA damage accumulated during waking hours." *ScienceDaily*. March 5, 2019. www.sciencedaily.com/releases/2019/03/190305170106.htm.

Benedict C et al. Gut microbiota and glucometabolic alterations in response to recurrent partial sleep deprivation in normal-weight young individuals. *Molecular Metabolism*. Dec 2016; 5 (12): 1175-1186.

Fischer G, Kokoschinegg PJ. The treatment of sleep disturbances and meteorosensitivity by pulsed magnetic fields of low intensity. *J Bioelectr* 9(2): 243, Third Symposium on Magnetotherapy and Magnetic Stimulation, 12-14 October 1989, Hungary, 1990. Doi: 10.3109/15368379009119812

Fulz NE et al. Coupled electrophysiological, hemodynamic, and cerebrospinal fluid oscillations in human sleep. *Science*. Nov. 1, 2019; 366 (6465): 628-631.

Ghaly M, Teplitz D. The biologic effects of grounding the human body during sleep as measured by cortisol levels and subjective reporting of sleep, pain, and stress. *J Altern Complement Med. Oct10, 2004; (5):767-76.*

Hafner M et al. Why sleep matters — the economic costs of insufficient sleep: A cross-country comparative analysis. Santa Monica, CA: RAND Corporation, 2016. https://www.rand.org/pubs/research_reports/RR1791.html.

Haghayegh S et al. Before-bedtime passive body heating by warm shower or bath to improve sleep: A systematic review and meta-analysis. *Sleep Medicine Reviews*. Aug 2019; 46: 124-135.

Hurley S et al. Sleep duration and cancer risk in women. *Cancer Causes & Control.* July 2015; 26 (7): 1037-1045.

Ibarra-Coronado E et al. The Bidirectional Relationship between Sleep and Immunity against Infections. *J Immunological Research*. Aug 31, 2015. doi: 10.1155/2015/678164.

Irwin M. Effects of sleep and sleep loss on immunity and cytokines. *Brain, Behavior, and Immunity*. Oct 2002; 16 (5): 503-512.

Li Y et al. The Role of Microbiome in Insomnia, Circadian Disturbance and Depression. *Front. Psychiatry*, December 5, 2018 doi.org/10.3389/fpsyt.2008.00669

Mulligan JM et al. Sleep loss and inflammation. *Best Practice & Research Clinical Endocrinology & Metabolism*. Oct 2010; 24 (5): 775-784.

Ober Clint, Sinatra Stephen T, Zucker Martin. *Earthing-The most important health discovery ever?* Laguna Beach, CA: Basic Books, 2010.

Parkar SG, Kalsbeek A, Cheeseman JF. Potential Role for the Gut Microbiota in Modulating Host Circadian Rhythms and Metabolic Health. *Microorganisms* 2019; *7 (2):* 41. pii: E41. doi: 10.3390/microorganisms7020041.

Pawluk William and Layne Caitlyn J. *Power Tools: How Pulsed Magnetic Fields (PEMF) Can Help You.* Victoria, BC: Friesen Press, 2017.

Pelka RB, Jaenicke C, Gruenwald J. Impulse magnetic-field therapy for insomnia: a double-blind, placebo-controlled study. *Adv Ther* Jul-Aug 2001; 18(4):174-180. Pilcher JJ et al. Interactions between sleep habits and self-control. *Front. Hum. Neurosci,* May 11, 2015 doi.org/10.3389/fnhum.2015.00284.

Repaying your sleep debt-Why sleep is important to your health and how to repair sleep deprivation effects. *Harvard Women's Health Watch.* www.health.harvard.edu/ newsletters/harvard_womens_health_watch/2007/july

Rosselot AE, Hong CI, Moore SR. Rhythm and bugs: Circadian clocks, gut microbiota, and enteric infections. *Cuur Opin Gastroenterol.* Jan 2016; 32 (1): 7-11.

Sigurdardottir LG et al. Circadian Disruption, Sleep Loss, and Prostate Cancer Risk: A Systematic Review of Epidemiologic Studies. *Cancer Epidemiol Biomarkers Prev. July 2012; 21(7): 1002–11.*

Sigurdardottir LG et al. Sleep Disruption Among Older Men and Risk of Prostate Cancer. *Cancer Epidemiol Biomarkers Prev. May 2013; 22 (5): 872–879.*

University of Rochester Medical Center. "Not all sleep is equal when it comes to cleaning the brain." *ScienceDaily,* February 27, 2019. www.sciencedaily.com/ releases/2019/02/190227173111.htm

Van Erde W, Venus M. A Daily Dietary Study on Sleep Quality and Procrastination at Work: The Moderating Role of Trait Self-Control. *Front Psychol.* Nov 2, 2018 doi. 10.3389/fpsyg.2018.02029.

Xie L et al. Sleep Drives Metabolite Clearance from the Adult Brain. *Science.* Oct 18, 2013; 342 (6156): 373-377.

Zada D et al. Sleep increases chromosome dynamics to enable reduction of accumulating DNA damage in single neurons. *Nature Communications,* Mar 5 2019; 10 (1) doi: 10.1038/s41467-019-08806-w

Chapter 9

Adachi M, Rode CLE, Kendle AD. Effects of floral and foliage displays on human emotions. *Hort Sci.* 2000;10:59–63.

Coleman CK, Mattson RH. Influences of foliage plants of human stress during thermal biofeedback training. *Hort Technology.* 1995;5:137–40.

The Inside Story: A Guide to Indoor Air Quality. www.epa.gov/indoor-air-quality-iaq/ inside-story-guide-indoor-air-quality

English J. The Positive Health Benefits of Negative Ions. *NutritionReview.org*; Apr 22, 2013.

Hickey, H. Toxic chemicals found in common scented laundry products, air fresheners. University of Washington, July 23, 2008. www.washington.edu/news/2008/07/23/ toxic-chemicals-found-in-common-scented-laundry-products-air-fresheners

Lohr, V. I. and Pearson-Mims, C. H.: 1996, 'Particulate matter accumulation on horizontal surfaces in interiors: influence of foliage plants', *Atmos. Environ.* 30 (14), 2565-2568.

Min-sun Lee, Juyoung Lee, Bum-Jin Park, Yoshifumi Miyazaki. Interaction with indoor plants may reduce psychological and physiological stress by suppressing autonomic nervous system activity in young adults: a randomized crossover study. *J Physiol Anthropol.* 2015; 34(1): 21.

Omasa, K., Tobe, K. and Kondo, T.: 2002, 'Absorption of organic and inorganic air pollutants by plants', in K. Omasa, H. Saji, S. Youssefian and N. Kondo (eds), *Air Pollution and Plant Biotechnology: Prospects for Phytomonitoring and Phytoremediation.* Springer, Tokyo, Berlin, Ch. 8, pp. 155-178.Reilly T, Stevenson IC. An investigation of the effects of negative air ions on responses to submaximal exercise at different times of day. *J Hum Ergol* (Tokyo) 1993 Jun;22(1):1-9.

Chapter 10

Benson, Herbert and Klipper, Miriam Z. *The Relaxation Response.* New York: William Morrow Paperbacks. 2000.

Bruce M et al. Church attendance, allostatic load and mortality in middle aged adults. *PLOS One* May 16, 2017; 12(5): e0177618. doi: 10.1371/journal.pone.0177618. eCollection 2017.

Byrd RC, Positive therapeutic effects of intercessory prayer in a coronary care unit population. *Southern Med J* Jul 1988; 81(7):826-829.

Harris SH, et al. A randomized, controlled trial of the effects of remote, intercessory prayer on outcomes in patients admitted to the coronary care unit. *Arch Intern Med* Oct 25, 1999; 159(19):2273-2278.

Keeping the faith: UC Berkeley researcher links weekly church attendance to longer, healthier life. berkeley.edu/news/media/releases/2002/03/26_faith.html

Koenig HG, Pergament KI, Nielson J. Religious coping and health status in medically ill hospitalized adults. *J Nerve Ment Dis.* Sept 1998; 186(9):513-21.

Koenig HG et al. The relationship between religious activities and blood pressure in older adults. *Int J Psychiatry Med.* 1998;28(2):189-213.

Koenig HG, Larson DB. Use of hospital services, religious attendance, and religious affiliation. *Southern Med J.* Oct 1998; 91(10): 925-32.

Li S, Stampfer MJ, Williams DR, VanderWeele TJ. Association of Religious Service Attendance With Mortality Among Women. *JAMA Internal Medicine, June 1, 2016; 176(6):777-85.*

Zauzmer, Julie. Another possible benefit of going to church: A 33 percent chance of living longer. *Washington Post* May 16, 2016.

Conclusion

Rackow P, Scholz U, Hornung R. Received social support and exercising: An intervention study to test the enabling hypothesis. *British Journal of Health Psychology*, 2015; 20 (4):763.

About the Author and the Academy of Comprehensive Integrative Medicine

Larry Trivieri Jr is a recognized lay expert in the fields of alternative and integrative medicine, and a bestselling health book author. He served as editor and principal writer of both editions of the landmark volume, *Alternative Medicine: The Definitive Guide*. His other books include *The American Holistic Medical Association Guide to Holistic Health, Outstanding Health* (with Michael Galitzer, MD), *Chronic Fatigue, Fibromyalgia & Lyme Disease* (with Burton Goldberg), *Juice Alive: The Ultimate Guide to Juicing Remedies* (with Steven Bailey, ND), *The Acid-Alkaline Food Guide* (with Susan E. Brown, PhD, CNN).

He has also written over 200 articles for Internet-based health sites, including *Integrative Health Review*, the online health journal of the National University System, *HuffPost.com, MariaShriver. com, and Newsmax.com/Health*, as well as articles for *Alternative Medicine, Natural Health, Natural Solutions, Yoga Journal*, and other health magazines.

The Academy of Comprehensive Integrative Medicine (ACIM) was established with the goal of shifting the healthcare paradigm toward wellness by restoring hope, empowering people, training and supporting practitioners, conducting research, implementing therapeutic innovations, and creating a new global wellness care community among the lay public, both in the United States and around the world. With more than 5,000 members, ACIM is recognized as the leading organization of its kind due to the caliber of the physician trainings it provides via conferences, seminars, and online tutorials and webinars. Under Dr. Cowden, ACIM has also created the most in-depth wellness coaching training and certification program in the United States.

About the Contributors

Zach Bush, MD, is a triple-board certified physician in Internal Medicine, Endocrinology and Metabolism, and Hospice and Palliative Care, and the medical director of the M Clinic in Charlottesville, Virginia. He is an internationally recognized expert and educator on the microbiome as it relates to health, disease, and food production, and the developer of the ION*Biome health products. His focus is on developing root-cause solutions for human and ecological health and extending his passion for educating others on topics such as the state of our soil, including the need to eradicate toxins such as glyphosate from our farming chain, and the importance of gut/brain communication as a vital part of our overall health and wellbeing.

W. Lee Cowden, MD, MD(H), was board-certified as an internist and cardiologist in 1985 and is internationally known for his knowledge and skill in practicing and teaching integrative medicine. He has contributed to many health books (in addition to the six books he has co-authored), written numerous articles on integrative medicine, and has pioneered successful treatments of cardiovascular diseases, cancer, autism, Lyme disease, chronic fatigue syndrome, fibromyalgia, and many other illnesses. Dr. Cowden is also a recognized leader in the practice of evaluative kinesiology, electrodermal screening, homeopathy, orthomolecular and herbal therapies, German neural-therapy, electro-cutaneous stimulation, photonic (light) therapies, as well as fixed-magnetic, electromagnetic, and detoxification therapies. In 2008, Dr. Cowden co-founded the Academy of Comprehensive Integrative Medicine and serves as the organization's Chairman of the Scientific Advisory Board and is an Academy Professor. Dr. Cowden is the co-author of *Foods That Fit A Unique You, Create A Toxin-Free Body & Home Starting Today, BioEnergetic Tools For Wellness, An Alternative Medicine Definitive Guide to Cancer, Longevity: An Alternative Medicine Definitive Guide* and *Cancer Diagnosis: What To Do Next.*

Dr. Cowden has treated many patients who were sent home to die by allopathic doctors but are still alive decades after their terminal prognosis. He accomplished this by restoring hope in the minds of those patients and helping them to call on the power of God for their healing. Dr. Cowden believes that the source of all healing is the one-and-only living God and believes (and has overwhelming scientific proof) that the entire Bible is the inspired Word of God. In addition, Dr. Cowden has had personal experiences that confirm God's love for him. Even though Dr. Cowden is imperfect and there is evidence that God is perfect, because of God's infinite grace and mercy, God made arrangements for Dr. Cowden, and any other human who desires such, to have a relationship with God through acceptance of God's Son Jesus. For Dr. Cowden, spirituality can be distilled down into a statement made by Christ Jesus, "Love the Lord your God with all your heart and with all your soul and with all your mind and with all your strength…[and] love your neighbor as yourself." (NKJV Mark 12:30-31)

Dr. Cowden's personal website is www.DrLeeCowden.com.

Bob Dennis, PhD, is scientist, engineer, inventor, and a tenured associate professor at the University of North Carolina, Chapel Hill who is dedicated to developing and marketing new technologies that will benefit everyone and will be made available at a reasonable price to anyone in the world who needs them. He is also the founder of Micro-Pulse, LLC, the manufacturer of the ICES-PEMF products he has developed, and the co-founder (along with Mark Tommerdahl, PhD) and chief engineer of Cortical Metrics, LLC, the manufacturer of the Brain Gauge.

Jennifer Gramith, ND, is a doctor of naturopathic medicine accredited by the American Naturopathic Medical and Accreditation Board, Inc., with a 17-year background in the medical field in internal medicine. She is also the founder and president of Rightway Health and Wellness LLC, and a Lymphatic Decongestive Practitioner and Instructor certified through the Academy of Lymphatic Studies in Manual Lymph Drainage and Complete Decongestive Therapy. Dr. Gramith specializes in nutritional counseling, lymphatic decongestive therapy and low level laser detoxification therapy. She is also the founder and president of the Foundation for the Advancement of Energy Medicine Technology (FAEMT), an organization dedicated to research and support of this emerging field.

Angelique Hart, MD, oversees the Holistic Medical Clinic in Albuquerque, New Mexico. She has received extensive training in Internal Medicine, Anestheisology and Pain Management, and a wide range of Integrative Medicine modalities, including Detoxification Therapies and Functional Medicine, Regenerative Medicine modalities including PRP Stem Cell Injection Therapies for Pain Management and Aesthetics, Bio-Identical Hormone Therapy, and Live O2/Exercise with Oxygen Therapy (EWOT). Dr. Hart is also certified in Chelation Therapy and Spinal Epiduroscopy, and participated as a Clinical Investigator for the National Institutes of Health (NIH) funded national study: TACT (Trial to Assess Chelation Therapy).

Steven Hines, ND, NE, is both a naturopathic physician and a naturopathic endocrinologist, and founder and director of the Hope Wellness Center in San Angelo, Texas, and its treatment facility in Ciudad Acuňa, Coahuila, Mexico. Dr. Hines specializes in the treatment of allergies, cancer, gastrointestinal disorders, lupus/fibromyalgia/chronic fatigue syndrome, Lyme disease, and other advanced degenerative diseases, as well as the use of diet, nutrition, and life style management to normalize the function of the endocrine system. In addition to co-authoring the book *The Road To Health* with Laura Shroeder, Dr. Hines created a 4½ hour DVD series on gastrointestinal function and the treatment of gastrointestinal disorders. This definitive work is now part of the curriculum of naturopathic colleges and other educational curriculums across the U.S.

Doug Kaufman is the host of the daily national television show *Know The Cause*, which he developed after 22 years of clinical nutritional work in physicians' offices. The show has enjoyed tremendous success for more than two decades, based on a simple concept that most physicians remain unaware that certain fungi that we humans are regularly exposed to make poisonous byproducts that can cause or mimic many autoimmune diseases and cancer. This void leaves Americans searching for medical answers. With the many integrative physicians that Doug's show interviews and introduces within the 80 million households in his TV audience, Doug has helped thousands in their search for more natural physicians and more effective approaches to health care.

Doug was a US Navy Corpsman trained in emergency medicine and was attached to the 7th Marines in Vietnam in 1970-71. Based on that experience, and also suffering from an array of symptoms upon homecoming, Doug became outspoken on fungal diseases after discovering that fungus was the cause of his own health problems. While his TV show teaches the lay public, Doug has been blessed to be asked by physicians to offer medical training on toxic fungi within various medical communities. These courses have been well attended and accepted. In 2014, the cancer journal, *Oncology News*, published his paper, *Fungi and Their Mycotoxins: An Underappreciated Role in Cancers,* scientifically linking fungus to cancer. He has authored 12 books on the fungus link to health problems and has a strong social media presence in addition to his lectures and TV shows.

Doug knows that it is by the Grace of God, that he has enjoyed such tremendous success during his 50-year career. Grace did not stop there for Doug, however. The many blessings bestowed upon him by his wife Ruth for 40 years, their sons and their sons' wives and families, and their newest Kaufmann family additions, grandsons

Berkley and Rex, have all confirmed God's continued Grace and love to him.

James Lemire, MD, has been practicing medicine for nearly 50 years. He is the founder and medical director of the Lemire Clinic in Ocala, Florida, a full-service family practice "from cradle to grave", where he educates his patients about diet and nutrition, lifestyle changes, and stress and sleep management. His treatment offerings include diet, nutrition (including nutritional IV therapy), ultraviolet IV therapy, homeopathy, Chinese medicine, detoxification therapies, energy medicine, occupational therapy, exercise therapies, and other integrative modalities. Dr. Lemire's diagnostic testing and treatment protocols are designed around each patient's unique individuality.

Nuris Lemire, MS, OTR/L, NC, she holds six college degrees, ranging from Early Childhood Education to Psychology, and has a Master's Degree in Occupational Therapy. She holds numerous certifications as a Nutrition Consultant, Lifestyle Changes Educator and Advisor, Acupuncture therapist, lymphatic drainage, and Craniosacral and Heart Center Therapy. She is also an accomplished Reiki Master Practitioner, and a Wudang China External Qi Healer. She educates and assists patients along with her husband, Dr. Lemire, at the Lemire Clinic.

Brad Nelson, DC, is a holistic chiropractor and medical intuitive, and one of the world's foremost experts in the emerging fields of Bioenergetic Medicine and Energy Psychology. He is also the creator of The Body Code™ System, which includes The Emotion Code®, and the bestselling author of *The Emotion Code* book. An acclaimed public speaker, since 1995, Dr. Nelson has lectured internationally on alleviating chronic diseases through energy work, and restoring balance to the 6 key elements of health in the body. Dr. Nelson and his staff operate an international network of certified Emotion Code and Body Code practitioners , and The Body Code System is being used successfully by doctors and laypeople alike to improve the health of thousands of people all over the world.

William Pawluk, MD, MSc, is a previously board-certified family physician with additional training in acupuncture, homeopathy, hypnosis, energy medicine, and bodywork. He has had academic faculty appointments at a number of universities including Johns Hopkins and was the Clinical Director of the University of Maryland's Complementary and Alternative Medicine Program. In addition, he was formerly Vice President of the North American Academy for Magnetic Therapy, and is an international expert in the medical use of medical use of electromagnetic fields, including pulsed electromagnetic field (PEMF) therapy and PEMF devices, with over 25 years of experience. He regularly teaches practitioners about the appropriate use of magnetic therapies, as well as educating the public about this technology. Dr. Pawluk currently practices functional and holistic medicine in Baltimore, Maryland.

Dr. Pawluk is also the author of ***Power Tools For Health: How Pulsed Magnetic Fields (PEMFs) Help You.***

C. Norman Shealy, MD, PhD, is President of Shealy-Sorin Wellness Institute and Holos Energy Medicine Education. He created the concept of Holistic Medicine in 1971 with the introduction of spinal cord stimulation and TENS. He is also the editor of the *Journal of Comprehensive Integrative Medicine*, and the founding President of the American Holistic Medical Association. Dr. Shealy hold 14 patents in Energy Medicine, and has has published 36 books and over 350 articles. Dr. Shealy's innovations include Electro-acupuncture, Spinal Cord Stimulation, Transcutaneous Electrical Nerve Stimulation (TENS), the RejuvaMatrix ® for rejuvenating telomeres, and Transcutaneous Acupuncture, which also rejuvenates telomeres; Chakra Sweep Gamma PEMF for stress reduction and opioid addiction, Sapphire Enhanced Scalar for remarkable biochemical reduction in stress. and Biogenics Retraining of the Nervous System based on his PhD in Humanistic Psychology. His clinical work includes comprehensive holistic management of pain, depression, anxiety, and chronic disease. Dr. Shealy is still active in clinical work, research, writing, education and is a highly sought after keynote speaker at a number of National and International Conferences. He is also the recipient of a number of lifetime achievement awards in the fields of Medicine, Holism, Wellness, Innovation and Education and advancement in Science and Humanitarian aspects.

Dr. Shealy is also a prolific author. His books include *90 Days To Self-Health, Living Bliss, Blueprint For Holistic Living, Medical Intuition, Energy Medicine: Practical Applications and Scientific Proof, Life Beyond 100, Nutrition For Energy, Sacred Healing, Soul Medicine, The Healing Remedies Source Book,* and *Third Party Rape: The Conspiracy To Rob You Of Your Health Care.*

Stephen T. Sinatra, MD, is a board-certified cardiologist, a fellow in the American College of Cardiology and the American College of Nutrition, and an Assistant Clinical Professor of Medicine at the University of Connecticut School of Medicine in Farmington, Connecticut. Dr. Sinatra pioneered the field of metabolic cardiology, and is also a certified bioenergetic psychotherapist, and nutrition and anti-aging specialist, as well as the founder of HeartMDInstitute. com, an informational website dedicated to promoting public awareness of integrative medicine. In addition, Dr. Sinatra is one of the world's leading authorities and researchers in the emerging field of grounding, or "earthing", documenting the significant health benefits grounding provides. He is also the bestselling author of numerous health books, including *The Great Cholesterol Myth, The Great Cholesterol Myth Cookbook, Reverse Heart Disease Now, Heartbreak & Heart Disease, Nutritional and Integrative Strategies in Cardiovascular Medicine, The Sinatra Solution: Metabolic Cardiology, Lower Your Blood Pressure In 8 Weeks, Earthing: The Most Important Health Discovery Ever!* (with Clint Ober), and *The Healing Kitchen.*

Sergey Sorin, MD, is a board certified physician with extensive experience in Urgent Care, Occupational Medicine And Emergency Medicine, and serves as CEO and Medical Director of the Shealy-Sorin Wellness Institute. Previously, he served as Medical Director at the Bath, NY VA Hospital as well as several other organizations including Physician Weight Loss and Wellness Center, Tri-State

Surgical Weight Loss Practice and Delphi/Workfit Healthcare. After a life-altering diagnosis and successful treatment of colon cancer in 2007, Dr. Sorin's focus has been on the broad field of Holistic Medicine. Together with Dr. Shealy, he is actively involved in clinical research projects as well as several upcoming patents and scientific developments, and is a faculty member at the Holos University Graduate Seminary and the Graduate Institute in Bethany, Connecticut.

Mark Tommerdahl, PhD, a neuroscientist and faculty member at the University of North Carolina, Chapel Hill, and the President of Cortical Metrics, the company he co-founded with Dr. Bob Dennis. Cortical Metrics is actively developing sensory testing technology that can be widely distributed, including the BrainGauge. Dr. Tommerdahl's broad range of research interests center on cortical mechanisms of information processing that led him to develop novel human sensory perceptual testing methods and technologies to research across a broad spectrum of neurological disorders. Neurological areas of interest to Dr. Tommerdahl include concussion/TBI, developmental disorders (e.g., autism), aging and chronic pain.

Acknowledgments

This book could not have been written without the support I received from each of the wonderful health experts whose recommendations appear within it. The work they continue to do in service to others is some of the most important work in the entire field of health care. I am humbled to have been able to create this book with them. So my sincerest thanks and deepest gratitude to Zach Bush, Bob Dennis, Jennifer Gramith, Angelique Hart, Steven Hines, Doug Kaufman, James and Nuris Lemiere, Brad Nelson, William Pawluk, Norm Shealy, Stephen T. Sinatra, Sergey Sorin, and Mark Tommerdhal.

I also am very grateful to and wish to thank Joseph Mercola for writing this book's Foreword, and for the many years he has devoted and continues to devote to educating and empowering others via Mercola.com, the world's largest and best online health resource of its kind.

Finally, and most especially, I want to thank Lee Cowden. Lee was the first doctor I approached about this project. From the start his support and enthusiasm for it have been strong and unwavering. Lee's contributions to this book go far beyond the recommendations he shares within its pages. He helped me to fine tune the Table of Contents and chapter-by-chapter outline I initially created, put me in touch with many of the above contributing experts, and reviewed and edited each chapter in the book, making key suggestions and improvements throughout. Thank you, Lee, for everything!